IRISH LITERARY PORTRAITS

IRISH LITERARY PORTRAITS

W. B. YEATS : JAMES JOYCE : GEORGE MOORE
: J. M. SYNGE : GEORGE BERNARD SHAW :
OLIVER ST JOHN GOGARTY : F. R. HIGGINS
: AE (GEORGE RUSSELL)

Edited by W. R. RODGERS
from his broadcast conversations
with those who knew them

Taplinger Publishing Company : *New York*

First published in the United States in 1973 by
TAPLINGER PUBLISHING CO., INC.
New York, New York

Copyright © 1972 by the Contributors and the
British Broadcasting Corporation.
All rights reserved. Printed in the U.S.A.

Library of Congress Catalog Card Number: 72-7790

ISBN 0-8008-4249-9

ACKNOWLEDGMENTS

Copyrights from which permission to quote has been granted:

The contributions of St John Ervine are reproduced by permission of the Society of Authors.

Oliver St John Gogarty. "Non Dolet," "The Phoenix," "Ringsend," "To Petronius Arbiter." Reprinted with permission of Devin-Adair Company from *Collected Poems* by Oliver St John Gogarty. Copyright 1954 by Oliver St John Gogarty.

The contributions of Frank O'Connor are reproduced by permission of Cyrilly Abels, literary agent.

Æ (George Russell). "Salutation." Reprinted with permission of A. M. Heath and Co. Ltd. from *Collected Poems of Æ*.

William Butler Yeats. "He Wishes for the Cloths of Heaven." Reprinted with permission of Macmillan Publishing Co., Inc. from *Collected Poems* by William Butler Yeats. Copyright 1906 by The Macmillan Company; renewed 1934 by William Butler Yeats.

William Butler Yeats. "The Mask." Reprinted with permission of Macmillan Publishing Co., Inc. from *Collected Poems* by William Butler Yeats. Copyright 1928 by The Macmillan Company; renewed 1956 by Georgie Yeats.

William Butler Yeats. "Easter 1916." Reprinted with permission of Macmillan Publishing Co., Inc. from *Collected Poems* by William Butler Yeats. Copyright 1924 by The Macmillan Company; renewed 1952 by Bertha Georgie Yeats.

William Butler Yeats. "All Souls' Night," "1919," and "The Tower." Reprinted with permission of Macmillan Publishing Co., Inc. from *Collected Poems* by William Butler Yeats. Copyright 1928 by The Macmillan Company; renewed 1956 by Georgie Yeats.

William Butler Yeats. "Beautiful Lofty Things," "High Talk," "The O'Rahilly," "Politics," "Three Songs to the One Burden," "Under Ben Bulben," and "What Then?" Reprinted with permission of Macmillan Publishing Co., Inc. from *Collected Poems* by William Butler Yeats. Copyright 1940 by Georgie Yeats; renewed 1968 by Bertha Georgie Yeats, Michael Butler Yeats and Anne Yeats.

CONTENTS

INTRODUCTION

In a land of 'good talkers' there was one good listener – Bertie Rodgers. Not that he wasn't himself a good talker – with plenty of stamina – when he felt like it, but listening was his social speciality, his craft. It had once been an important part of his job, as a Presbyterian Minister in Co. Armagh, and there was always something a little pastoral, as well as a little clinical, about his listening. It was indeed a rather disconcerting thing to be listened to by him. He seemed to listen with his eyes. These were large, prominent, lustrous, suited to a hypnotist, or a Swami. They also seemed to be, in some strange way, turned off, not looking. They had the quality often referred to as 'inward-looking', they were in fact rapt in the contemplation and analysis of spoken words. He never watched, as detectives or criminal lawyers are said to do, for the movements of hands or features that 'give away' the truth concealed by the patter. Partly, that kind of alertness would have reduced his effectiveness as an interviewer; his air of sympathetic abstraction and absent-mindedness put people at their ease. Partly, it was that the kind of truth the detective or lawyer, or even historian, is interested in, interested him only marginally (though sharply enough). But mainly, I think, it was that he didn't need to look; the spoken words, and the way they were spoken, told him all he needed to know. So he listened like a blind man.

As he puts it himself, in the preface to this collection: 'I knew very well before I finished how far any man's statement was trustworthy or factual, but truth is not the whole of life, or facts the whole of truth, and these people were, like myself, as honest as the day is long, and no more.'

He would have made a good spy, in the sense of being able to find out an extraordinary amount about the people among whom he moved, but a very bad spy if required to report anything that could harm the people in question. He was in fact – and this comes through in the present collection – exceptionally careful to avoid hurting people's feelings. Dubliners – and most of those whose talk is recorded here are

Dubliners, by birth or adoption – are generally less careful about this. Dublin's malice –

'The daily spite of this unmannerly town', (Yeats) –

has often been exaggerated, especially by writers, but it is a constant presence, electric and reductive. It is a style, a way of going on, a habit which some would like to shake off but can't. It is mild and persistent, chronic rather than acute, seldom takes brutal forms, is usually present as a generalised corrosive irreverence – perhaps in part a release from the reverence obligatory on certain subjects, and at certain hours and places, in this Catholic city. Dublin's malice is egalitarian, almost impersonal. Writers have suffered from it – Yeats and Joyce especially – for several reasons. 'Men of letters,' as Edmund Burke observed, are 'fond of distinguishing themselves', and it is Dublin's unwritten law that its citizens are not, with impunity, to be allowed to distinguish themselves. Writers are a favourite target because a number of vocal Dubliners feel themselves *to be* writers, whom only cruel fate or a conspiracy holds back from actually writing. Writers who actually write, and are published, *and paid for it*, are in fact defrauding the men of integrity, the non-writing writers, and deserve to be punished for this. Some writers resent this disproportionately and take it out on Dublin in their writing. Dublin rather enjoys this.

Bertie Rodgers appreciated, with his usual discretion and delicacy, the full range of Dublin's malice. It is part – a rather considerable part – of the savour of Dublin conversation, and Bertie had to come to some kind of terms with it, in his editing of the stupendous quantities of talk and gossip he listened to in Dublin. Dublin's malice is enjoyably present in these portraits, but the average level of malice is distinctly – and acceptably – lower than the average level of malice in Dublin talk. The filter of Bertie Rodgers's mind has been interposed: a mind drawing on Calvinism's bottomless fund of pessimism about human nature, but deriving also, from a long personal experience of pain, an unusual determination to avoid inflicting it on others. This interposition does not detract from the value of the portraits: on the contrary. The ordinary level of Dublin's malice is distorting, if entertaining. By tuning out superfluous malice – as I believe him to have done – Bertie Rodgers has, as we should expect, produced a better, clearer picture. There is still plenty of entertainment.

There are three distinct sets of portraits in this fascinating and protean book. There are the portraits of the subjects: Yeats, Joyce,

George Moore, Synge and the rest. And there is a set of miniatures – the little self-revelations which Bertie encouraged his talkers to provide of themselves. As the talkers include the most notable writers of the post-Yeats generation – Austin Clarke, Brinsley Macnamara, Sean O'Faolain, Frank O'Connor, Patrick Kavanagh, Rodgers himself and others – this set of portraits too will be of importance to the literary historian, as well as entertaining to the general reader. One man, Oliver St John Gogarty, is present both as talker and talked about, a play of mirrors. And Bertie Rodgers's own self-portrait, as a practitioner of the craft of listening and editing, is here in his Preface, one of the most interesting parts of this book.

Bertie Rodgers was an Ulster Presbyterian who sought and enjoyed the company of Southern Catholics. The case is not unique: it remains unusual. He had a great affection and admiration for the late Monsignor Paddy Browne (whose death he mentions in his Preface). My wife, who was a niece of Paddy Browne's, remembers meeting him in the street not long before his death and being greeted with the words: 'Come and have a drink. I'm worn out keeping the poet Rodgers from becoming a Catholic.'

Bertie Rodgers would have suffered greatly had he lived to see the present state of Catholic-Protestant relations in the North. He would have suffered all the more because there is nothing in this that would be entirely new to him. Mr Darcy O'Brien in his brilliant and sensitive *W. R. Rodgers (1909–1969)*[1] tells what he heard from Bertie of his family's reaction to the day-to-day news of the killings of the early twenties: 'Every night his father would spread open the *Belfast Telegraph* and scan the list of casualties. "Woman dear," he would say to his wife, "this is terrible. Eight Catholics. Nine Protestants." And the family would shrink from the window at the crackle of distant rifle fire. But the next night Justice would right the balance. Again the paper was spread. "Eight Protestants. Nine Catholics." Providence could be counted on, eventually.'

People – Catholics and Protestants, North and South – are reading their papers with precisely these (or corresponding) sentiments in this year 1971 – fifty years later.

Would Bertie Rodgers be as welcome now in Dublin, in these tense times, as he was when he came to prepare for the recording of these programmes? The answer, I think, is 'Yes, if he kept to the right

[1] Lewisburg (USA): Bucknell University Press, 1970.

pubs'. In the wrong pubs he might well, these days, be taken for a real spy. The thought, and its appropriateness on a metaphysical plane, would have gratified him. He liked to listen, in the right pubs, to what people were said to be saying in the wrong pubs. He was, among so much else, a very good Dubliner and Dublin loved him, in all its right pubs.

CONOR CRUISE O'BRIEN

PREFACE

It was in Dublin, 'the most oral city in Europe', that in 1942 I got engrossed in the gossip and minutiae of Irish literary history. The Second World War had started, W. B. Yeats had died, and the seas of Dublin small-talk were in turmoil again. How to capture this talk, in all its staring contradictions, its instant regurgitations of living memory, its fascinating paradoxes that would not lie flat on the page of history, continued to exercise my mind.

At the time I was Presbyterian minister in Loughgall, County Armagh. In 1941 my first volume of poetry, *Awake! And other Poems*, was published. This brought me in contact with other writers, and in 1946 Louis MacNeice persuaded me to join the BBC in London. Sound radio was expanding, experiment was in the air, and with the inception of the BBC 'Third' Programme a sort of Indian summer of the imagination evolved. Under Laurence Gilliam a group of writers and producers and skilled engineers were encouraged to explore the possibilities of sound in all its aspects on the air. We invented a new audience in England, a 'Third' audience that was assumed to be robust in its ability to accept unusual and provocative ideas, language, presentation. Also, budgets were liberal, departmental chiefs enlightened, journeys abroad were freely undertaken and people and views appeared illimitable. We saw and met people then that we shall never meet again without fear or favour.

When asked to contribute new ideas to this programme, I realised at once that here was the opportunity to collect and record in Dublin 'those things which seem to be nothing', as St Simon said, and yet which make history. I had many good friends in literary Dublin, and I was fascinated by the way they twisted in wordy wedlock, trying to get things straight. Most of the older men had taken part in the Irish Literary Movement and their talk centred on the great figures of Yeats, Joyce, George Moore, J. M. Synge, AE, as well as the more peripheral writers. Their reminiscences were curiously and characteristically at variance, and their stories uncensored. Listening to them I wondered if one could ever discover the reality from the myth, if any pattern of truth could emerge from such highly personal accounts. Perhaps by recording all the Dublin gossip and opinions about Yeats, say, or Joyce, a rounded portrait of the man might emerge. But how to get the essential Dublin talkers to speak freely with all the paraphernalia of recording gear and engineers on the scene (these were the days of 'disc' recording, before tape made it possible for everyone to do his own recording) was a problem. I decided to start on W. B. Yeats and proposed to make a symposium consisting of the voices of all the people still alive who knew him and had things to say about him. The BBC programme planners accepted the idea and I embarked on a task more formidable than I ever anticipated and which, in fact, occupied and engrossed me for the next twenty years.

'A literary movement,' said AE once, 'consists of half a dozen writers living in the same city who cordially detest one another.' Many of my talkers were not on speaking terms with one another and were inclined to frequent separate pubs. The only answer, I decided, was to record them separately and then edit and juxtapose the results. I remember asking Frank O'Connor if he would be willing to talk with another of my Dublin friends whom he had long known. 'I wouldn't be found dead in the same room with him,' said Frank. 'You'll be surprised,' I said, 'when you listen to the broadcast to hear yourself conversing with him, as it were, face to face.' As for getting Dubliners to talk freely for public broadcast, this was a continuous difficulty that could only be got over in time. Many months, and, in some cases, years, were spent in getting to know the contributors to these broadcast 'portraits', and this not because of strategy, but because one got fond of the people themselves primarily, and confidence usually followed, often most relevant when least sought for. And if, in such litigious country as Ireland, I got away with broadcast material which might have given offence in certain quarters, I owed this indulgence to the fact that I had the goodwill of my contributors.

It must be remembered that these contributors were not just the hangers-on and edgers-in of centre-pieces like Yeats, Joyce, etc.: they were rather the air and sounding-boards, the social meaning of the period. In the end I was as well-informed about the contributors as I was about the subjects I discussed with them. I could tell fairly well how trustworthy or untrustworthy each one was on a particular point. As a Presbyterian clergyman I had learned to listen to a husband's and a wife's talk, each contradictory in every respect, yet each compulsively true and equally convincing. Everybody's story, I decided, was true, the only thing wrong was 'relationship' – the only thing that mattered. These radio 'portraits' are really studies in relationship, and a 'lie' therefore could be as informative as the 'truth', and the myth as substantial as the reality. I knew very well before I finished how far any man's statement was trustworthy or factual, but truth is not the whole of life, or facts the whole of truth, and these people were, like myself, as honest as the day is long, and no more.

In general, contributors were not scripted, but spoke 'off the cuff', in this way being less likely to censor themselves when talking. But more often than not they would then have second and safer thoughts after recording, and would ask to see a script of the actual recording in order to cut it. But in the event there was little that was cut in this way. 'You may indeed have a script of what you have said,' I remarked to Maria Jolas after she had recorded an impromptu and admirably sympathetic account of Lucia Joyce's illness, 'and you may blue-pencil anything you care to blue-pencil in it. But remember, if you leave only the words "yes" and "no", I can put them in such a context that your best friends will never speak to you again.' Being an experienced newspaper correspondent, she laughed and let the matter go. In the broadcast of the first part of 'Portrait of James Joyce' St John Gogarty told the story of how he had lent Joyce a dress-suit and Joyce's sister Eva had come to collect it. As she didn't want to be seen in broad daylight carrying a gent's suit, Gogarty offered to see her home and carry it. Gogarty then described the father as a drunkard and said that the stairs seemed to have been broken up for firewood. Eva afterwards resented this and denied it strongly. 'You treated us very hard in that broadcast, Mr Rodgers,' she said. 'Yes,' I agreed, 'I did treat you hard, but you know I gave you every chance of saying your say, and if you want to contradict Gogarty I'll gladly let you do it in the next broad-cast. But I do want the truth.' She looked at me a moment and then simply said: 'James would have liked you.'

This anxiety on the part of the contributors to retrace and possibly retract their first statements was entirely understandable, since personal relationships were at stake. Also it would have been so fatally easy, in the final editing and juxtaposing of statements, to have coloured or misrepresented a contributor's words or intention, that one had to take the greatest care and give the strongest assurances. Hence too the need to make every effort to know people properly and

to let them know oneself. Needless to say, in the close, gossipy atmosphere of Dublin I was frequently warned by contributors to be wary
of the word and the motives of other contributors, and given all the
reasons therefor. All this – rule number one – I ignored, and the very
fact that one prejudged no man's word and approached him without
bias was self-asserting and resulted in many good recordings by
unlikely people. Some contributors were all too keen to tell me their
best stories on first meeting, and then, if I had no recording facilities,
I would have to check them; 'Keep it till I ask you in front of the
microphone,' I'd say, for the story would never be as fresh on second
telling.

It was not only the well-known writers who had contributions to
make; one is forever being surprised in Dublin by the high standard of
knowledge displayed by ordinary citizens in any walk or on any level of
life. I had many instances of this; as he pulled me a pint, a Dublin
publican said to me on 'Bloomsday' 1962, when the Martello Tower
was opened as a commemorative museum to James Joyce, 'I wish
Joyce had been alive now to finish the book. All that grand crowd up
there at the Tower today, he could have polished them off.' 'There's
gravel in that,' I said. 'I'll tell you something,' he said. 'I sent some of
them word last spring that there was a great old Dublin character by
the name of Ted Keogh dying in one of the hospitals there. They took
no notice. Oh there was a picture of him all right in one of the evening
papers after his death, but not a word to say that he was the man on
whom Joyce based that famous character, Blazes Boylan in *Ulysses*.
Not a word. Just teetotal indifference.' 'You've read *Ulysses*?' I asked.
'I bought it in Miss Beach's shop in Paris in 1928. The nice-looking
edition with a white cover and blue letters. It was the only book in the
window. A wonderful book that, especially for Dublin people. I think
that for other people Joyce will always be a hard one to make out.' Not
that Irishmen in general are voracious readers of books. They are not.
The late Dr Best of the National Library who appears in the library
scenes in *Ulysses* told me he had never read the book. Yeats admitted
to never having finished it. Bernard Shaw wrote me that he had never
had time to decipher *Finnegans Wake*. Synge did not read Yeats or
Shaw. James Stephens and George Moore at first meeting were aware
that each had not read the other's work. 'You and I,' said George
Moore to Dr Best, 'can be very good friends without your having to
read any of my books.' And Joyce, writing to Miss Weaver, said, 'I

have not read a work of literature for years.' All of a piece throughout. The truth is that the Irish are too fond of the spoken word to bother overmuch about the written word. 'Architecture,' said Carême, the famous French chef, 'is but another form of pâtisserie.' In the same mood Irishmen tend to look on writing as just an architected kind of talk. Ireland's best exports, in fact, are her talkers, and her best imports are listeners, and she usually manages to show a credit balance. Talk is a national industry, and always it is dramatic and colourful talk with the thrust-and-parry of debate in it.

So in this respect I couldn't have found a better hunting-ground than Ireland. After my programme on Joyce had been broadcast it was said that a new form of radio had emerged and this type of dove-tail editing of spontaneous interviews was later in BBC circles called the 'Rodgers technique'. It seemed a good way to collect biographical material and other producers tried it for programmes on English personalities. But they admitted to me it was uphill work; to get spontaneous comment and reminiscences out of any Englishman except the professional speaker or broadcaster needs a good deal more ingenuity than the odd whiskey or glass of beer. Nor does the average Englishman have the prodigious memory for the minutiae of his own history that the Irish have to a truly obsessive degree. As an official Irish church history says, 'The Irish have a great sense of history, but little sense of perspective.' Ireland carries a memory in her mouth as softly as an old retriever bitch carries an egg without breaking it. And this goes for all sorts and conditions of Irishmen, from navvies to scholars. The contrast with England is well illustrated in the following incident that happened to a friend of mine, a Dublin poet, who got a call from an English television producer. She explained that she was preparing a documentary on the Easter Rising. Was there, she inquired, any sort of inscription on the statue of Cuchulain in the Dublin GPO. The poet told her that it bore the name of the seven men who pro-claimed the Irish Republic. 'D'you think I could interview any of them?' she said. 'I'm afraid not,' said the poet, 'they're all dead.' 'Oh, did anything unusual happen to them?' 'They were executed,' replied the poet. 'But who executed them?' she asked. '*You* did, ma'am,' said the poet. There was a silence, and then she said, 'I'm so sorry.'

What makes the Irish memory so tenacious? For one thing, it is an oral memory, and Dublin, as I said, is the most oral city in Europe. The spoken word is King in Ireland which still holds the last remnants of the medieval Gaelic storytellers, whose fantastic memories (they could neither read nor write) were the repositories of the unwritten libraries of Europe. Now the storytellers are vanishing because the printed word has taken away their memory, just as television and films have replaced the fireside pictures that were once seen in the glowing peat of the hearth. I remember going to visit a Gaelic storyteller who was reputed to be the only man left in his district who could tell in the traditional manner *The King of Ireland's Son*, a tale that took him two weeks of nights in the telling. He was not at home; I found him in his enemy's house, the local cinema, watching a Wild West film. For a long-impoverished nation, with no rich urban heritage of culture, words were both portable and inexpensive, requiring only a mouth and an ear. And because the word is the only medium of communication which can convey tense and time and history, it conserves memory more than anything else. Exile tends only to sharpen the word and the memory. 'When I first came to London,' an old friend told me, 'every Irish barman had one book under the pub-counter which formed his sole reading. It was called *Speeches from the Dock* – the last words of the condemned patriots of Ireland.' Preserved in the deep-freeze of memory, they moulded the minds and attitudes of generations of Irishmen.

If I was fortunate in my speakers, I was even more fortunate in my choice of subject. The Irish Literary Movement was a most compact movement both in place and time. Dublin was the centre of its activities and the period can roughly be said to have started in the late 1890s and to have ended with the outbreak of the Second World War. Not that all of its members actually lived in Dublin or even Ireland, for it is a great characteristic of Irish writers to go into exile. The list of great Irish writers who left their motherland is long; Swift, Burke, Goldsmith, Sheridan, Farquhar, Wilde, and, in the period with which I was dealing, Yeats left Ireland when he was twenty-one, so did Shaw, and though Yeats's self-imposed exile was only temporary, Shaw never returned to live in Ireland. 'As for Ireland,' said Shaw, 'I left Ireland because I realised there was no future for me there . . . Ireland was a desert.' James Joyce left at twenty-one in 1905 and spent the remaining thirty-eight years of his life abroad. But to a friend he wrote, 'Every day and in every way I am walking the streets of Dublin.' Sean O'Casey left in 1925 after the storm over the first production of *The Plough and the Stars* and decided to stay away when the Abbey turned down his next play, *The Silver Tassie*. St John Gogarty, Frank O'Connor, Samuel Beckett, Sean O'Faolain, Denis Johnston and Padraic Colum spent many years away from Ireland. In most cases the physical reason was the need to earn a better living, but there is also for Irishmen the psychological need to distance themselves in order to enable them to turn the telescope on their native country. They leave Ireland, but Ireland never leaves them. Presented with a new country they are like the Australian aborigine who, given a new boomerang, spent the rest of his life trying to throw the old one away. With the possible exception of Shaw; he solved the problem by dropping the boomerang and leaving it where it lay.

If it is true to say that the health of a nation's literature is not to be judged by its peaks, but by its lesser heights, then Dublin had a greater concentration of 'lesser heights' than any other city, and I was lucky to know so many of them before they too, alas, passed on. Through these years of talking and recording it was often quite uncanny how I would manage to get a vital interview with someone just in the nick of time. I remember particularly when I went to see Monsignor Patrick Browne to ask him for his memories of St John Gogarty. He received me in his flat in Dublin and he told me how it was Gogarty who had brought him back to reading the classics – especially Dante. 'He gave me,' he said, 'a post-scholastic introduction to literature.' From a man as erudite as Paddy Browne this was tribute indeed, and the whole interview was, in fact, one of the most lucid and constructive recordings I ever made. But just as we had finished and the tape-recorder was switched off, Dr Browne slumped in his chair; he had had a seizure. I helped him on to a couch and called for his housekeeper. We gave him some brandy and when the doctor had been sent for I left my old friend, hoping the attack would not prove fatal and promising to visit him again when I had completed my other recordings. Three weeks later, when I was back in Dublin, I called to see him. There he was, still sitting on the same couch exactly as I had left him; it had not been possible to move him after his attack. Looking at his face drawn with pain, the only words I could find to say were, 'It's a battle, Paddy!' 'And you, Rodgers,' he replied, 'are a battlement!' A few days later he died.

So far I have spoken only of the collecting and recording of the material. But this is, of course, only part of the work involved in building a radio 'portrait'. For each of the programmes (most of which last one hour on the air) there will be anything from five to thirteen hours of recorded talk to sift and edit and finally to juggle and juxtapose into the 'spontaneous conversation' which astonished even the participants. Here is an extract from *George Bernard Shaw* to illustrate the technique. Lady Hanson knew the Shaw family well from when GBS was a child. She is speaking about his sister Lucy. Juxtaposed are St John Ervine's memories of Lucy. The two recordings were made separately.

LADY HANSON: Lucy was the star and heroine of our childhood and her coming was wildly welcomed by us young ones. We delighted in her ribald talk and her often Rabelaisian humour.

ST JOHN ERVINE: Mind you, Lucy was a pretty hard woman herself. She treated GBS very badly when he first came to London, and implored her mother to turn him out of the house. But she was a very able woman, she had great vivacity. Oscar Wilde and his brother Willie were both in love with her. And she might have married what's called well, but for some reason or another she married a second-rate actor who was no earthly use to anybody.

LADY HANSON: I retain in my memory the picture when Lucy and he swayed to and fro, his arm round her waist, to the waltz tune which recurred through the opera:

> 'I swear to be good and true
> To the maid whom I fondly adore.'

But it turned out otherwise, for he proved to be incapable of fidelity and the marriage came to an end; she sternly divorced him and no more was heard of him until, in the closing years of her life – when she was dying of a deadly consumption – he, alone and forlorn, was permitted to spend each Sunday afternoon at her house with an assignment to wind all her clocks!

ST JOHN ERVINE: The odd thing about it was that that man's family were very fond of her; a curious woman – Shaw never liked her.

The linking narrative is very important to the shaping and elucidating of the programmes, and I found that each subject imposed a different style on my narration. But I learned the hard way; for the first programme, *W. B. Yeats*, I was so anxious to let the talkers do their own talking that I kept the narrative interruptions to a minimum. The disadvantage was, of course, that listeners, except native Dubliners, found it difficult to distinguish the speakers. Added to this was the unfamiliarity to English ears of the Irish accent, a fact we soon discovered when the transcriptions of the individual recordings came back from the telediphone room with many blank spaces to indicate unintelligible words. The producer, Maurice Brown, and I then had to decipher the missing words from the recordings ourselves.

It must be emphasised how much I owe to the co-operation of Maurice Brown, who not only assisted me on most of the recording trips, but produced the whole series of programmes in the studio. Without him and all the expert and willing engineers the job could not have been done. Many patient hours were spent in small, hot studios working out the cuts and exact cues for each recorded insert. When the narration and inserts were finally 'married', the whole programme was recorded again before being broadcast.

Looking at these edited symposia of talk which I made on the heels of the events, I notice that they have one thing in common; they are shaped by my preoccupation with people and with poetry. It was not enough to record these oral memories separately and relegate them to the library shelf for correlation by future generations of scholars. However much I wished to be objective I was bound to attempt my own correlation and summing-up of them while they were still open to contemporary comment and correction. Also, I had rubbed shoulders with these raconteurs, had breathed their breath and shared their hesitancies. I knew the weight of their spoken and unspoken words in a way that no succeeding generation would know them. Therefore any assessment I might make – and editing involves assessment – would provide a useful springboard for future literary historians who might wish to reassess these pieces of oral history or put them in a new context.

Created in the first place to be *heard*, these broadcasts may offer the listener some advantage over the reader, for it is the way people say things that betrays their bias, and the overtones, hesitancies and pauses that give them away. But it is my hope that the reader may find compensation in having all the programmes under one roof, as it were. This will give him a unique opportunity to build up a composite picture of Ireland as it was more than half a century ago, of the literary renaissance which flowered so magically and died as mysteriously, and of the tragedy of the Rebellion which followed so hard on its heels.

W. B. YEATS

But names are nothing. What matter who it be,
So that his elements have grown so fine
The fume of muscatel
Can give his sharpened palate ecstasy.
No living man can drink from the whole wine.
I have mummy truths to tell
Whereat the living mock,
Though not for sober ear,
For maybe all that hear
Should laugh and weep an hour upon the clock.

Before Dante, the poet, went forth on his journey, Virgil, his guide, girded him with a reed, a reed that grew between land and water – symbol of the creative struggle. For it is on this fringe of struggle that life grows. And from this quarrelsome foreshore, Yeats's poetry sprang. He was born on debatable ground – of Anglo-Irish stock. He was reared between the ebb of Victorian faith and the flow of scepticism. He swayed and swithered between the deep sea of dream and the devil of action. And out of that dramatic clash was fashioned a character which still excites debate amongst Dubliners.

FRANK O'CONNOR: There was a peculiar sort of innocence about the man – an extraordinary innocence.

SEAN O'FAOLAIN: I confess I never warmed to him because I felt there was an absence of *bonhomie* and simplicity about his nature, at any rate as he presented it when one met him. Whether that was part of a pose or of a mask that he put on I don't know, but it kept one at a certain distance. I respect that. Certainly there was no reason why he shouldn't go masked if he wanted to, but you would sometimes wish that he'd drop it and say 'Hello', or talk in a natural way, as we talk among ourselves.

O'CONNOR: But I think he did. I never felt any of that difficulty that you seem to have felt with him at all. Yeats only posed when he was shy or embarrassed. I kept on telling people, 'Now for God's sake don't call him sir, because if you call him sir he'll start posing.'

W. K. MAGEE: It would be very hard to say whether he was simple or not, but I don't think he was a poseur – certainly not consciously.

O'FAOLAIN: I remember once Edward Garnett told me how, when he was very young and they were both poor (in the days when W. B. used to have to black his heels so as to cover up the holes in his stockings), they'd walk from his digs to Edward's digs and back again, and back again, all night long, absolutely forgetting everything in the most natural way. And once Edward invited him down for a week-end to his country cottage, and he arrived with nothing but a toothbrush and a bit of soap. Edward said he was absolutely innocent. That was quite evident, there was no pretence about it, although he had seen the same man in the box at – I forget what theatre – when a play of his was on, standing up as he used to do in the Abbey Theatre at the head of the stairs, looking around. On view. Clearly an actor.

AUSTIN CLARKE: He'd also something else we couldn't copy, that was a marvellous black lock of hair; when he spoke and chanted and waved his arms, the lock of hair would fall over his brow, and with a gesture he would fling it back, and then it would fall down again. Well, we didn't know how he had trained it.

O'CONNOR: I remember when I was first in Dublin, going to a party and being very shy. Mrs Yeats signalled to me to come and sit beside her. She said, 'I knew you were shy, because you did exactly as Willie does when he's shy, you ran your hand through your hair.' And after that I just looked to see what he did with his hands and I saw that the man was frequently shy.

O'FAOLAIN: Let's try and get an example of this alleged pose which I say he had. Was it a habit or was it conscious? The way he had of not recognising people, who themselves felt that he must really know them perfectly well. A way of saying 'Hello Tierney' when it was really Binchy, or of saying when he meets Mary Colum in the street – she told me herself – intoning 'I hear a voice from across the seas. It is a girl's voice but I do not know whose it is'.

O'CONNOR: Yes, he would say that, if he knew the person concerned.

When he went into a room it was always a toss-up whether he would behave as a shy man and go up to Tierney, as you say, and say 'Hello Binchy', trying to pretend that he knew him, or whether, as he more often did, with me at any rate, he would just hold out his hand and say, 'Who have I?' That was the admission that he was blind, which he didn't like to make normally.

DOSSY WRIGHT: That is quite right because he has passed me time out of number in the street. If I didn't want to speak to him I didn't bother, but if I had to speak to him I went up to him, and he knew me at once, but otherwise his head would be in the air and he'd pass anyone. His thoughts were miles away.

BRINSLEY MACNAMARA: I remember one such meeting with him myself. He brought me walking round Stephens Green. And as we went around he told me lots of things about plays, and he finished up by saying something which may have some bearing upon what we're trying to work out now about whether it was a pose or not with him. He said, 'A man, an author, should always try to keep the company of his superiors, never of his inferiors.'

O'CONNOR: A very wise remark. Very wise.

DR RICHARD BEST: Well, he was always very dignified, and he wasn't without a sense of humour, but when he said something humorous, because he saw the humorous side of things, he bent his head and clasped his hands together as if he were washing them in invisible soap and laughed slightly, but always in a most dignified way. Yeats, so far as I can remember him, was always in full dress, as it were; he never let himself down. I used to think that, if he had been called upon to play the part of Pontifex Maximus, he would do it most naturally, without ever having to act. He was always like that. But to tell you the truth, I never felt quite at my ease with Yeats, as I did with George Moore, let us say, and other people, because Yeats was always on a plane, as it were, above me; he always lifted the conversation into a higher plane.

MACNAMARA: The only thing he never really got used to was the fact that poets and writers might be found sometimes in the public houses of the town, and he never ventured into one of them. There's a story that Yeats once approached Fred Higgins and he said, 'Higgins, do you know I have never been in a pub in my life and I'd like to go into a pub.' So Higgins came to me and he asked me what was the most likely pub now to which we might bring Yeats without horrifying him too much by what he'd see there in the shape of literature and other things. And we decided on one pub, and Higgins went along with him there, and they called for some mild drink and Yeats looked around and he said, 'Higgins, I don't like it. Lead me out again.'

O'FAOLAIN: There's no trouble about meeting O'Casey or O'Flaherty in a pub, and talking to them and chatting as man to man, which you never could do with Yeats. It seemed to me he did put a barrier between himself and his fellow men by the technique that he employed.

O'CONNOR: You see, the real problem is that Sean [O'Faolain] is assuming all through that it's necessary and desirable that poets should sit in pubs and call one another, as we do, Sean etc. I don't think that's proved.

O'FAOLAIN: I don't think it's necessary, I think it occasionally happens – I personally very rarely go into pubs, but I'm capable of doing it on occasions, and I think if it *never* happens then a poet is liable to be thrown into an extraordinary kind of isolation, and may develop what I can only call a sort of fake Brahminism. And it seems to me that that poet's technique of protecting poetry may result in a fake Brahminism that must infect his own work.

O'CONNOR: Well, I maintain that infect is the wrong word, and that poetry *is* Brahminism – it's the soul of a man alone with himself.

O'FAOLAIN: That is a nineteenth-century romantic conception of poetry.

O'CONNOR: Very well, it *is* a romantic conception of poetry, but it is none the less a conception of poetry.

O'FAOLAIN: That takes Yeats back to William Morris, and Ernest Dowson, and Francis Thompson, and Pater, and Dobson, Lionel Johnson, and to Beardsley . . .

O'CONNOR: And to Dante?

O'FAOLAIN: To all that Yeats grew up with as a young man during fifteen of the most influential years of his life in London towards the end of the century, years during which he wrote some of his most mannered and artificial poetry. His great triumph was to shake off that influence. It took years and years.

MACNAMARA: But didn't the bulk of Yeats's poetry come out of that romantic conception of poetry, or out of the period when that was the conception of poetry that it maintains?

O'FAOLAIN: That's true, and I have no doubt that probably Yeats sitting at his desk and writing his poetry was, as it were, perfectly natural and innocent with himself so long as he didn't let that thing infect him. The outward signs were in his manner of dress: the cane, the lovely grey suit, the carefully chosen colours, the long hair, the flowing tie. All that theatrical pose must have come between him and his own natural self.

O'CONNOR: Bless my soul – that a man's taste in shirts stands between him and his own natural self – where is art getting to?

O'FAOLAIN: Down the drain of *fin-de-siècle* romanticism.

O'CONNOR: Well, the other thing is just getting down the drain of sloppy democratic feeling – I mean, you just be dirty because everybody else is dirty.

O'FAOLAIN: Oh come, come! There's no need to go to that extreme. T. S. Eliot wrote his poetry absolutely personally, absolutely originally, in a rolled umbrella and a bowler hat coming out of a bank.

O'CONNOR: Well, don't you feel that *that* poetry had been infected, in your own word, by the umbrella?

O'FAOLAIN: No, I do *not*. I think it was necessary for Eliot to live like a Londoner in order that he should get down to the reality of his time, place and self.

CLARKE: Well, I think that it is a great pity that the poet, like the soldier, the clergyman and many others, hasn't some specific dress, or at least part of a dress to distinguish him, say, from the businessman. As a young poet I wore an enormous bow-tie – it was of shimmering gold and green – and I was very proud of it. The reason I wore that bow-tie was because in Dublin all the poets wore a bow-tie. Yeats, appearing frequently at the Abbey Theatre, had a magnificent black tie, which we could copy in other colours. But when I came to London for the first time I found that poets no longer wore any specific sign or symbol of their art. They were all dressed in hard stiff white collars, like businessmen. It was the time of the Georgian school, and I think it would have been better for the Georgian poets if they had worn flowing ties. It might have saved them from the terrible rush and pressure of the modern world. It might have protected their art. Look what happened to the Georgian school. I attribute that solely to the fact that they did not wear flowing ties, like the Irish poets!

O'FAOLAIN: Do you never get the feeling that Yeats is an old-fashioned poet belonging to an old-fashioned period?

MACNAMARA: But yet he was able to go on and adapt himself to the new realistic time and the new conception of poetry. You consider Yeats's later work – it's altogether in contrast to the earlier, and to that romantic conception of poetry.

O'FAOLAIN: The gods were good to him. They let him live long into his maturity. But he is a nineteenth-century poet. Our last romantic.

MACNAMARA: I think he was always pretty near to the realistic quality of his own country. Even when he was living in the days of pose, in the big tie and a velvet coat in London, he could write very realistically about the death of Parnell, and the effect it was going to have upon his country.

O'FAOLAIN: You mentioned the name of Parnell. Probably Parnell and old John O'Leary the Fenian were his two great heroes, men who, like himself, had gone down into the gutter. But you remember in his autobiography he says, 'You must *not* go down into the gutter if you want to have authority over people. You must keep yourselves from them.' He did live a remote and isolated life, and the result of it was that he *could* speak with the voice of authority. AE didn't, and he did not speak with the voice of authority. Nobody today has the same authority that he had.

O'CONNOR: That was really what motivated his kind of Fascism; it wasn't Fascism, it was a worship of dictatorships, of authority.

MRS ISEULT STUART: One day he presented me to an extremely vulgar lady with a title, whom I, being very young, snubbed, not out of snobbishness but out of extreme shyness. He was extremely indignant about that. He thought that to snub a person with a title – no matter how obtained – was a horrid thing and not at all correct. Nevertheless, although he had this love of titles, although he thought it was a great thing to be a senator, he did love real nobility.

O'CONNOR: He used to jeer at my Socialism. 'Damned Utopianism,' he'd say.

> How can I, that girl standing there,
> My attention fix
> On Roman or on Russian
> Or on Spanish politics?...
> And maybe what they say is true
> Of war and war's alarms,
> But O that I were young again
> And held her in my arms!

LENNOX ROBINSON: Well, Frank, my impression of Yeats, of course, is about twenty years or more earlier than yours, when I came up from the wilds of County Cork, not knowing anything, only having written a couple of plays and meeting Mr Yeats at the Nassau Hotel with Lady Gregory. I'd never met either of them before. It was afternoon and Mr Yeats was late; he came in not in the magnificent way that you're talking of, but remember this is twenty years earlier...

O'CONNOR: Twenty years humbler. You must remember that when I met Yeats first, he was an old, very authoritative, rather Olympian figure: very tall, very dignified, all his gestures were sweeping, his voice had a soft, oratorical cadence which comes back into my ears even now. There must have been another and very different Yeats when he was younger, because I remember AE describing him with a sort of longing in his voice, the boy with a beard, as AE used to say, who used to come into his bedroom at two o'clock in the morning to recite some new poem which he'd written.

MAGEE: I was at school with Yeats. He was a much older boy than I – he seemed to me quite a young man, he had a beard. I got to know him quite well and we were friends. We used to sit together in class and I even used to cog from him in examinations. He was a little uncertain, I think, with the headmaster, Mr Wilkins. He wanted to start a naturalist club in the high school, and I remember sitting opposite the two of them when they were talking and noticing the smile on Wilkins's face while Yeats was talking. He didn't take him seriously.

And he used to call him 'the flighty poet'. He came in quite casually and went off whenever he wanted. He would announce that he wouldn't be there tomorrow and so on, in a way that excited my envy. I remember being greatly struck by his making friends with a very unpopular boy, walking up and down with him, and I was wondering what they were talking about. And I think it was simply a sort of interest in the soul of this boy that made him talk to him.

O'CONNOR: 'Soul claps its hands and sing and louder sing
For every tatter in its mortal dress.'

BEST: I remember hearing Yeats give a lecture – it may have been an Irish Literary Society lecture – I think it was the late Dr Sigerson who was in the chair, and I was tremendously impressed by Yeats's final remarks, where he quoted something of an Italian poet who described the way he was being tossed about in a storm and he saw amid the waves a flame, and he recognised that that flame was his own soul, and if the waves overwhelmed it then he was lost for ever, but gradually the storm subsided and the flame burned bright, and Yeats said, 'That is Ireland,' and he wound up his address in this most impressive way. That was Yeats at his very best, I remember. Old John O'Leary came in . . .

Beautiful lofty things: O'Leary's noble head;
. . . Maud Gonne at Howth station waiting a train,
Pallas Athene in that straight back and arrogant head:
All the Olympians; a thing never known again.

MAUD GONNE MCBRIDE: I was twenty, and William was twenty-one when we first met, and it was through John O'Leary. Willie's father was painting his picture and I never saw a more beautiful head than John O'Leary had. Willie and I had the deepest admiration for him. As I said, Willie was then twenty-one and I was twenty, and he was extremely proud of that one year's seniority. He looked much younger than I did, because he was rather a dishevelled art student – for he intended to be a painter like his father. John O'Leary used to say, 'Your vocation is to be a poet. You have that in you,' and then he would make him read some of his early poems.

Had I the heavens' embroidered cloths,
Enwrought with golden and silver light,
The blue and the dim and the dark cloths

Of night and light and the half-light,
I would spread the cloths under your feet:
But I, being poor, have only my dreams;
I have spread my dreams under your feet;
Tread softly because you tread on my dreams.

MADAME MCBRIDE: 'Don't you understand in the spiritual world, in the faery world here,' he would say, 'everything is the reverse. Therefore your poems are children, and I'm the father and you're the mother.'

I am like the children O my beloved
and I play at marriage – I play with images of the life
you will not give to me O my cruel one.

'My real use to Willie,' says Madame McBride, 'was that I kept him in close touch with the people.' But as always with Yeats, hand and head were divided. In the struggle for Young Ireland 'one part of me,' he said, 'looked on, mischievous and mocking.'

MADAME MCBRIDE: Willie and I fought very hard; he went on all those committees really to help me more than anything else; but he was wonderful at a committee meeting and used to be able to carry things very often.

O but we dreamed to mend
Whatever mischief seemed
To afflict mankind, but now
The winds of winter blow
Learn that we were crack-pated when we dreamed.

Between the deep sea of dreams and the devil of deeds, Yeats swung for many years. When Maud Gonne at last went from him, the withdrawing wave of love left him high and dry in 'the desolation of reality'. More and more, as a result, he became a realist. The firm man of affairs, the alert leader. Always on the spot – or was he?

MRS STUART: I have known him to be wonderfully on the spot when he absolutely had to be, when there was nobody, no grown-up, extrovert grown-up, to take the burden, but when there were tiresome things like, when travelling together, seeing to the luggage, or getting a cab or anything like that, then Willy would fall into a great abstraction, from which I learnt a great lesson myself, not to be there on these occasions.

ROBINSON: Look at his connection with the BBC. He gave certainly three recitals for the BBC, every time they loved him more and more, and they gave him more and more money, and in the end they wanted to give him the best battery, the best whatever they could do to his home in Rathfarnham, and they said, 'Have you got electric light in the home?' He had to wire back to his wife to find whether they had electric light in the home – he hadn't.

ANNE YEATS: We acquired a wireless. For a long time he wouldn't have one, he didn't like them, then when we acquired one, the first evening it was turned on, he was listening to it, and he couldn't hear very well, so he put his hand to his ear, and said, 'I beg your pardon?'

O'CONNOR: Yes, I can well believe he was impractical.

ROBINSON: He wasn't impractical! He could do a balance sheet better than anybody I know.

WRIGHT: But he was an extraordinary man in that way meeting with the company. He would be talking of the Greek gods or something, and then he'd suddenly say, 'Well, we've heard all these figures, but what I want to know is what we have lost and what we have gained in pure simple words.'

BERTIE SMYLLIE: I think I was the first person, certainly the first person in this country, to know that Yeats had won the Nobel Prize. I was on duty at the *Irish Times* office that night, when the message came over the Creed machine to say that for the first time an Irish poet had won the prize, which amounted to quite a considerable sum, I think between seven and eight thousand pounds. I was rather friendly with Yeats at the time, and it was fairly late in the evening, getting on to eleven o'clock I suppose, and I rang him up at his house, hoping that he didn't know the news. He came to the phone himself – he *didn't* know the news. I said, 'Mr Yeats, I've got very good news for you, a very great honour has been conferred upon you,' and I was rather enthusiastic and gushing at the time, and I said, 'This is a great honour not only for you but for the country,' and I could tell that he was getting slightly impatient to know what it was all about, so I said, 'You've been awarded the Nobel Prize, a very great honour to you and a very great honour to Ireland,' and to my amazement the only question he asked was, 'How much, Smyllie, how much is it?'

ROBINSON: Well, I say he was tough. I say that from the moment I met him he was tough, and he was tougher and tougher as his years went on; and when he was a senator and when he had this position and when he defended divorce and when he defended censorship he said, 'Nobody can touch me, because I'm so important.' And on this question of censorship he said, 'I want to read all the dirty English Sunday papers because I will read the last words of every murderer. Whereas, if I buy the *Observer*, I will read the last words – alas! not the *last* words – of St John Ervine on the theatre.'

MRS STUART: I remember Yeats telling me that the greatest prose line that was ever written which had its own particular prose rhythm – which was as great as verse rhythm – was in Emerson: 'The stars, the stars everlasting are fugitives also.'

ARTHUR HANNAH: I can remember Yeats well, he came into our shop quite a lot. As a matter of fact, all he bought from us were detective novels. On one occasion he came into me, reprimanded me, said I had sold him a detective novel in which there was far too much detection. Well, then I sold him an Edgar Wallace and he went out very happy.

ANNE YEATS: Detective stories and Wild West might not seem to come under the category of what I call guided reading, but father read a great many of them, though mother always had to vet them to make quite sure that they had happy endings. But about the Wild Wests, too; when he was ailing in Majorca, he was very ill at the time, and delirious, I remember he was telling mother, 'George, George, call the sheriff!'

> Two natures in him mixed,
> One fugitive, one fixed,
> The innocent and the tough
> Were one and the same stuff;
> Between contraries he grew. He knew
> That only in soil the soul grows, and drew
> Clouds from the clod, and strength from each rebuff.

MACNAMARA: He began to be altogether more natural, and towards the end of the period when he was a senator here, he spoke and acted rather like any ordinary man. He played golf and went around.

SMYLLIE: Well, of course, the idea of WB taking up golf was rather amusing to us who knew him, and he came to me and suggested that possibly I might help him, so I did. I was a member of a Club called Camikmines, and of course the Great Man left everything in my hands; there was another young man called Duncan, and we had to provide all the clubs, we had to do everything. I'd a small car, a little MG, and the first day we were going up, I handed WB his bag, and he said, 'Smyllie, this is my quiver' – he always insisted on calling his golf bag his quiver. However, we started off, we played several times, and he'd make a wild swipe at the ball, let the club fall on the ground, and walk off with his hands behind his back in the characteristic Yeatsian fashion, leaving myself and Duncan to pick up the quiver and the club and to look for the ball, which was very important – for the ball was very rarely to be found. He used to drive the ball into a clump of furze bushes or into a ditch or anywhere, about, say, ten yards from the tee, and we lost several balls this way. But a rather characteristic thing about this was that the next game we went out to play, WB noticed we had been losing all these balls and we had been providing him with new ones – not new ones, actually, we knew too much about it for that – but old ones. The next day he came out, and every time he hit the ball and lost it, he used to produce a half-crown from his pocket, and hand the half-crown either to myself or to Duncan in compensation for the ball that had been lost.

ANNE YEATS: We used to play croquet quite a lot in Rathfarnham. He was a very good croquet player and he used to hit a ball at the far end, seemed to concentrate a lot on it, and I don't think he played to win, but I think he liked winning the game like anybody else. I remember somebody came to tea and cheated to let him win, and he never played with her again.

Norah McGuinness remembers taking part.

NORAH MCGUINNESS: That was a singular honour, because very few people I think were asked to play croquet with him. I believe he took the game very seriously indeed and really enjoyed winning a game, so I feel that I did what I was supposed to that day, because he won the game, but then I'd never played croquet before.

MISS MACNIE: He was very anxious to play it, and one time they took a house out in the country and there was a croquet lawn there, and he was very anxious to come up against some competitor. So he asked a friend of mine if she could produce some person to play a game with him. She produced a young daughter of hers who had never played a game in her life before. However, she played the game with WB and it was impossible not to win because WB's shots were not the best in the world. At the end of the game he looked very disconsolate and, as my friend put it, if it had been announced to the world that he was the worst poet in the world he couldn't have looked more dejected. And he walked across to my friend and he said to her: 'You must have had her trained.'

MRS STUART: Willy walked on land rather like a swan or a pelican without too much certitude but was very different in the water. He was a wonderful swimmer and could swim for ages under water and reappear after a great distance. When we were bathing together, I was always struck by the extraordinary agility and ease he had in the water and athletic power. He was also very fond of kites. We had bought one which he said was inadequate, and he himself altered this thing, and used to run along the shore on a windy day, and the kite flew at a great height and that was a great pastime.

SEAN MCBRIDE: He used to come and spend some time with us in the summer at a house at the seaside in Normandy – a place called Colville, not very far from Bayeux. He used to be very keen on flying kites, and we used to spend hours together on a long strand flying them. He was able to get kites to a marvellous height. He'd apparently always been keen on it, because I remember he told me that his father in Sligo made some kites which he flew. After that, my next vivid recollection of Yeats was when my mother was in prison in England in 1918. I went to stay with Yeats and Mrs Yeats in Galway, outside Gort, near Coole, near Lady Gregory's house.

O'CONNOR: Oh, Lady Gregory was a terrifying old lady, and I was once telling Mrs Yeats how terrified I used to be of her, and she said, 'Oh well, Willie was the same. After we got married we went to stay at Coole, and Willie felt it was really time to assert himself. I suppose he was getting on for fifty at the time, he was a famous man, a most distinguished man, and a married man, and he felt he simply must break the rules of Coole House. Now one of the rules was that you could not have animals in the house, and WB, being famous and married and middle-aged, decided that he must defy the laws of Coole House and bring Pangur. So Pangur was duly brought on the train, and loaded on to the side-car to take them to Coole House. But half-way up the drive to Coole, the famous public man suddenly got cold feet at the thought of the frosty visage of that old lady in the big house, and he tapped the driver on the shoulder and said, 'Drive to the stables,' and Pangur was put into the stables and late that night, when the old lady was fast asleep, WB went down in his slippers and rescued Pangur and brought him up to his bedroom, so that he never really succeeded in asserting himself against the old lady up to the day of her death.

Now, Anne, tell us something about what it's like to be the child of a famous man.

ANNE YEATS: I think chiefly, almost the first thing I remember – at least, I don't remember, I was told it – was calling him Willie when I was still in my pram, and a voice coming out of the window, firmly saying, 'You are not to call your father Willie!' and then I replied, 'Willie Dada, Willie Dada,' which I take it didn't go down very well, either.

MAGEE: I don't wonder because everyone in Dublin called him 'Willy' and I think it rather irritated him. The name that he said was the finest name was Michael, I think. I was rather interested when he called his son by that name.

MISS MACNIE: Even people who knew him a great deal better than I did have never mentioned that he was a perfectly splendid father, and that Mrs Yeats was an equally splendid mother and wife. But to me, meeting him as I sometimes did at teatime, when he came in, he was perfectly delightful with his children. And it really was a very amusing thing to watch WB coming in with his head well up as he always held it, and with his hands clasped behind his back followed by Michael who, by the way, never spoke until he was about four years of age, and who at that time was about two feet high; he used to walk in after his father in the most sedate manner possible, with his hands clasped behind his back and keeping pace with his father, exactly like his father, just a miniature image of him. It always used to make me laugh every time he did it. Anne was very amusing too. She was wiser than Michael, and when her father would come in after he had played bears or elephants with Michael, he used to lie down flat on a sofa between the two windows and this was part of a game apparently, because Anne would always run across the room, open the door, go outside, shut it, then bang it open and rush across the room and jump flat on her father's prostrate body on the sofa.

There was another side, too, when it mattered.

MISS MACNIE: Oh yes. Anne and I discussed a point about that at one time. I said to Anne, 'Were you afraid of your father?' And she said, 'I was terrified of him.' And I said, 'Well, what an extraordinary thing, so was I.' He was the only person in the world I ever was frightened of, and I was, I was afraid of her father. I said, 'Why was it?' 'I don't know,' said Anne, 'there's no explanation so far as I'm concerned, because he never laid a finger on us, he didn't believe in corporal punishment, and he never touched either Michael or me – never punished us in any way – and yet I was afraid of him.'

ANNE YEATS: We had to be frightfully quiet really about the house generally; I remember once Mike and I were fighting, rather more than usual, and mother couldn't cope with us, so she sent father in. He just sat down in the chair, and intoned in full voice, 'Let dogs delight to bark and bite' and then got up and went out of the room. He was rather awe-inspiring, I think, on the whole. You always had to stay rather quiet, and then he was writing quite a lot.

MRS YEATS: Yes. He had to be absolutely alone, so completely alone that even when an infant was in the room and silent, he had still to be alone, because no personality must be there at all. It wasn't a matter of merely being spoken to or interrupted or anything else, but he had to be in absolute isolation in a room wherever he was writing.

O'CONNOR: He was one of the hardest workers that I have ever come across. I know George Moore jeers at this business about his writing four lines in a day and his reaching his record of seven lines. But if you'd seen exactly how much labour those four or seven lines had cost him, you wouldn't think it was anything like a bad day's work; because he would recite a single line hundreds and hundreds of times in succession. Even in the middle of a conversation with you – he would be talking about politics perhaps, and quite suddenly he would lift the right hand and would begin to beat time and you would hear him recite a line a couple of times and then the hand would drop again and he'd go on with the conversation, just as though nothing had happened.

'My poetry costs me endless labour,' said Yeats. *'Other people write fine poetry with no trouble at all to themselves.'*

MRS STUART: For most poets it seems to me that concealment and secrecy is necessary before their work can come to anything, whereas with Yeats, it was quite different. He had to exteriorise everything he wrote before he wrote it in talk and discussions, and even ask for advice, and then he would begin to write the first draft and talk it over more, and the second and so on.

> Everything he wrote was read,
> After certain years he won
> Sufficient money for his need,
> Friends that have been friends indeed;
> 'What then?' sang Plato's ghost. 'What then?'

ROBINSON: He was an awfully human person, because he loved his children, he loved birds.

> All his happier dreams came true –
> A small old house, wife, daughter, son,
> Grounds where plum and cabbage grew,
> Poets and Wits about him drew;
> 'What then?' sang Plato's ghost. 'What then?'
>
> 'The work is done', grown old he thought,
> 'According to my boyish plan;
> Let the fools rage, I swerved in naught,
> Something to perfection brought';
> But louder sang that ghost, 'What then?'
>
> What shall I do with this absurdity –
> O heart, O troubled heart – this caricature,
> Decrepit age that has been tied to me
> As to a dog's tail?
>   Never had I more
> Excited, passionate, fantastical
> Imagination, nor an ear and eye
> That more expected the impossible –
> No, not in boyhood when with rod and fly,

Or the humbler worm, I climbed Ben Bulben's back
And had the livelong summer day to spend.
It seems that I must bid the Muse go pack,
Choose Plato and Plotinus for a friend
Until imagination, ear and eye,
Can be content with argument and deal
In abstract things.

SMYLLIE: You know, I never believed that WB knew anything much about philosophy, though he talked a great deal about it, but he invented a philosophy of his own, which was rather amusing. One very interesting and amusing thing occurred, when he was expounding this highly esoteric theory of his one night up in the Arts Club. And among those present was a little man called Cruise O'Brien, a very brilliant journalist, and one of the very few people who could be rude with impunity to WB. WB gave him, as he very often gave me, a fool's pardon. This night, at any rate, he was expounding this philosophy of his which was connected in some queer way with the phases of the moon; he was telling us all about the twenty-eight phases of the moon and he had equated every phase against some historical figure. He said, 'Number one – the highest phase – is perfect beauty.' With a respectful silence for a few seconds we all listened, and then he said, 'Number two was Helen of Troy – the nearest approximation to perfect beauty.' And he went right round the twenty-eight, or rather twenty-seven, phases and finally he came to the last, and then he said that the lowest form of all is Thomas Carlyle and all Scotsmen. This shook us all a little bit and Cruise O'Brien spoke up at once, 'WB,' he said – he'd a very mincing voice, Cruise – 'have you ever read a word of Carlyle? You say Carlyle is the lowest form. Oh come! Have you ever read a word of Carlyle?' 'Carlyle, Cruise, was a dolt,' said WB. 'But I insist, WB, did you ever read one single word of Carlyle?' 'Carlyle, I tell you, was a dolt.' 'Yes, but you haven't read him.' 'No, I have not read him, my wife, George, has read him and she tells me he's a dolt.' That was the end of the philosophical treatise for the night.

MRS STUART: I think the main idea was that the human cycle was similar to lunar months but divided into twenty-eight periods of successive reincarnations. But I really think I'm not quite the person to talk about the phases of the moon, because Yeats gave me such a very flattering position in it, placing me phase fourteen, which is one of as near complete beauty on earth as can be attained, and as near complete subjectivity also, because at phase fifteen you do not incarnate on earth. Similar in beauty but beginning to work towards objectivity is phase sixteen at which he placed my mother, but there the first impulse is towards action again. I had a cat, a black Persian, in Normandy at the time when the thought of the phases of the moon was beginning to take shape in his mind and this cat used to dance wonderfully in the moonlight, take huge leaps. And in a queer way, I think that gave the kind of poetic urge to the idea which otherwise would have been a little bit too coldly philosophical.

In the half-light, between reason and unreason, Yeats's imagination leaped and circled. 'I cannot explain it,' he said once, 'but I am certain that every high thing was invented in this way, between waking and sleeping.'

But it was Mrs Yeats – herself a remarkable medium – who supplied him with the impulsive images which he elaborated into his highly mystical metaphysical system. 'George's ghosts,' he said, 'educated me.' And he built his philosophy into a book called A Vision. *'I don't know,' he wrote, 'what my book will be to others – nothing perhaps. To me it means a last act of defence against the chaos of the world.'*

NORAH MCGUINNESS: His book, *A Vision*, had just been published, and he started talking about it over dinner. I think it was even at the first course he started talking about it. So I said to him that unfortunately I hadn't read his book, I'd only heard it discussed. I don't know what sort of kink Mr Yeats had, but he got it into his head that I'd read his book. I even hesitate now when I think of that dinner, because there were about five courses to be got through and Mr Yeats started asking me my opinion on various aspects of the book, about various passages, and I tried to assure him again, 'No, I haven't read it, Mr Yeats.' He seemed to ignore that, but fortunately for me when he asked me a question he didn't seem to expect an answer. So I struggled through the fish and the entrée and fruit, whatever it was – and I felt at the end I had come through fairly well, because I hadn't given away the fact that I hadn't read the book, seeing that he'd made up his mind that I had.

Well, it was one of his famous Monday evenings, which as everyone knows were very sacred evenings, inasmuch as women were never admitted to these evenings. I thought that perhaps I'd be released when I left the dining-room, but not at all. Mr Yeats said, 'Come up to the study.' So I thought, 'Oh well, it's only for a few minutes and I'll be asked to go.' So I went up to the study and there were several young men whom I was introduced to. I don't remember who the young men were, except one who was Sean O'Faolain, and years afterwards he told me it was also his first visit to Yeats, and he was really more in awe of me than Mr Yeats, because he thought I was the blue-stocking of all the world at that time.

MISS MACNIE: There was a young man who came across here from England, a rather objectionable and pushing young man, who came uninvited to one of WB's evenings. He was announced by the maid and found himself in the room with WB and George Russell standing at the mantelpiece talking busily to one another. WB saw him, I think, but he took no notice whatever. He was an uninvited guest and as such WB didn't acknowledge him. The young man walked across the room, stood beside WB and George Russell for a moment or two and then went across and sat down in a chair beside a friend in the corner. WB paused for a moment or two, looked across at the corner and then very slowly and very, very erect walked forward to the corner and said very politely to him, 'Sir, you have not been invited. You are not welcome. Will you please go.' And he walked across the room and opened the door and closed it after this young man.

CLARKE: So far as the younger generation of poets are concerned, here in Ireland, Yeats was rather like an enormous oak-tree which, of course, kept us in the shade, and did exclude a great number of the rays of, say, the friendly sun; and of course we always hoped that in the end we would reach the sun, but the shadow of that great oak-tree is still there.

O'CONNOR: He lived a deep interior life and all the outside things counted practically for nothing – unless he concentrated on remembering them. I remember his once quoting to me a lovely poem of Eleanor Wylie's and he quoted it with an intensity of passion that I never heard him give any other poem. 'Live with a velvet mole: go burrow underground.' And he burrowed underground quite a lot. I got the impression that right up to the end he remained a very shy, gentle creature.

MRS YEATS: Yes, a great many people thought this. I often felt it was very sad that there were so many people that he himself would have liked to meet. I will just give you one example only, and that was Arnold Toynbee. He only met him in the last year of his life, and he was introduced to him one lunch by Miss Hilda Matheson. He'd longed to meet him for, I may almost say, years, because he thought that his thought was part of his own scheme. And you see, that meant a great deal to him, that meeting. But he would never have written to Toynbee to ask him if he might go and see him. That was a curious kind of shyness on his part that he wouldn't approach the great man.

CLARKE: Well now, that is rather curious. I'd gone down to the Seven Woods at Coole as a very young enthusiast in a romantic way, and I crossed a wall into the domain, and came into a dark wood which was surely the Wicked Wood of the poem, in which there was a witch, and then I saw another bright wood ahead, and I moved towards that. Suddenly through the leaves I saw a glimpse of blue, and for a moment, being very young, I almost felt here was an elemental spirit; and then I said no, if this is the great domain, it's a peacock. I crept forward, I looked through the leaves, and there, crossing the grass towards a Georgian house, I saw a tall figure in a marvellous sky-blue watered silk raincoat holding fishing-rods and lines and all that fierce tackle of the country gentleman, and I said to myself, I'm in the wrong domain, this cannot be the Seven Woods. Then I looked again, and I recognised dimly from those frontispieces of the books that it was the poet himself, disguised as a great country gentleman and sportsman; as a young romantic poet of the Irish movement, I was shocked and disappointed.

> Between land and water he grew,
> Between low and high,
> To both the man ran true,
> Arrogant, shy.
> Enough that out of the two
> (And their commotion)
> The salt root rose and grew
> Into a green reed, a wavering blade
> That between land's night and sky's light
> Saw red, ran wild, and tongued the imperturbable ocean.

Malachi Stilt-Jack am I, whatever I learned has run wild,
From collar to collar, from stilt to stilt, from father to child.
All metaphor, Malachi, stilts and all. A barnacle goose

Far up in the stretches of night; night splits and the dawn
    breaks loose;
I, through the terrible novelty of light, stalk on, stalk on;
Those great sea-horses bare their teeth and laugh at the
    dawn.

JAMES JOYCE

PART I: A PORTRAIT OF JOYCE AS A YOUNG MAN

James Augustine Joyce, author of Ulysses *and* Finnegans Wake, *was born in February 1882 in Dublin City. He was born between two worlds and two ages – the Age of Faith, in which men brought rabbits out of a hat, and the Age of Reason or Science, in which they bring habits out of a rat. Faced by this dilemma, Joyce's answer was enigmatic and inclusive. He was at once a traditionalist and a revolutionary. He was the most devout literary craftsman of his century; yet he was the playboy of the Western word. He had one subject only – himself; and one setting – his native city: yet he made himself the measure of mankind, and he made Dublin the mirror and manifold of the world.*

NIALL SHERIDAN: That's very curious, because I was trying to trace down some information about Joyce in Dublin, and I was reduced to going to the local Civic Guards' barracks – the Guards are always very knowledgeable men. I went in, and discovered the station sergeant who was on duty, and of course he was straight out of 'Lady Gregory', an enormous man, very comfortable-looking. So I inquired about the whereabouts of this address which was connected with Mr James Joyce, the well-known writer, who was recently dead. And this man scratched his head, and said, 'Would he be from Connemara?' So I explained that he had antecedents in Connemara, but this man was a well-known writer who had died in Zürich. 'Was he a teacher?' said he. 'I knew a Joyce, a teacher, that died foreign. Would that be him?'

And, says Niall Sheridan, the same thing happened with the undertaker, Corny Kelleher, who figures in Ulysses.

SHERIDAN: I asked him about John Stanislaus, Joyce's father, and he was a bit vague, and then I said, 'Do you remember James Joyce?' 'Ah,' said he, 'I buried so many Joyces in my time. I couldn't be bothered,' said he. 'I don't know. I don't know. I might have seen him.'

Who did see him? Let us go back fifty years, with George Roberts. He and a friend were looking at a pamphlet in a newsagent's window in Sackville Street, Dublin.

GEORGE ROBERTS: It was an essay by our mutual friend Sheehy-Skeffington. But our interest was on a second item entitled 'The Day of the Rabblement' by one, James Joyce. 'Who in the hell is Joyce?' I asked Seumas, who replied, 'That's the man that wrote the essay on Ibsen before he was eighteen.'

'The Day of the Rabblement' attacked writers like Yeats for sponsoring an Irish National Theatre. Apart from that pamphlet, says Richard Best, the Librarian, Joyce hadn't written much.

RICHARD BEST: We all thought that there was great promise in Joyce. I remember AE telling me how one day Joyce came to his house, and he didn't know him. A young man came in, and sat down, so shy that he couldn't explain the nature of his business. So, AE told me, 'I said to him, well I have many interests. For instance, I'm interested in the Co-operative Movement, in Plunkett House. I'm interested in ancient religions from Maharater or the Bagva Gita and then I'm interested in poetry.' 'Ah,' said Joyce at once, 'that is where I come in,' or some remark like that; and Russell said he took out of his pocket a great roll of expensive writing-paper. No doubt Gogarty had supplied this paper, because he was a friend in need to Joyce, and he unrolled it. And there in the very centre of each page were two or three little lines of verse, and Joyce read out these lines to him, and that was the beginning of Joyce, I think, as a poet.

It might have been the end. 'Young man,' said AE to Joyce, after reading the careful, mannered poems, 'you have not enough chaos in you.'

ROBERTS: Having published so little there was no wonder at the attitude of most people to him. Moore didn't understand this young fellow who approached him as an equal, or rather I should say, looked down on Moore as an inferior. As for AE, he had his own following of satellite poets and looked askance at any who was not of his own constellation. Joyce looked on the work of AE's poets, of whom I was one, as beneath contempt. However, this didn't prevent me from forgathering with Joyce. I used often to await him at the 'Pillar' till he would appear, a conspicuous figure wearing a white yachting cap and white canvas shoes to match, stalking along with the ever-present

American-cloth case under his arm, such as schoolgirls use to carry their music. His case contained the poems subsequently published as 'Chamber Music'.

Oliver St John Gogarty remembers first meeting with Joyce in a tram.

OLIVER ST JOHN GOGARTY: I met him I think in the year 1901. We were both in a tram and there were very few people on the tram and he was sitting on my left-hand side, a young man without glasses, with smoke-blue eyes and more or less chestnut-coloured eyelashes, which were rather noticeable, and, which was much more noticeable, a slight golden beard, like a haze. I've forgotten how we got into conversation – at any rate, it was very formal and staid; and under his arm he carried a roll of vellum which turned out to be copies of his poems written in his beautifully clear handwriting in the very middle of the page, leaving a large margin.

ROBERTS: About this time his published work consisted of the article in the *Fortnightly Review* on Ibsen, and a few pages entitled 'The Day of the Rabblement'. Yet nevertheless he had the absolute assurance that he would take his place as a famous writer in the long run, and conducted himself accordingly. Looking back, there was something uncanny in his certainty, which he had more than any other writer I have ever known, that he would one day be famous. It was more than mere wishful thinking. It governed all his attitudes to his compatriots, and accounts for what many referred to as his arrogance. He was never really arrogant, but seemed to have a curious sense of his own powers and wouldn't tolerate anyone who didn't wholly appreciate his work.

Apropos of which, Gogarty recalls an incident:

GOGARTY: We both lived on the north side of the city, and we were going up Rutland Square, I think it was a horse-drawn tram in those days. I happened to mention that thing that the newspapers were full of – that it was Yeats's fortieth birthday and that Lady Gregory had collected from his friends forty pounds with which she bought a Kelmscott edition of Chaucer by William Morris. Everybody knew it was Yeats's birthday. But when I made an epiphany, so to speak, and told Joyce this, at the first tram stop he got out. Yeats was lodging in the Cavendish Hotel, in Rutland Square, and he solemnly walked in and knocked at Yeats's door. When Yeats opened the door of the sitting-room he said, 'What age are you, sir?' and Yeats said, 'I'm forty.' 'You are too old for me to help. I bid you goodbye.' And Yeats was greatly impressed at the impertinence of the thing.

'Never,' said Yeats, 'was so much presumption with so little to show for it.' W. K. Magee, alias 'John Eglinton', remembers Joyce gate-crashing a party at Lady Gregory's.

w. k. MAGEE: Oh yes, he made up his mind to visit everybody – Dowden, Yeats, of course. Once I remember he heard that Lady Gregory was having a party in the Nassau Hotel, and it was more or less all the prominent members of the literary circle, and he determined he would be there. I remember seeing Joyce coming in rather timidly but still with his usual audacity. He was received by Lady Gregory, and then he turned away.

> *There once was a kind Lady Gregory,*
> *Who said: Come all ye poets in beggary,*
> *But she found her imprudence*
> *When a swarm of wild students*
> *Cried: Ask me, I'm in that category.*

Joyce's limericks were many. Dossy Wright knew him in those days when the young Irish National Theatre was beginning to take shape under Yeats and Lady Gregory.

DOSSY WRIGHT: Indeed I did. In the very early days, he was very young and I was young. He was one of the boys in those days. He'd remind you of Fred Higgins, and he could take a drink; but I don't think the drink took to him very well, they went to his head fairly quickly. He used to come down, like all the other people that were interested in literature, to the Camden Hall, and come in there talking to us. But he generally visited a few of the houses before he came and, perhaps because he spoke a little bit too much, Lady Gregory and Yeats didn't realise the brain that was there behind all this, because he didn't show it – he was really, more or less, like the type of carefree medical students that took years to get through.

Joyce was an Arts student at University College. But Art and Nature, Life and Letters, met.

GOGARTY: Joyce bore the distinction of being what they called a medical student's pal, and therefore a lot was forgiven them. Medical students were never attacked even in the red light districts, because that would have meant cutting off all the medical aid to the residents or denizens.

'Yes,' says Dr Kerrigan, a contemporary of Joyce at the College, 'those were the happy days.'

DR KERRIGAN: Those were the happy days when one could get royally happy for a shilling – plain stout cost a penny. It was Joyce's usual drink. He was not a heavy drinker – he could not carry much drink.

GOGARTY: No, he always suffered from inanition and you see, he was drinking while probably on a thirty hours' fast. Whereas the medical students were drinking on solid food.

KERRIGAN: Even when he drank he kept a quiet reserve that all who knew him remarked. Even the crowd he went with he regarded, as he wrote of them, detachedly; he looked on them as foils. He was capable of strong, but few, friendships.

CON CURRAN: Yes. He maintained this aloofness; I'm sure there was something deliberate about it. It was an aloofness that the more serious students respected; it didn't mean any diminution of friendship – there was nothing unfriendly about it. But amongst his old class-fellows a different sort of Joyce appeared – a Joyce who loved burlesque, loved getting into and out of difficult situations, loved parody. In those days, in Dublin, we had a passion for charades, and Joyce took great pleasure in acting these. One house we used to go to freely on Sunday evenings – in the old Dublin fashion the house was open – there might be a little dancing, there might be games, but inevitably we had charades. I remember Joyce in two or three roles in such plays. One as the Queen in *Hamlet*, in that terribly sad scene when the mad Ophelia came in scattering cauliflowers about the drawing-room floor, and the Queen, suffocating with emotion says, 'Ah, the poor girl, the poor girl.'

But Mr Curran lifts the curtain on another and a studious Joyce. He recalls a certain English class in University College.

CURRAN: Father Darlington opened that class in English with some reference to Aristotle's *Poetics*. I pricked up my ears, thinking that this was the sort of stuff I'd come to College for. This was the real stuff. But I also had the idea that English literature had ended with

Tennyson and Browning. Father Darlington suddenly asked the question: 'Have any of you gentlemen read this new play by Stephen Phillips?' (Phillips had just written a play called *Paolo and Francesca*. I had never heard of it.) The lecturer asked the question a second time, and then added: 'Have you read it, Mr Joyce?' And I heard a voice coming from behind me, a very cool, casual, and indifferent voice, say, 'Yes.' I looked round to see who this extraordinary man was who had heard of Stephen Phillips and had read his books. And I saw my first poet. Joyce at that time was a slim and elegant young man, with very blue eyes, thin lips, and a rather square chin. He carried his head always in almost an arrogant fashion, with his chin pushed out, and he had a very graceful carriage. These things I gradually found out in the next few weeks because he was a figure that fascinated me from the very beginning, and I didn't lose sight of him, I suppose, for forty years after that. I found that he lived rather much to himself in the College. He had three or four particular cronies.

He was also rather fastidious in his choice of classes. He was taking the Modern Literature course, but it so happened that the classes started at nine o'clock, at half past nine, or ten o'clock in the morning, and therefore it was not an hour that was convenient to Joyce to appear. He came to the College with a peculiarly formed and mature mind. I happen to have some books that he had at that period. But I find them both autographed and dated from 1899. That is to say, when he was seventeen years old; and the books are characteristic. They include two theses by Ibsen, five or six plays of Maeterlinck, a play of Hauptmann's, *Pamela*, three by d'Annunzio, and more surprising, an anthology of verse written by Paul with a paper from Randall – a figure that has always seemed to me to resemble Joyce.

Dante, Tasso, Guido, Cavalcanti, Castiglione, Flaubert, numerous Rosicruscian books – Joyce's reading was unusually wide.

KERRIGAN: I remember his giving a paper in the Literary Masonical Society on Mangen, and the notable thing was that Mangen was to Joyce, then nineteen years old, more European than merely Irish.

CURRAN: Eliot has said that his style has been influenced by Newman and Pater. I'm not so sure about Newman, Pater certainly, but he had put Pater behind him years ago. One book that he seemed to attach some importance to at that time, at least it cropped up frequently in his conversation, was Henry James's *Portrait of a Lady*.

Joyce's brother, Stanislaus, adds:

STANISLAUS JOYCE: In the course of his reading in Italian he had come across *Le Vergini delle Rocce*, of d'Annunzio, and read with profound interest the imaginary portrait of Socrates in the first chapter. The exaltation of an ardour of life in diversity by the development of native energies appealed strongly to him at this early stage of his own development. The thought expounded in these pages is that the elect are those few spirits who, conscious of their gifts, endeavour by a self-imposed discipline to become the deliberate artificers of their own lives, and that they owe obedience only to the laws of that style to which they have willingly bent their free natures in pursuit of a personal idea of order and beauty.

Was it this feeling of being an elect and single spirit that made Joyce 'arrogant'?

GOGARTY: No, only in his attitude in literature. He liked to think of arrogant people, but he was a very meek person when you met him face to face or in company.

BEST: I can't say that Joyce, any more than Synge, had what is called conversation. If you made a remark about some literary man to Joyce, let us say you said, 'Oh, I think that Meredith is a wonderful writer,' he might say, 'Ho, ho, ho, ho,' like that; he had a way of guffawing.

CURRAN: In a sense he talked a great deal about books, but not in the way that students do. He talked much more about the principles of aesthetics. His talk about books was always by way of allusion, very flattering allusions of course, because he assumed that you had read all that he had read, and perhaps one concealed one's ignorance for the time being, and then looked up the book in the National Library or elsewhere.

BLAKE: Well, forty-five years ago, when I was a junior in the National Library of Ireland, it was a free-and-easy place: it was a sort of discussion centre for poets, students, and intellectuals. I remember James Joyce as a regular visitor to the Library during the years 1899 to 1904. In appearance he was a tall, willowy young man, dressed in a double-breasted reefer jacket, and with a blue yachting cap. He was rather given to striking poses, and would sometimes stand at the desk staring around him at the other people in the waiting-room. I do remember on one occasion supplying him with F. H. Meyer's *Human Personality* and the *Survival of the Body After Death*. This work was in two volumes. It had been published in 1903, and it seemed one of the books in which Joyce was especially interested.

Which reminds Mr Magee, then of the Library, of a conversation he had with Joyce.

MAGEE: Yes, I remember distinctly. At one point he said, 'If I knew I were to drop dead before I reached that lamp-post, it would mean no more to me than it would mean to walk past it.'

This man overtook me and began talking to me in a sententious way. I had just noticed his figure in the street, but we fell into conversation and we walked right across the town, I remember, and we talked all the way about different things – literature, I suppose, and I should think theology entered into our conversation a good deal, because he seemed to be very well grounded in Catholic theology. We talked a little about Luther even, and I recall his saying that the only Protestant he cared about was Luther. I remember the way he described the Mass – with emotion, almost. And he described how the bell was rung, and the candles, and so on. And the ceremonial of the religion was most important and most impressive with him. Of course, I – as he said in his limerick – was merely a Presbyterian.

> There once was a Celtic librarian,
> Whose essays were voted Spencerian,
> His name is Magee
> But his essays to me
> Have a flavour that's more Presbyterian.

Was Joyce deeply or at all religious? His sister Eileen says –

MRS SCHAUREK: I think that all Jim's loves really were created in the love of God. As a child he was very very religious. He was a Child of Mary and a Prefect of the Jesuit College in Belvedere.

'My brother,' says Stanislaus Joyce, 'was not intensely religious. He had been in early youth.'

CURRAN: But his real love of course, in those days, was singing.

GOGARTY: He had a supreme, light tenor voice. His physique was not able to carry an organ, but it was clarion clear, and he would have easily got first in that grade in all Ireland in the thing they call the Feis, which is equivalent to the Eisteddfod in Wales.

Yes, Joyce entered for the Feis Cecil competition in singing.

CURRAN: The year before, I think in 1904, McCormack got the Gold Medal for tenor singing. Joyce only got the bronze medal. He ignored the sight-reading test, which was arbitrary. It threw up an amusing scene. I had something to do with that. I was interested in the theory of the piano and his training at that time. He appeared on the platform in spotless linen and with a butterfly tie, he was young, but he looked even younger than his age, and he fascinated an old lady who was sitting behind me. 'Oh, what a nice boy,' she said to me. Joyce sang the recitative, I remember, splendidly – 'Whom the Lord Chasteneth', and an aria by Sullivan, 'Come Ye Children'. Then the sight-reading test was presented to him, and he gave one look at it, jumped off the platform, and took refuge in a hostelry adjacent to forget. We had to console him.

Joyce was bitterly disappointed. Gogarty says he flung the bronze medal into the Liffey. His cousin says he flung it, in passing, into the area of a Dublin house. Eva Joyce, his sister, says –

EVA JOYCE: I don't know how the disappointment at the beginning of his life, as regards his voice, came about, but he never seemed quite to recover from it. He was set on a musical career; and I think it frustrated his life all through, the fact that he was a sort of failure at this. That seems to me the beginning and end of the whole situation of his life and death, turned into his writings in the fashion that he did. He had a hard life through devoting himself to writing, because writing is a very different thing from making a living through natural singing.

Few people ever took a hurt to heart so much as the young and sensitive Joyce. 'I felt compelled,' he says, 'to assume the enigma of a manner.' A reticent manner, an arrogant manner. He blistered into wit: and blistered even before he was burnt. 'What is imagination?' he said to Budgen long afterwards. 'What is it but memory?' His sister Eileen says –

MRS SCHAUREK: One morning coming from church when he went to ask for a drink of water he was refused it. Jim got a very bad feeling that never left him. He was a very sensitive child and a very sensitive boy and a hurt was a kind of a wound that never healed with Jim. And that's why his early life, even as a child in Clongowes, started his feeling against life and against the Jesuits, as he has written, you know.

GOGARTY: His memory was stupendous, but he would withdraw from company, and I'm sure that must have been for note-taking because, in latter days, you told me that he did take notes.

Memory! Imagination! Joyce's memory was stupendous. It was pointed by foreboding and barbed by afterthought. Forty years after a conversation, says Con Curran, he'd expect you to remember the very words he had used. Once, as a lad at the Jesuit College, Belvedere, the Rector questioned his memory of certain history notes. Whichever was wrong was to write out the correct answer three hundred times. In the event Joyce was right: the boys cheered, the Rector wrote his imposition, 'and Joyce,' says a schoolfellow, 'kept those notes, I believe, all his life.'

'What a little thing to remember for years, To remember with tears.' An eternal moment; or, as Joyce himself used to call it, an 'epiphany'.

GOGARTY: Epiphany was a kind of joke of his. It was profanity, really; epiphany is the church festival, the presentation of the Divine Child, or the Star over Bethlehem. But Joyce used 'Epiphany' where you presented your mind against your will to the superior intelligence which had detected some little thing you were holding back. For instance, if he wanted to borrow half a crown, and you'd say you couldn't lend it him, then later in the day, some conversation brought out the fact that you had five shillings, he'd suddenly shout 'Epiphany!' In other words, you showed yourself forth in shame, that you'd withheld the half-crown when you really had five shillings.

Oliver Gogarty shared Joyce's poverty sometimes, just as Joyce occasionally shared his plenty.

GOGARTY: One morning we were in the Martello Tower as is recorded in *Ulysses*; and the milk-woman, whether she had a deliberate purpose or not, called rather early and collected her two shillings and it was the last two shillings we had. But we had to get to Dublin and that meant walking seven miles on foot. So, as we set out – it was very early, for the light was still slanting – we beheld the gangling, gaunt figure of the father of Yeats, the poet; he must have been about seventy at this time and he was having his morning constitutional. He was about 6 foot 4 inches, brown-faced with great eyebrows and deeply recessed bright eyes. He was swinging along with a stick and Joyce, whenever he wished to make a joke, assumed an attitude of great seriousness and he said, 'It is your privilege to touch the elder Yeats who is now approaching.' And I said, 'Quickly! What do we want?' 'Well, we want threepence each for the tram, that's sixpence, and we want a shilling for drinks this evening in "The Ship", that's one shilling and sixpence each.' Well, you could get a pint of porter for twopence in those days, so by the time I stopped the elder Yeats I got awful timid, and I reduced the sum. I said, 'Mr Yeats?' 'Yes, sir, what do you want?' I said, 'Could you oblige us with a loan of ninepence?' 'Make it a shilling, Gogarty,' whispered Joyce. I said, 'Even a shilling?' 'Certainly not,' Yeats answered. 'First of all I haven't got such a thing and secondly, you and your companion there will spend it on drink.' Then Joyce came forward and said, 'Might I interpose a moment? By the rules of logic, by the razor of Occam – who was a thirteenth-century monk, and lived in Surrey – you're not allowed to have a second explanation if the first is adequate. You have stated that you haven't got a shilling and at the same time you begin to prognosticate what would happen if you had it. It is not allowable to discuss the fate of a thing that doesn't exist. I bid you good morning, sir.' So we had to foot it to 'The Ship'.

MAGEE: Oh yes, Joyce was quite impecunious. The only instance I remember of his appreciation of money was when I paid him for his poem that he contributed to the little paper I was editing. And he chortled, I remember, when he pocketed the half a sovereign.

And Mr Best, the Librarian, remembers –

BEST: Joyce, when I first met him, had already graduated, though I don't think he was earning any money. I think his friends used to help him a little. I myself wasn't endowed with this world's goods then and I wasn't able to respond to one of his demands upon me, but I don't think he bore me any grudge about that.

Mr Best remembers another visit from Joyce, years later.

BEST: During the conversation he put his hand in his breast pocket and took out a big, thick wad of bank-notes and held them up to me without saying a word, and then put them back.

The aloof, sensitive Joyce, who used the bolts of silence and bars of wit to lock out the rebuffs of the world, had found another line of defence. He and Gogarty had retired into the Martello Tower, an early nineteenth-century fortification built on the seashore as a buffer against Napoleon. They rented it for eight pounds a year.

GOGARTY: The newly founded University was called the National, and it was filled with young men who were in a rebellious condition, and that included getting away from the parents and also getting away from the accepted canons.

From this tower Joyce and Gogarty surveyed Dublin, and sallied forth into the 'seventh city of Christendom'. On one of these forays they visited AE's Hermetic Society but found it was not in session. They did find, however, a portmanteau of ladies' lingerie belonging to George Roberts, a Dublin friend and publisher. George had a side-line as a traveller at the time.

GOGARTY: So Joyce took the portmanteau with him as a memento and he distributed the undies to a lady friend, and threw in the portmanteau as good value because she tried them on without any reticence or modesty. Oh yes, and when leaning over the bed, admiring the undies and the fit, his toe struck the nightjar and it rang, and about two hours later, when we were returning to the seaside, he said – when he wanted to make a joke he would assume a great seriousness and ritual – 'I have got now the title for my book of lyrics.' And the lyrics were the ones which were on the shelf taking over possession as furniture for the Tower. I said, 'What is the title?' 'Obviously,' he said, 'Chamber Music.'

But to return to the Tower – even here Joyce's defences failed.

ROBERTS: Joyce himself told me the story of being turned out of the Tower in a downpour of rain at midnight and left without shelter. This was the sort of treatment Joyce got from the man that tried to reinstate himself with the public when Joyce got at last his due recognition.

Gogarty, however, recalls having brought over a man called Trench from Oxford and having invited him to stay in the Tower.

GOGARTY: Well, at two in the morning, Trench, whom we didn't know very well, got a frightful nightmare, screamed, 'There's the black panther,' and produced a colt revolver and shot off two bullets in the dark, greatly alarming Joyce. Well, I knew it was one of these night-mares that might recur, but I took the precaution of stealing the revolver, and sure enough Trench woke in another twenty minutes and screamed again. I said, 'I can take care of the menagerie,' and I deliberately shot down the fish kettle and all the other tin cans that were over Joyce's bed. He rose solemnly, dressed himself in his faded trousers, pulled on his shirt and his white yachting cap and his tennis shoes, took his ashplant and left the Tower and never came back.

MAGEE: Curiously, Joyce had come into the library that morning and told me that he had been chucked out of the Tower.

Exile again, and Mr Magee further remembers that that was the morning of the famous library conversation about Hamlet.

MAGEE: I have a sort of feeling that there was a talk about Hamlet and that I may have said something as ridiculous as what he credited me with in *Ulysses*.

Who, we may ask, was this dispossessed, proud, suffering, eternally brooding, betrayed young man? This Joyce, Hamlet, call him what you will? Where did that recurring pattern of hurt and estrangement – silence, exile and cunning – come from? His father?

GOGARTY: His father was, in his latter days, a miserable provider. The landlords often paid the Joyce family to clear out because they used to burn the banisters in the winter for kindling. Once I was in Joyce's home in St Peter's Road, Cabra, and it was miserable. The banisters were broken, the grass in the back-yard was all blackened out. There was laundry there and a few chickens, and it was a very very miserable home. He spent most of his time in the National Library. I think he went home rather reluctantly. He couldn't desert his mother and he found her caught in the middle of this misery and that burned and made him very miserable. But the idea of distaste for the home as home didn't exist, because his mother was there and she was the home, but the misery of her surroundings made him more indignant with life because it included his mother, whom he dearly loved.

Joyce's father had *been a provider – at least for Joyce – therefore the more memorable the hurt. John Stanislaus Joyce was a prodigal Dublin 'character'. A man of much address and many addresses: sportsman, musician, wit, boon-companion, and politician – liked by everyone. The feckless father of a large family of whom James Joyce was the eldest. He sent his son to the Jesuit Schools of Clongowes Wood and Belvedere – a training of which James remained proud. But James at school, and later at university, felt the pinch of poverty. Still, as his sister Eileen says of their father –*

MRS SCHAUREK: He was absolutely the real meaning of Jim's success, giving him everything that he desired. From boyhood he gave him everything – absolutely everything. He deprived the rest of the family to give to Jim. He saw in him a genius.

Eva Joyce, another sister, bears this out.

EVA JOYCE: He thought the world of Jim, and there was no one else according to him – 'Jim's coming in,' 'Jim's going out,' 'Jim's coming home,' all the preparations were for him, and all the visitors coming, and the state of excitement, and happy and delighted with himself to have him home again.

My father was the most outstanding man as regards his brains and intellect, and Jim got his intellect from him, and his love of music more from his mother. The two combined made him what he was. He was a very lonesome boy. He was the greatest favourite in the family. Father and mother idolised him, and all the brothers and sisters seemed to be quite happy that he was the one that got the most attention. He was a very gentle child, indeed I never remember seeing him in a temper about anything – in fact, he always laughed everything off.

A kind and a good boy as they say in Ireland, meaning a religious boy. Like all her family, Mrs Joyce was devoutly religious. Like all devout religious Irishwomen she hoped in her heart that her boy would be a priest.

EVA JOYCE: He was a very religious boy. He was holy, as a matter of fact. He wrote a lot of very beautiful verse, holy verse; things to the Blessed Virgin, and things that his mother thought a lot about. I don't know why, or where they disappeared to, but I believe he destroyed them himself later. He changed in his attitude towards the Church, but he didn't change in his feelings towards religion, as far as I could judge him in after life. He didn't practise his religion, if that's what they call it here, but he had the religion.

'When the soul of a man is born in this country,' said Joyce, 'there are

*nets flung out to hold it back from flight. You talk to me of nationality,
language and religion. I shall try to fly by those nets.'*

EVA JOYCE: Of that I have no idea. I only know that he got a terrible
shock when he turned against his religion – well, I can't say he turned
against his religion, but when he ceased to practise it – because to the
very last I say he believed in God.

*In November 1902, Joyce, in the midst of frustration and dereliction,
wrote to Lady Gregory explaining that he was going to seek in France
the freedom which the Church had denied him in Ireland.*

*'I want,' he said, 'to have a medical diploma which will allow me to
devote myself to my work with every freedom. I want to work out my
destiny, be it large or small, for I know that there is no philosophy or
heresy that the Church disapproves more of than that of being a human
being.*

*'I am going alone, without friends, to a strange country and I write to
you to ask you if you can help me.'*

*So Joyce left mother, Mother Church, and motherland. Not for long.
He received a telegram saying his mother was seriously ill, and he borrowed
the money to come straight home.*

EVA JOYCE: He undoubtedly was her favourite. She absolutely lived
for him, and when he went away it seemed to be the breaking up of her
life. She didn't seem to last long after he went, in fact she seemed to
fade out altogether.

GOGARTY: He never let you know when he was wounded. I hurt him
tremendously by calling him to go and pray beside his dying mother's
bed. He refused to bend a knee and he never forgave me for being
right.

*So says Gogarty. But 'it pleases me,' says Joyce's brother Stanislaus, 'to
destroy a legend. I have read in several articles on Joyce that his dying
mother asked her son to pray for her and that Joyce refused. It is said that
the remorse of this refusal tormented him for the rest of his life. That is
not so. The command, which was preremptory, came from an uncle, and
was not a legend. Our mother was already unconscious.'*

GOGARTY: All the same, that woman was taught by her religion to
believe that she brought into this world a soul that would be damned
for eternity, and that was the soul of her beloved son who wouldn't

bow down and pray with her. Then she passed into unconsciousness. And he did it defiantly. He was very defiant about religion. When he lost his faith it was a shock to him and his answer was defiance.

KERRIGAN: He went the pace all right for a short period just between his mother's death and his departure from Ireland: but he really couldn't hold any great quantity of liquor. He was too slight physically, and he was too temperamental.

GOGARTY: Oh, he had no money . . . One day I met him and I said, 'I haven't seen you for two days.' 'No,' he said. I said, 'Were you ill?' 'Yes,' he said. I said, 'What were you suffering from?' 'Inanition.' And it was perfectly true. I had a place near Glasnevin, about a mile from Joyce, before you come to the Botanic Gardens. A place called 'Fairfield', and it had about seven acres and a kitchen garden, and in the kitchen garden there was an orchard. I remember the blossoms were pink and white, because it made Joyce recite his poem, 'My love is in a lighted tower', and there were some birds in the apple-trees, and they rose and Joyce said, 'By the way, I hear you have a ·22 rook-rifle?' I said, 'Yes, I believe I have.' 'Are you using it?' I said, 'I never use it.' 'In that case I'd like you to lend it to me.' So, hoping there was some turn for sport, if not for the best or the better, I lent Joyce the rook-rifle. He put it under his arm at the 'ready' and departed. Next day when he met me he produced a pawn-ticket for eight shillings and said, 'Here's your rook-rifle. Here's the licence for it, at least.'

In the autumn of 1904, the year of his mother's death, Joyce left Ireland for good. The towers had fallen. But within all those towers was an inner keep of self-integrity, an irreducible pride. 'I will not serve,' said Joyce, 'that in which I no longer believe, whether it call itself my home, my fatherland, or my church: and I will try to express myself in some mode of life or art as freely as I can, and as wholly as I can, using for my defences the only arms I allow myself to use, silence, exile and cunning. Old father, old artificer, stand me now in good stead.'

STANISLAUS JOYCE: My brother's unquestioning devotion to his art would have been not unworthy of the artist as priest, as Carlyle conceived him. It was a service to which he felt himself called by the chance of having been born with talent.

It was a service, also, to which he was impelled by his solitary cast of character. What bitterness was it that turned the young Joyce in on himself, that made him a stranger to his mother's faith, his father's politics, and his country's hopes? And why – being by birth that most social of beings, a Dubliner – did he choose to stand apart from his fellows, in silence, scorn, and nonconformity. What Judas kiss had life given him? We do not know: no more than we know what song the Sirens sang.

James Stephens once heard Joyce sing a certain song.

JAMES STEPHENS: He told me at table that he was the only person living who knew a certain folk-song. He had learned it from his grandfather, who has asserted that it was a lost song, and that it was the best love-song in the world. He sang it to me in his careful tenor voice.

At that time I had a gift which has since deserted me. If I heard a song that I liked, thereupon that song, its music and words, became my property. Because of that small talent here is the song that Joyce sang to me, on the Champs-Elysées, in a lovely tenor voice.

> I was walking the road one fine day
> Oh, the brown and the yellow ale,
> When I met with a man who was no right man
> Oh, Oh, love of my heart!
>
> And he asked if the woman with me was my daughter
> Oh, the brown and the yellow ale,
> And I said she was my married wife
> Oh, Oh, love of my heart!
>
> And he asked would I lend her for an hour and a quarter
> Oh, the brown and the yellow ale,
> And I said I would do anything that was fair
> Oh, Oh, love of my heart!
>
> So you take the high road, and I'll take the lower,
> Oh, the brown and the yellow ale,
> And we'll meet again at the ford of the river
> Oh, Oh, love of my heart!
>
> I was waiting there for a day and a quarter
> Oh, the brown and the yellow ale,
> When she came to me without any shame,
> Oh, Oh, love of my heart!

When I heard her tale I lay down and I died
Oh, the brown and the yellow ale,
And she sent two men to the wood for timber
Oh, Oh, love of my heart!

A board of holly, and a board of elder
Oh, the brown and the yellow ale,
And two great yards of sacking about me,
Oh, Oh, love of my heart!

And if it wasn't that my own little mother was a woman
Oh, the brown and the yellow ale,
I'd sing another pretty song about women
Oh, Oh, love of my heart!

'The best love song in the world', and Joyce the only living man who knew it. A song of betrayal, hurt and loss. The motif of Joyce's lonely mind and life.

STANISLAUS JOYCE: My brother suddenly made up his mind to leave Ireland. The decision was regarded in his circle of aspirants to literary careers as just another of his escapades and in the bars he had frequented too assiduously, the comments of his former companions, at least so far as his career was concerned, were rather in the style of an obituary notice. He had spurned what he called their temporising and poltroonery, their attitude of timid, covert revolt on all issues not purely national, their fear to be the same in act and valour as they were in desire. And they, for their part, with the patient memory of many a jibe, took offence at his hectoring manner.

ROBERTS: Joyce's lack of money at last became unbearable to him and having a flair for languages he took a job in the Berlitz School in Zürich and circulated a letter to all his friends – and some of his enemies – requesting money to raise the fare. In the letter I received the fare was multiplied by *two*, he wasn't travelling *alone*. To free Dublin from his presence seemed very cheap at the price, so most of us heartily subscribed.

'He wasn't travelling alone.' *No. In the year that his mother died Joyce met the girl from Galway, Nora Barnacle.*

GOGARTY: I only met Miss – she was then Miss Barnacle – once.

She was pale-faced with beautiful, what they call auburn, hair, really a chestnut colour, that's all I saw. I saw her thirty or forty yards off.

MARIA JOLAS: When one thinks how young they both were – I am speaking now of Joyce and his wife – when they first met on that 16 June 1904, it seems extraordinary that both he and she should have known it would be 'till death us do part'. For, in reality, and it was she herself who told me this – that is the significance of this date, the date Joyce fixed for all time in *Ulysses*. It was on that day that he first met Nora Barnacle.

FRAU GIEDION: It was in 1904, at the age of twenty-two, that James Joyce came to Zürich for the first time. A hotel porter directed the young couple to a hotel in the Lagerstrasse, whose proprietor – a special joke for Joyce – bore the name of Dubliner. For three weeks Joyce explored the possibility of giving English lessons, but with no success.

He quickly went to Trieste, as English teacher in the Berlitz School. There he was to stay for ten years. Once, to better himself, he tried to get a pass degree in English at Padua University, but failed. And once he attempted a job in a bank, in Rome. But for Joyce all roads – especially cul-de-sacs – lead from Rome, and he soon returned to Trieste. And here his son Giorgio and his daughter Lucia were born. Here he tasted the bitterness of exile. Here he brought his brothers and sisters from Dublin. For in his quarrel with the world the family was to be his sheet-anchor and still centre.

STANISLAUS JOYCE: When my brother invited me to come and join him at Trieste, he spoke of a comparatively short stay, but I knew that he wanted me to remain and second him in his struggle. I accepted with my eyes open.

EVA JOYCE: He really wanted to have as many members of the family with him out there as he could possibly manage. He had already brought Stany out and then he brought me out, and then he thought I was a bit lonely and he brought another sister out so that we could all be together. He was lonely himself and he understood that. And if, when we went out there first, we were a bit lonely, he quite understood, because it was the one thing that had been outstanding in his life.

MRS GRIFFIN: Yes, he was a very lonely person. I remember one time my sister Nora came to Ireland, here to Galway, and he sent her a letter which said, 'Dear Nora, I want you to come back next week. I am like a man looking into a dark pool. Everything is so lonely without you.'

Dublin, for Joyce, had been 'the centre of paralysis' of silence, of impotence. He was too close to it, too warmly engaged, too mothered and smothered by it. In fact, he was Dublin. And only by estranging himself from that city could he come home to himself. Only by denying himself sight of it, as of some Medusa's head seen only in the mirror of a shield, could he escape paralysis. 'In tearing out my eyes,' says Oedipus to Theseus in André Gide's fable, 'in this cruel act I was driven by some secret need of pushing my fortune to the limit, and of accomplishing a heroic destiny.' In darkness, in exile, in Trieste, Joyce began to accomplish his destiny. Dubliners, Portrait of the Artist, Exiles, *and the opening of* Ulysses, *followed in turn. The saga of the city and himself.*

MRS SCHAUREK: He wrote at night mostly, and he lay always across the bed on his stomach when he wrote. He had a huge blue pencil, like a carpenter's pencil, and a white coat on to reflect on the paper because his sight was so bad. He always wrote with a white coat on – it gave a kind of white light.

Music always touched him, and if Jim had an inspiration the piano was his call. He would go and give vent to feeling by singing – even sitting in the dark and magnificently singing. You'd hear Jimmy's voice coming through the doors and the windows of Trieste and the people all standing and clapping him – they just thronged outside. His voice was absolutely marvellous at the time. At other times he would be quite a blank. His life would be slow, he'd be depressed and he'd be singing sacred music and would stay very much alone.

'I may not write again for ten years,' he would say. Eileen recalls a discussion –

MRS SCHAUREK: – a very hot discussion – about the publication of the book and the manuscript had come to grief, and I arrived to find it burning on a charcoal fire. I rushed to it, scattered it about and saved it from burning. And I remember my brother saying to me, 'Some parts of it I'll never write again, Eileen.'

'In a fit of petulance, because the manuscript of Dubliners *had again come home to roost, my brother,' says Stanislaus, 'threw it into the fire.'*

GOGARTY: He was greatly handicapped by the miserable publisher we had, a fellow who really did more to curtail the outcome of the Irish renaissance in literature than anybody. He burned all Joyce's first edition and gave him but one, of *Dubliners* . . .

ROBERTS: I resent vehemently Gogarty's comments nearly forty years after the book was published. After all, what did Gogarty do when Grant Richards published *Dubliners*? I have no recollection of him hailing it as a masterpiece.

And George Roberts, the publisher in question, goes on to explain –

ROBERTS: I had started and was managing director of a publishing firm called Maunsel and Co. Joyce sent me the manuscript of *Dubliners*. I had some doubts about it, for books of short stories were very difficult to sell, especially by an unknown author, as Joyce was then. Still, I liked the stories and was loath to turn them down. And at last I agreed to publish *Dubliners*. I should mention that I was quite unaware of the fact that Grant Richards had already turned it down after a lot of correspondence. Well, when the page proofs were submitted the proprietor of the printing works took objection to some passages. At this stage, if Joyce hadn't been so pigheaded and had agreed to make a few changes that the printers requested, all might have gone smoothly. But nothing would persuade him and I – thinking time might persuade him – put the proofs aside and let him cool down.

Legal opinion was taken by both sides. And Dubliners *fell between both stools. Both opinions supported the printers against Joyce. But Joyce – well, as his brother says –*

STANISLAUS JOYCE: The bickering and unexpected eleventh-hour disappointments sapped his energy. The recalcitrant Dublin publisher, who went back on his contract, could not altogether crush him under the weight of defeat, but he could and did spoil another book of stories and delay Joyce's appearance in print. That was one of his feats. When *Dubliners* did at last appear, the First World War had just broken out, and the reading public had more preoccupying matter to claim its attention.

Joyce, with his family, found asylum in Zürich. But, in fairness to George Roberts, one must point out that no English publisher was eager to touch Joyce's early books. Still Joyce was singularly fortunate in the support which he got from ungrudging women friends. In 1914 Miss Harriet Weaver, who edited a progressive review, The Egoist, offered to publish Joyce's Portrait of the Artist, when no other publisher could be found.

HARRIET WEAVER: I first became in touch with Mr Joyce in the autumn of 1914 when I had occasion to write to him in Trieste to suggest a way in which he could send, by a friend in Switzerland, the final chapters of his first novel *A Portrait of the Artist as a Young Man*, which had been running as a serial in *The Egoist*, but had been held up when war broke out. As Mr Joyce consistently refused to make any alterations at all in it, *The Egoist* with his approval ventured to embark on the publication of the complete text in book form, though it had never before published any book. But again difficulties cropped up. No British printer could be found willing to print it intact, with the result that printed sheets had to be imported from America.

It was Miss Weaver's generous benefactions that enabled Joyce to devote himself wholly to writing. The finishing of Ulysses and the undertaking of Finnegans Wake we owe to Miss Weaver.

HARRIET WEAVER: I should like to mention that Mr Ezra Pound was extremely helpful to Mr Joyce, as to many young writers in a number of ways, and Mr Joyce was very grateful to him.

A relative of mine had left me some money and as I really didn't need it I made it over to Mr Joyce to be a help to him. He was no financier and greatly exaggerated the amount; he didn't understand at all.

The line of Joyce's ascent is interesting. As I see it, it was Yeats who introduced him to Arthur Symonds, who got his poems published; Symonds who brought him to the notice of Ezra Pound, who got his novel published; Pound who interested you, and Pound, too, who, after Zürich and the war years, took Joyce to Paris.

HARRIET WEAVER: Yes, he got him to go to Paris actually. He went to see him in Trieste, rather they met in Italy and he induced him to come over with his family; it had only been for a temporary stay, so Mr Joyce thought, but he never returned afterwards to live in Trieste again, and Mr Pound introduced him to all kinds of people in Paris, literary people who were a help to him.

Sylvia Beach, first to publish Joyce's Ulysses, in Paris.

SYLVIA BEACH: It was in the autumn of 1920 that I went to a party with Adrienne Monnier to the house of the poet André Spier in Neuilly. When we got there we found Ezra Pound and he had brought James Joyce and Mrs Joyce. André Spier had come rushing up to me and told me in great excitement, 'The Irish writer, James Joyce, is here!' I was quite overwhelmed; it was so unexpected for me to come suddenly face to face with one for whom I had such a deep admiration, and I was quite trembling. After lunch I got up the courage to speak to him, however, and he soon put me at my ease. He was a very easy man to talk to. His manners were so courteous and he was very gentle, slightly humorous, and rather melancholy at the same time. I thought he was delightful; his musical voice, his long fingers, with several rings on them (and somehow they didn't seem to make him look effeminate either), his fair skin – he was always blushing, and his very small feet, and his way of drooping against a bookcase.

STANISLAUS JOYCE: My brother came back to Trieste for a year after the First World War, but I had just returned from close on four years in various internment camps, and I had not the energy to tackle him again. To be my brother's keeper was a whole-time job and very exhausting. After he went to live in Paris I saw little of him, and our correspondence fell off because I quarrelled with him about *Finnegans Wake*. It seemed to me that the indispensable controls which had held so firmly before the war failed to act in the French capital, where he was surrounded by a too admiring group and where deference to originality tends to run to a cult of the eccentric.

Miss Beach was interested in Ulysses.

SYLVIA BEACH: Soon we began to talk about *Ulysses*, for that was uppermost in my mind. I was following, as far as I could at such a distance, what was happening to *Ulysses* in New York. It was appearing in the *Little Review*, edited by Margaret Anderson and James Heep, and had been suppressed already four times when I met Joyce. He would sometimes come to see me to tell me how it was progressing. Finally, one day he said that the *Review* had been completely suppressed, that the editors had been dragged off to court, and their thumb-prints taken, and they had been fined a hundred dollars, although the well-known Irish-American lawyer, John Quinn, had defended them. So Joyce seemed very much concerned at this – *consterné*, as the French say. We talked together about it, and I began to feel that the work that had been begun in London by Harriet Weaver, and had been carried on by Margaret Anderson in New York, must be continued and somehow finished up by me in Paris. So then it was arranged for me to bring out *Ulysses* in Paris. I consulted what Joyce called the business adviser of Shakespeare and Co., that was Adrienne Monnier, whose famous library was across the street.

So Adrienne Monnier met Joyce with Sylvia Beach and Ezra Pound.

ADRIENNE MONNIER: Ezra Pound et James Joyce que je ne connaissais pas du tout. Sylvia Beach naturellement les connaissait très bien et en voyant James Joyce elle manifesta aussitôt une émotion qui me parut extraordinaire. Elle me dit, Mais tu sais, James Joyce est là. Quand je lui ai dit, 'Mais qui est James Joyce?' elle me dit, 'Mais James Joyce, le plus grand écrivain de langue anglaise – enfin moi, c'est ce que je pense.'

'At last,' says Mlle Monnier, 'Sylvia Beach got into conversation with Joyce, and I watched them. Joyce was sitting on a sofa. She was very animated – Joyce reserved and laconic . . .'

Adrienne Monnier advised her friend to go ahead with the publication of Ulysses.

BEACH: She advised me to go ahead, and also she recommended her printer in Dijon, a man who had printed Huysman's work, and that interested Joyce very much. And we went ahead with the preparation for printing, although I had no money, and the printer was very trusting about that, and said it could be paid for when the subscriptions came in. Joyce, of course, said there would be no subscriptions, meaning that nobody would buy such a dull book. I felt entirely confident about it, and I issued a prospectus that I began to send out all over the world. Everybody gave me addresses, 'Oh, you must send to this person in India, and to that person in Canada, and to somebody else in China.' I told Joyce I was going to send a prospectus of *Ulysses* to Bernard Shaw. Joyce bet me a box of his favourite cigars, Voltigeurs, that Shaw would refuse to subscribe, but I was quite hopeful. Once Mrs Desmond Fitzgerald, who used to be a secretary to Mr Shaw, told me of his benevolence, and I thought, 'Oh, he couldn't help but be interested in this case of a fellow-countryman,' and so I sent him the prospectus. I received a reply from Mr Shaw saying that he had read several fragments of *Ulysses*, which he called a 'revolting record of a disgusting phase of civilisation'. Shaw wrote as follows:

'*I have read several fragments of* Ulysses *in its serial form. It is a revolting record of a disgusting phase of civilisation, but it is a truthful one; and I should like to put a cordon round Dublin to round up every male person in it between the ages of fifteen and thirty, force them to read it, and ask them, whether on reflection they can see anything amusing in all that foul-mouthed, foul-minded derision and obscenity. To you, possibly, it may appeal as art. You are probably (you see, I don't know you) a young barbarian beglamoured by the excitements and enthusiasms that art stirs up in romantic youth; but to me it is all hideously real: I have walked those streets, and known those shops and heard and taken part in those conversations. I escaped from them to England at the age of twenty, and forty years later have learned from the books of Mr Joyce that slack-jawed blackguardism is as rife in young Dublin as it was in 1870. It is, however, some consolation to find that at least one man has felt deeply enough about it to face the horror of writing it all down, and using his literary genius to force people to face it. In Ireland they try to make a cat cleanly by rubbing its nose in its own filth – Mr Joyce has tried the same treatment on the human subject. I hope it may prove successful. I am aware that there are other qualities and other passages in* Ulysses: *but they do not call for any special comment from me. I must add, as the prospectus implies an invitation to purchase, that I am an elderly Irish gentleman, and that if you imagine that any Irishman, much less an elderly one, would pay 150 francs for a book, you little know my countrymen.*'

BEACH: Joyce was jubilant, of course, and he got his box of cigars.

ARTHUR POWER: One day when we were leaving Larbel's flat together, Joyce casually pointed to the concierge's son who was playing on the steps and he said to me, 'One day that boy will be a reader of *Ulysses.*'

BEACH: And on 2 February 1922, the conductor from the express from Dijon brought me personally the two first copies. This was Joyce's birthday. There was a long stream of people, all the way down in the Rue de l'Odéon, waiting for a copy. They'd heard of it. It had got about, and there was only a copy in the window for them to look at, but nobody could have one. And there was no miracle of loaves and fishes, either.

The broadcast ended with Joyce's own voice, reading the speech of John F. Taylor from the Aeolus episode of Ulysses:

He lifted his voice above it boldly:

'But, ladies and gentlemen, had the youthful Moses listened to and accepted that view of life, had he bowed his head and bowed his will and bowed his spirit before that arrogant admonition, he would never have brought the Chosen People out of their House of Bondage nor followed the pillar of the cloud by day. He would never have spoken with the Eternal on Sinai's mountaintop nor ever have come down with the light of inspiration shining in his countenance and bearing in his arms the tables of the law, graven in the language of the outlaw.'

He ceased and looked at them, enjoying silence.

JAMES JOYCE

PART II: A PORTRAIT OF THE ARTIST IN MATURITY

FRANK BUDGEN: I suppose that Joyce was a great autobiographical artist; that's been commented on by quite a lot of people. But I always wondered if he really gave the whole of himself, and I suppose having painted a few portraits myself, self-portraits, I'm wondering whether he didn't miss some of the angles; after all, whatever mirror we look in, whether it's made of quicksilver or whether it's our own memory, we're likely enough to miss at least 180 degrees of the all-round thing. Now, the thing that I always liked in Joyce and never saw in his self-portraits was something infinitely boyish and gay, not like a bad, but like a good boy, gay and full of spirits, and when there was a convivial atmosphere, it would express itself in song and dance and dressing-up – not because he wanted to hog the limelight or anything, but just because he felt very gay.

NINO FRANCK: The first impression people had on seeing Joyce was that he was a very serious and cold man, but in fact he was very simple and gay, although it was very difficult for him to become gay. I had a feeling that there was a very cool air, a very strange thing in Joyce, I always remarked it; he made around himself a big zone of silence. It was a very special and very deep silence, so the first feeling when I met Joyce was a cool feeling, but after some time I was convinced that it was a very, very extraordinary youth, that was not the youth of an old man; it was the youth of a young man. I had the feeling that Joyce was fixed in his adolescence, that was the age of Stephen Daedalus perhaps.

Madame Leon, whose husband was Joyce's close friend for the last twelve years of his life, recalls –

MME LEON: At six o'clock my husband would start pacing the room. rather restlessly, and I would say, 'What's on? What are you expecting?' And he would say, 'Why, the old man is due.' He used to call Joyce the old man. It was a loving and affectionate nickname he gave him. But

Joyce said to me one day, 'You know, Mrs Leon, I am not old. You should tell your husband not to call me old.' The word for 'old man' in Russian, because my husband was Russian, is *sturik*. Joyce knew several Russian words but he resented this word very much.

I used to overhear some of the readings because my husband used to read to Joyce and correct proofs with him, and sometimes my husband was puzzled by the sense and he would say to Joyce, 'Sir,' because they were always very formal with each other, 'this may be art and this may be genius, but don't ask me to understand it.'

And talking of formality, says Mrs Jolas –

MARIA JOLAS: One never felt that he was any more formal with one person than with another. He was naturally of a formal nature, and at the same time capable of extraordinary intimacy. For many Americans, who are apt to call each other by first names before they know the last, his attitude of formality seemed to them a form of coldness. I was brought up in the South in America, and we have perhaps retained a certain formality ourselves, so it didn't shock me as it did certain people. Though Joyce was certainly a close friend for many years I never called him anything but Mr Joyce, and he never called me anything but Mrs Jolas. If he liked the men well, he called them by their last names without the mister. But the women he always called Mrs or Miss.

As Arthur Power says, the notable thing about Joyce – this man who could write with the savage indignation of a Jonathan Swift – was his gentleness.

ARTHUR POWER: Joyce was very easy-going and he hated any unpleasantness. In fact if it occurred, Joyce would disappear and never reappear. And if unpleasantness did occur, or a tension between people, Joyce would give a great display of manners. He'd practically bow to the ground, and more or less efface himself before it. It was a form of defence really.

'My brother,' says Stanislaus Joyce, 'worked with illimitable patience, above all, patience. Once he was talking angrily to me about somebody and I said to him, 'Is that the patience of which you boast?' 'Oh,' he said, 'but I haven't written that.' And he added ironically, 'when the poet begins to write he intellectualises himself.'

Joyce reserved and kept himself for his writing. So much so, that his patient mask of gentleness, and reticence, made him seem boring at times.

POWER: One might say perpetually boring. I remember once he came to a studio party I gave, and an American journalist came there to meet him; he got Joyce in a corner and got nothing out of him and then he turned to me afterwards and said, 'Oh, everything he has to say has gone into his book.'

NIALL SHERIDAN: I felt he was a person withdrawn entirely from the real world, and when he was asked a question, before answering it, he would lie back in his armchair behind his enormous double glasses and seemed to disappear completely, and then came out with a studied answer which was deliberately dull.

Austin Clarke used to meet Joyce in a Paris café in the twenties.

AUSTIN CLARKE: Indeed, in depressed moments I can still remember the drabness of that place. It was a narrow by-way lit by gas and over-shadowed by the black wall of St Sulpice. I think Joyce chose that gloomy side-street because it reminded him somehow of Dublin. Always at six o'clock he was there before me, a tall, melancholy, bearded figure in black; fretting, impatient, striding up and down before the Holy Wall or standing despondently at the kerb.

We went into the same cheap little café, which was usually empty at that hour, and sat there in a strange silence. What could I say to him? What could anyone say to him? I felt like a small boy in the presence of a kind but very dejected schoolmaster. As he sat there, gazing abstractedly through the thick lenses of his spectacles and sighing to himself, I was oppressed by the silence that I daren't break and by his misery.

FRANCK: I think Joyce liked life. He was not so unhappy as one would imagine, but his happiness was a very special one. He really played with words, and only with words. That was the only one reason of happiness he had.

And speaking of words, Frank O'Connor remembers on one occasion visiting Joyce in Paris.

FRANK O'CONNOR: There was a tiny print in the hall which I noticed on my way out because it was a view of the river at Cork. It was a very pleasant little print and it had a very curious frame; I'd never seen anything like it before. So I put my hand on it and said, 'Oh, that's rather nice, what's that?' and Joyce said, 'That's cork'; and I said, 'Oh, yes, I know it's Cork but what's the frame made of?' and Joyce said, 'That's cork.' Then he said, 'I had great trouble getting the French framemakers to make it; they said they'd never made a frame of cork before.' I felt just a little bit dizzy after that one and it struck me that the man was suffering slightly from associated mania – a thing I was quite familiar with owing to a certain young lady who had an awful tendency whenever I was speaking about George Moore to turn the conversation on to Dartmoor.

Words, words, words. Joyce's appetite for them grew with eating. For him words were things: *the word was flesh. Frank Budgen got to know Joyce in Zürich.*

BUDGEN: Well, as I got to know Joyce better, his method of composition seemed to me to be to collect words. He invented them himself; he put them down himself, but then he was always listening and listening for every crumb of talk he could get from anybody – at the table, anybody in the street, anybody on the tramcar. He wanted words and words and words.

He'd always got a little tablet in his vest pocket – I should think about two inches square, and on any occasion that seemed to him to warrant it, he'd drag out this tablet and put down a word. It doesn't matter what it was, he'd put it down, one word, two words, a whole series of words if he could get them on it. And he'd always got that in his vest pocket in the restaurant where we used to eat every evening and drink.

In the beginning, it was Life that led Joyce to 'the Word'. In the end it was the Word that led him back to Life. Nino Franck recalls Joyce taking a taxi one day to the Bois de Boulogne –

FRANCK: In the last years before the war Joyce was working very hard on *Finnegans Wake*. Once he told me that during the whole afternoon he was working on his book, and so he was very tired. He'd taken a taxicab and gone into the Bois de Boulogne. And when he was in the Bois de Boulogne, he wanted to take a little walk. And he had been working on and making jokes about words all afternoon. So when he spoke to the chauffeur he called him 'chou-fleur' – that's cauliflower, and naturally the man was astonished and a little insulted, and Joyce paid and went out laughing. When he told me that he said, 'You know, I looked in and really he had the head of a cauliflower.'

For Joyce, words were magic. With them he could make or unmake a world. Nino Franck for a time worked with him, translating a part of Finnegans Wake *into Italian.*

FRANCK: He would read me one line of the book and naturally I would not understand entirely. But he explained to me all the jokes and all the significations of the line. Then we were trying to find an Italian equivalent but it was very shocking for me. He was never interested in an exact translation. He just tried to have an adaptation. Perhaps, for instance, he had said that the pencil is yellow and in Italian he would take just other words, such as 'the stilograph is green', just because sounds or jokes were better with those words. And that shocked me always, but he explained to me that he was not interested in truth. He said that it will be delivered from history.

In words, Joyce was free. But in fact, he was confined and consumed by his past. He left Dublin, but Dublin never left him.

CON CURRAN: Ah yes, over and over again, of course. In later years, asked when he was coming back to Dublin, his invariable reply was: 'Have I ever left it?' His love of Dublin was as great as his friendship for the people he knew in his youth in Dublin. To be a Dubliner of his generation was the passport to his house in Paris, or wherever he lived, in his later years.

POWER: If you asked him if he'd see anybody, his first question was always, 'Do they come from Dublin?' And if they came from Dublin he would always see them. His wife told me that his room was full of Dublin papers, and I remember once a friend arriving from Dublin and Joyce spent the whole evening arguing whether the price of bread had gone up, or down, because the friend said it had gone up, and Joyce maintained that it hadn't.

SHERIDAN: Occasionally he'd say, 'Has the number nine tram been taken off yet?' and he'd talk about Dublin, and then say, 'I'm tired of Dublin, I want to talk about something else.' He'd talk about the general situation again, and in a few moments another intimate question about Dublin. The obsession with Dublin was there all the time. As we were talking he pointed at a rug on the floor. It was a woven affair with some sort of pattern in the middle of it, and he asked me whether I recognised the pattern. I didn't and he said, 'That's the Liffey from its source to its mouth, given to me by an American admirer.' And then he added, 'Much more than any of my countrymen has ever done for me.'

MME LEON: Joyce was a great traditionalist so far as feast-days and saint's-days are concerned, and St Patrick's Day meant a great deal to him. He always liked to wear a sprig of shamrock in his coat lapel, and I remember once I was in London and they were in Paris and I bought a little pot of shamrock and airmailed it to Joyce; I understand he was quite, quite delighted.

POWER: I remember one day we were driving up the Champs-Elysées in a fiacre and I said to him, 'Are you proud of being Irish?' And he replied, 'I regret the temperament it gave me.'

But he loved Ireland – at a safe distance. In London, says Mrs Joyce, he liked to stay at the Euston Railway Hotel, the terminus for the Irish boat-train that had once carried him into exile. And Robert Lynd remembered Joyce going to a Belfast shop in London to buy Irish linen collars, and recalled Joyce's disappointment on finding there were no 13½ collars in stock. 'If I were to go back to Ireland,' he said to Lynd, 'I should live in Belfast.' He admired the busy industrial North just as he feared the easygoing South, and Dublin with its weight of paralysing memories. Fascinating memories. He used to question the poet Austin Clarke about the Dublin school at which they had both been students.

CLARKE: When he questioned me about the streets and the shops of the north side of Dublin, he was testing his own amazing memory and I knew that it gave him pleasure to use me as what one might call a kind of walking directory. But when I told him of premises and shops that had changed hands, or places that had vanished or perhaps had been rebuilt, he would sigh to himself and relapse into silence. That dream city, that vision of Dublin in which he was absorbed, was static to him and I could feel how deeply the sense of change and of new generations affected him – of life going on there all the time. And during those long intervals of silence I was back again myself in Dublin, back again at school, and I could hear the murmur of classes, the grating of the chalk on the blackboard and see even those brass candlesticks in the school chapel which had reminded Joyce of the battered mail of the fallen angels.

Fallen into Space, and Time. Delivered over to 'the nightmare of history'.

CLARKE: One evening Joyce must have been stirred by kindness or conscience, for suddenly he asked to see my first book. It had been published a year or so before in Dublin. With some hesitation I sent for it to Dublin. It was a romantic narrative poem about legendary lovers wandering through the Irish glens. And when I met him again, in great expectancy, he told me that he couldn't read it because it was much too long.

FRANCK: I had often occasion to speak with Joyce about English or American writers of his time, and I often asked him his feeling about them. I remember once I spoke to him about Eliot, and he just made a grimace, so I understood he was not interested. Another time I heard that D. H. Lawrence was in Paris, so I asked Joyce if he would be interested – for a quarterly that I was publishing – to include something of Lawrence, and then he said, 'Oh, no, it's too badly written. If you want something of those people you might ask something from Aldous Huxley. He's best-dressed.' And other times we spoke – that was in '26 or '27 – about some young American writers who were in Paris at this time, that was Hemingway and others, and I think he did not know of their books. He had just heard about them, and he was not very interested. I had the feeling that he did not read very much. He could not; his eyes were really ill, and it was very difficult for him to read. But I don't think he was interested in writers of our time.

POWER: But the point that he was always interested in was whether they had broken new ground. And he didn't think much of a writer who followed after other writers or improved what other writers had done.

Joyce met Proust once at a literary dinner, and Proust asked Joyce did he like truffles, and Joyce said yes, he did, and I know Joyce was very amused afterwards. He said, 'Here the two greatest literary figures of our time meet, and they ask each other if they like truffles.'

Nothing else. Two absorbed figures, each in search of his own lost times. Joyce on his journey, his Odyssey –

BUDGEN: But he wasn't a Greek scholar, not as the word Greek scholar is generally understood; and that must have stuck with him in some sort of way because I remember walking with him – I think it was down the Bahnhofstrasse – and I said I regretted that my own education, which, by the way, finished at twelve years of age, hadn't included Greek, and then Joyce, from a listless air, became suddenly vehement and, regretting Greek himself, he said, 'But just think in my case how that world is one which I am peculiarly fitted to enter.'

Once in one of the flats that he lived in – I think it was one of them in Passey – we were alone and Joyce said to me, 'Have you ever noticed when you get an idea what I can make of it?'

Budgen – whom Joyce called 'the most naturally intelligent man' of his acquaintance – was in some ways helpful to him, in the writing of Ulysses.

BUDGEN: Oh yes, I was helpful to Joyce, I believe, in many ways. Oh, anybody else would have done it, I don't want to make a song about that, but while I was in London and he was finishing *Ulysses* in Paris, he got me to send him this, that and the other material. I suppose that every master-craftsman, which he was, wants a mate or a fetcher and carrier, somebody to go and take the can back, and fetch the can full, too. I was living in Camden Town at the time, and I searched the newsagents of that part of London for anything that might help Joyce in his composition of, say, the episode on sexual perversity. I lit on a whole lot of photo-bits. One of them was called 'Bits of Fun' or 'Fashions, Fads and Fancies'. It had a picture of a bathing girl and a banal joke on the cover, and I bought it along with the rest, but when I took it home I found that it was a journal used by tight-lacers, and heel-drillers and flagellants among themselves; the correspondence columns were full of it. I rushed down to buy up as many back numbers as I could, just in time, because the journal was suppressed a week after, with a forty-pound fine and publication stopped for obscenity. Well, it was very helpful, I think, to Joyce.

FRANCK: Joyce had the habit of reading each day four or five newspapers – just the best newspapers in Europe. He read *The Times*, *Le Temps* – also the *Neue Züricher Zeitung*, the Swiss newspaper, and especially the *Osservatore Romano* that was the Cité du Vatican newspaper. He was always a little against the Pope, but he was very interested in reading the Pope's newspaper, and I remember once he had read that morning the *Osservatore Romano* and he had the surprise to find in this newspaper an article about his work, and he was absolutely full of joy, because that was more interesting for him than other newspapers.

Budgen wrote a book about Joyce and his work. And Joyce said –

BUDGEN: Now he said, 'Just a word about one or two precisions that you ought to introduce into that book of yours. You allude to me as a Catholic,' he said, 'but for the sake of precision and to get the correct contour on me, you ought to allude to me as a Jesuit.'

Joyce was proud of his training in Scholasticism, though he carried it into other, and stranger, fields, proud of its precision, its logic –

BUDGEN: I met him, I think it was at the end of the Bahnhofstrasse, and we went for a walk along the Zeefeldstrasse towards the Zürich Horn. And then I asked him, just to start a conversation, 'How's the book going on?' 'Ah,' he said, 'I've written a whole sentence today.' And I thought that people sat down and did their thousand words, I didn't know, and he said, 'Yes, yes, it's been a bit of a strenuous day.' I said, 'What are you looking for, the mot juste, the Flaubert thing?' 'Ah, no,' he said, 'I'm not looking for the mot juste, I've got them all. What I'm looking for is the order of words in the sentence.'

Do you remember the sentence?

BUDGEN: 'Perfume of embraces all him assailed: with hungered flesh, obscurely, mutely he craved to adore.' I think that's it.

That passion for meticulous, microscopic, monkish precision distinguished Joyce's work, above all else. Mrs Jolas, who with her husband first published Work in Progress, *tells of Joyce picking up a facsimile of that early medieval illuminated manuscript – the* Book of Kells.

MARIA JOLAS: He realised that I was destined to have all his proofs go through my hands, and that perhaps it might be worthwhile for me to have some understanding of what it was about. But I remember he picked up a book – the *Book of Kells* – and he showed me one of its most intricate plates, a very beautiful plate, and after joking a bit about the quality of the figures – for instance I remember he laughed about the thirty-five-year-old Christ who looked as if he had just robbed the hen-house, who was sitting on his mother's knee – he took me down into the left-hand corner of this very intricate plate and showed me, through a magnifying-glass, the beauties of the design in the illumination, and he said to me, 'That's what I would like to feel that I am doing in my work – I would like it to be possible to pick up any page of this work and realise that this is this particular work. I want it to be as evident as this is. Nobody who is acquainted with early illuminations could possibly confuse those of the *Book of Kells* with others.'

The same scrupulosity Joyce extended to the last moment of his last work, Finnegans Wake.

MARIA JOLAS: Everyone knows that last exhilarating feeling when the final OKs have been given on a rather difficult manuscript. This was one Saturday evening. We had driven back home over eighty kilometres and were celebrating the event at dinner when Joyce phoned from Paris. With great hesitation and taking enormous precautions, so that what he had to say should not be a shock to us, he informed us that he had six more pages to add to the book. Well, he was accustomed to great indulgence on our part, and a great desire to help, but we did say rather painedly that the *bon à tirer* had been given, and he replied rather stubbornly, not the least bit excitedly, well, he thought we'd better get in touch with the printer because the six pages had to go in.

It was quite evident after a few minutes' conversation that we had lost and he had won, so we called our poor, long-suffering printer and told him to hold up the binding and by Monday morning we were back at Saint Cyr with our little Ford and the six pages had arrived. And they did get in, needless to say.

STANISLAUS JOYCE: There is no doubt in my mind – and I am quite willing to bear whatever odium may attach to this declaration – that if I had still been at his elbow, *Finnegans Wake* would never have been written in its present form. While it was appearing under the title of *Work in Progress* I attacked it bitterly in letters to my brother, asking him when he intended to take down the scaffolding, and whether it was likely to go on until somebody asked a question in Parliament about it. It vexed me to see how little its professed admirers understood it, even less than I did. I was exasperated by the obstinate waste over a period of seventeen years of such original talent in order to produce in the end the world's masterpiece of strenuous inertia, a kind of cross-word puzzlers' bible. For *Finnegans Wake* is not only unreadable but unprintable, as the thousand odd misprints after the first edition prove beyond dispute. I was there to prevent him, so to speak, from jumping off a roof in order to find out whether it hurts, and to apply such remedies as my limited means permitted when there were mishaps.

But how much did Joyce need protections?

BUDGEN: I remember saying to our friend August Suter once, 'Joyce reminds me very much of a goat – he's very sure-footed and he's very watchful but he's very curious and he's lured to the edge of something into which *he never falls.*' And oddly enough, you know, Joyce was rather fond of goats.

Joyce had his own protections, his fences and defences. In a world that was chaotic, Joyce kept the rounded and returning and retaining wall of routine. 'He lived,' says Louis Gillet, 'by an entire secret calendar, to which he attributed almost superstitious importance. To his daring mind, which had broken with all dogma, this private religion represented a liturgy from which he never departed. For nothing in the world would he have failed to celebrate Candlemas, which was his birthday, or 4 July, his father's. Those were his happiest days.'

HANS GASSER: He wore a great many rings with very flashing stones, a topaz and sapphire and as far as I remember, a ruby, and they were, as he explained, to protect him against evil – he attached magic power to these stones.

MRS GRIFFIN: Yes, he used to carry various charms. He got some of them from India, like stones and a rabbit's paw I once saw him with.

MRS SCHAUREK: He was slightly superstitious, as every Irishman is, and I think thirteen was one of his numbers that he didn't like. He also objected to an empty bottle on the table. He'd always kind of make a gesture if he saw an empty bottle on the table. He didn't like it, I don't know why, but it meant something to him.

Well, an empty bottle can never go the rounds. And the round, the circle, the recurring and reassuring routine, was all-important to Joyce, whether in Trieste, or Zürich, or Paris.

FRAU GIEDION: There was always in Joyce a hidden core of primitive nature. During thunderstorms, and we have many of these in summer, he would be seized by an elementary fear of mountains and would creep into his hotel in the Bahnhofstrasse, 'like the Pope in the Vatican', he mentioned once, refusing an invitation to tea. The Zürich mountain became a *mont noir* to him and when the heavens discharged their electricity he would not move from his safer shelter.

Arthur Power remembers an occasion on which Joyce ordered the taxi, which was taking him out of Paris, to turn back because of a thunderstorm.

POWER: And I believe that shortly after this incident in the taxi there was a thunderstorm and Joyce collapsed in his flat and had to have a doctor brought to him.

BUDGEN: Well, apropos of this, he was ill once in Paris, I remember, and I called on him and asked what the doctor's opinion was, and he said the medico had asked him – seeing him in a nervous state – 'What are you afraid of, Mr Joyce?' And he told the medico, 'I'm afraid of losing consciousness,' and I think he was tranquillised by reference to his pulse and temperature and so on, for he was extremely conscious as an artist – and very conscious of all that he did, said, thought. 'Great artificers have to be.'

Joyce hated to lose control. And, though drawn to the very edge of it, he feared the abyss of the unconscious. Doubtless that was why he disliked surrealism in art.

FRANCK: Yes, often I spoke with Joyce about surrealism, but he wasn't interested at all. And this I understand was because the Joyce way and the Surrealism way are opposite. Surrealism goes from unconscious to conscious and Joyce goes from conscious to unconscious.

Joyce's exploration of the underworld was always a deliberate one. 'I am like a man,' he said once, 'who is trying to tunnel from two sides of a mountain. Whether the ends will meet I do not know.' But they were conscious ends.

OLIVER GOGARTY: Mrs McCormack was a patron of his, she was the sister of Rodahy who owned the great meat-packing industry in Chicago – a woman of great wealth – and she had been occasionally a patron of Joyce's – giving him money – but she offered him a good deal more if he would submit to a psychoanalytical test by Jung in Zürich – and Joyce refused indignantly. (I once showed some of *Finnegans Wake* to a psychiatrist. He said, 'Obviously schizophrenia.')

BUDGEN: Zürich was the second city of psychoanalysis – I'm not sure it wasn't the first because, after all, Vienna was at war in these days, and

Zürich not. But Joyce would have nothing to do with it. I remember him saying to me once at the Restaurant Pfauen, 'What's all this fuss about the mystery of the subconscious? Isn't consciousness just as mysterious, and what do they know about that, anyway?'

But the most conscious artist must relax. And Joyce had his evenings off. He liked the cinema. Had he not once started the first cinema in Ireland?

FRANCK: Joyce liked very much to go to the pictures, and he had very special taste in cinema. He was a big admirer of Ibsen, and liked strong drama, very dramatic scenes and dramatic players. He liked Harry Baur who was a very dramatic French actor. I was always a little annoyed, I must confess, because we were obliged to sit in the first line of chairs.

– because of Joyce's semi-blindness. And Budgen remembers Joyce muttering to himself, 'Quelle vache! Quelle vache!' as he watched Marlene Dietrich playing the coy Venus in a cloudy bathing-pool. Opera was another relaxation, and Joyce was inordinately fond of Sullivan, the Irish tenor.

BUDGEN: You know I'm not musical at all, but there was a time when Joyce used to drag along old friends, give them tickets for the opera and so on, only to hear this tenor of all times. He regarded him, so he told me, as the greatest tenor since Tamagno.

MME LEON: John Sullivan, tenor, was one of Joyce's favourite singers – he was so enthralled with his voice that he absolutely inflicted Sullivan on to all his friends; he even brought us Sullivan records, and very often when he came to see my husband, he would have to play those records, which we disliked very much.

One evening my husband seemed rather despondent and I said, 'Well, what's wrong?' So he said, 'We have to go to the opera with the Joyces – Sullivan is singing in *William Tell.*' I said, 'Well, can't we get out of it?' and he replied, 'No, we can't, because everybody else has got out of it, so we have to go. Mrs Joyce has asked us to be there particularly, and we have to dress because Joyce is dressing.'

If Joyce got dressed up, we had to do the same and it was a great effort for my husband who disliked formal clothes very much, but Joyce in his flowing cape and white scarf and dinner jacket and his ebony-tipped cane – oh, he looked very, very swell and elegant.

We went to the opera and we had stalls in about the fifth or sixth row. Sullivan, of course, was on the stage, and when he finished his solo, I believe in the second act of *William Tell*, Joyce jumped from his seat in a terrific wave of enthusiasm and started waving his arms about and shouting at the top of his voice, 'Merde por Lauri Volpi.'

Of course, that is a word not generally used in public, except by taxi-drivers. There was a moment's silence then the whole house burst into howls of joy.

BUDGEN: The next day I called on him at his flat and he said, 'Well, what do you think of Sullivan?' Being non-musical, being a painter, I have to find pictorial references for everything, I suppose. I said his voice reminded me of the Forth Bridge. He thought to himself for a minute, then he threw his head back – it was something he was interested in, you know – and said, 'No, you're wrong. No, that voice isn't iron, isn't steel, it's stone; that voice is the voice of Stonehenge.'

FRAU GIEDION: The tenor seemed to him a gift of God, whilst the bass remained fettered by its healthy stability and the baritone by its beautiful naturalness.

The god-like, the heroic, attracted Joyce. It was part of the cyclic theory of history which he got from Vico. When he was in England his sister-in-law remembers –

MRS GRIFFIN: One Sunday afternoon we set out for Stonehenge. It was a very dreary day, and we could see nothing to amuse us but the wide open space of grass, and once in a while a soldier would come along on a motor-cycle. I said, 'Where are we going? This is a terrible place!' And he said, 'Kathleen, I am fourteen years trying to get here.'

MME LEON: Mr Joyce was a great lover of theatre, and also a great lover of music – they would all meet after the theatre, either at the Café Francis on Place l'Alma, or at Fouquet's, and there later on, when I was through with my own work, I would join them. And always find more or less the same group sitting there, sipping white wine. He was very fond of doing this – it ended his day in a very Latin way, because in France people generally end their day at a café.

And not only in France, but in Zürich.

GASSER: One evening we had a meal in one of those small restaurants around the lake. We went there in a car, and after that meal he lay on top of the car and was driven home in this way. He explained that he wanted to see the world pass by from this position.

'In vino veritas,' said a friend to Joyce. 'No,' said Joyce, 'in risu veritas.' Laughter was the link: the thing that made ends meet. The cunning, the punning, the double entendre of approach that tunnelled the mountain.

FRAU GIEDION: A regular meeting-place with friends was the Restaurant Pfauen, where the Sion Fondant wine, which Joyce christened Erzherzogin – Archduchess – because of its Erzgeschmack, or brassy taste, gradually converted the mood from one of quiet conversation to one of joking and fantasy. Joyce praised the white wine of Switzerland on all occasions, often to the sorrow of his French friends, as the wine *par excellence*, as the Midsummer Night's Dream. 'Red wine is like beefsteak,' he used to say, 'white wine is like electricity.'

BUDGEN: Joyce loved the white wine of Switzerland, or any other country for that matter – in France generally Chablis. But, on account of its acidity, it was not considered good for his system. However, in order to circumvent the rules of the doctor and the orders of his wife, he would resort to that 'silence, cunning and exile' that he proclaims in *The Portrait of the Artist as a Young Man*, and get planted in the vestibule to the men's exit a carafe of white wine and a couple of glasses. If he gave me the signal I would accompany him out, on account of his half-blindness, and we would knock back this wine and then go back to Mrs Joyce at the table, just as if nothing had happened.

François Quintin, maître d'hôtel at Fouquet's, says –

FRANÇOIS QUINTIN: Ah, oui, sa femme le freinait un peu – le freinait. Ah, il avait bien ce petit penchant – il aimait bien le vin un petit peu.

POWER: Joyce always dined at the Trianon Restaurant. I don't think he liked dining at any place where he wasn't known. People used to go there just to see Joyce, and he liked it.

SHERIDAN: As we walked into Fouquet's, the orchestra suddenly stopped playing and everyone in the restaurant stood up. I could see that Joyce took great pleasure from this, and his attitude seemed to suggest, 'Well, look at what they think of me in Paris; would this happen in Dublin?' Of course it wouldn't have.

QUINTIN: Ah, non, sauf ceux qu'il connaissait. C'était un homme qui s'était tout a fait éffacé, qui entrait tout doucement et s'asseyait et il mangeait.

'It was I,' he adds, *'who looked after him, who knew his habits, who brought him dinner, and who pressed him to eat, because without that he would have eaten nothing.'*

BUDGEN: One thing about Joyce was that he was always a very heavy tipper in restaurants, even in Zürich, but I'm thinking particularly of Paris –

JAMES STEPHENS: All waiters loved Joyce: he gave millionaire tips, and, better, he would ask a waiter which was best: the *sole chose*, or the *gigot quelque chose*, and would as eagerly ask whether the waiter preferred Racine to Corneille, or the other way about.

They loved him. He gave François Quintin a copy of Ulysses.

QUINTIN: C'est en '38 – il m'a fait cadeau d'un de ses derniers ouvrages qui s'appelle *Ulysse* – je le tiens précieusement chez moi. Ça me rappelle ces bons souvenirs.

MARIA JOLAS: He had that gift of inducing friendship – oh, to an extraordinary degree – in people of every walk in life. I don't know of anybody who showered as much affection, but real affection, among, for instance, head waiters, and the maids at the school. Whenever Monsieur Joyce came it was a special occasion, and they recognised that fact. They would run out to meet him, to take his cane and his coat, to do any errand he wanted; I don't think anyone who ever had that type of relationship with him had other than the most immense respect and affection for him.

A far cry from the timid but determined young man in Victorian Dublin who once saved up 12s. 6d. to go to a good restaurant to see how the well-to-do dined. And yet – was it? The mind's overcoat changes, the heart's underwear remains. Or does it?

BUDGEN: Talking about Victorianism, there's another angle that was very Joycean, another piece of him that was very Victorian, and that was his attachment – that's the right word I think – to the underclothing of the ladies of Victorian days. He regarded these articles of underclothing as being just as important to feminine allurement as the curves and volumes of the female body itself; he even went to the length of carrying a small pair, I might say, a miniature pair, of ladies' drawers, of Victorian pattern, in his pocket – tapes and all complete. And I've known him flaunt these around at the convivial table and when the laughter had died away he could go back to talking about Socratic dialectic and so on. But he waved these around just like a football fan might wave a rattle.

'Where,' Joyce would say, 'did Socrates learn his dialectic, but from Xantippe his wife? All those interrogations he got when he came home late at night.' 'You'll agree,' said Joyce carefully to Budgen, 'that women can do most things?'
'Yes,' said Budgen, 'I suppose so.'
'They have made a name in painting,' said Joyce. 'They even write. They can make music. But there's one world they have never entered.'
'What's that?' asked Budgen.
'You've never heard of a woman philosopher,' said Joyce triumphantly.

BUDGEN: Yes, he considered that Christ was imperfect in this sense; he thought that Christ was an imperfect figure because he had never had the great task of living with a woman, which is one of the greatest difficulties that male humanity is ever confronted with.

POWER: I don't think he liked women. He was frightened of them and you might say had almost a disgust of them. I remember asking him once – he lived of course a long time in Italy – what Italian women were like, and he said, 'Cold like all women.'

But definitely Joyce was not a man of taste. It showed in very curious ways. The Russian ballet then was very popular and very good and Joyce said he didn't care for it at all. In fact he went once and wouldn't go again. Also his flat didn't show any taste, it was just ordinary commercial reproductions of Breton furniture.

But Mrs Jolas got a different impression, and drew a quite different conclusion.

MARIA JOLAS: 'How curious!' I said to myself. 'Here we are in the home of the most original writer of the century, and yet no attempt has been made to translate this originality into an eccentric background.' On the contrary, the apartment was unobtrusively furnished, extremely comfortable and impeccably neat and clean. The tea and cakes were delicious, and Mrs Joyce's genuine friendliness made one feel immediately at home.

POWER: He was distinctly bourgeois. He hated Bohemians and he hated Bohemian cafés and anything to do with them. His life was very regulated and it was bourgeois in all its aspects. He was a great family man. The last time I saw Joyce he was living in a flat off the Champs-Elysées. I remember him sitting in the hall and shrugging his shoulders and he said, 'Well, I know *Ulysses* is a middle-class work.' And it seemed more than any other criticism I ever heard made against *Ulysses* that seemed to have gone home with him.

It was Wyndham Lewis, the iconoclast, who dubbed Ulysses *'middle-class'. Whereas Karl Radek, the Communist, castigated it as 'the dregs of capitalism'.*

MARIA JOLAS: There were certain persons that felt that his sympathy with the proletariat was not as great as it should be, and his comment on that subject was a very amusing one. As he said, 'I don't know why they should say that; there's no one in any of my books that has any money!'

Nor, on the other hand, is there anyone in Joyce's books who does any work. Joyce's world is a static world. But Mrs Jolas recalls a remark he made about Finnegans Wake –

MARIA JOLAS: Unless I'm dreaming, I remember a conversation one evening in which he explained that the apostrophe was left out of the title in the intention of giving it another dimension, which was to the effect that the Finnegans and the humble people of the world *do* wake.

But, for Joyce, the most important unit of society was the family.

BUDGEN: Well, he always said of the Jews that they were better fathers – and he said this with great emphasis; they are better fathers and better husbands and better sons than we are.

POWER: Joyce told me one day, when we were driving back along the Portsmouth road, that his grandson had been born. He seemed to regard it as a matter of great importance. And I was irritated at the time and I said I couldn't see why, that after all children were born every day to everybody, but he repeated with great insistence, it is the most important thing in the world, and I made some sarcastic reply and from that evening a coolness sprang up between us.

Joyce left no one in doubt of his feelings in this matter.

MRS SCHAUREK: Jim, you see, had Norah as a guiding star. If she hadn't come up to expectations, apparently it would have meant he couldn't write, he couldn't carry on.

MARIA JOLAS: As our literary ties grew closer with Joyce the writer, the ties of friendship also strengthened, and I was able to witness the absolutely essential role that Mrs Joyce played in his life. For Joyce, his wife and their two children were the organic, the permanent, the unbreakable relationships, the ones around whom his whole life rotated.

POWER: Mrs Joyce and Joyce always struck me as having great sympathy and great understanding between them. She was not literary in any way, and didn't pretend to be, and one admired her for it. But she was a very close companion, he never went anywhere without her, and he didn't like people who came and only paid attention to him and ignored Mrs Joyce. Generally such people he didn't care to see again.

MARIA JOLAS: Few of those who knew him, I imagine, realise to what extent she was not only interested in his work but contributed to it. She had always been a timid woman and, unlike many wives of artists, was quite content to remain in the background, when it seemed her role to do so. But it must not be forgotten that she was, even as a young girl, an extremely witty, gay woman; she shared Joyce's love of beauty, the operas he enjoyed, for instance, she knew by heart, and his works are literally filled with her original expressions and her humorous, penetrating observations. I recall once, while dining together, the four of us were discussing the word 'genius', which someone had applied to Joyce in a critical article one of us had just read aloud. The two men started a conversation of their own and Mrs Joyce turned to me, 'I don't know whether or not my husband is a genius,' she said, 'but I do know that he is absolutely unique. There is no one like him.'

Family celebrations were Joyce's happiest days.

MME LEON: Of course his memory was so remarkable that he never overlooked anybody's birthday or wedding day, and when his own came around, it was always celebrated with a great deal of pomp and ceremony, either at his son's and daughter-in-law's house, or at his own home. Sometimes the dinner would be at Fouquet's or at a restaurant, and it was always very gay, and generally the evening, if it didn't quite start with music, certainly broke into singing very soon. His daughter's birthdays, too, he never forgot, and on Lucia's Feast Day he always burnt a candle.

Lucia – Light! To Joyce, who was half-blind, light was all-important, the most cherished thing. Therefore he named his only daughter Lucia. His last years were entirely darkened by the mental illness of that daughter and unless one realises the immensity of the tragedy for Joyce, this total eclipse, one cannot measure the achievement of his last work or appreciate the courage and endurance that went with it.

MARIA JOLAS: The subject is, of course, a painful one, and since Joyce himself was extremely reticent about it, one hesitates, now that he is gone, to mention it. The fact is, however, that from 1932 on – when Lucia was first taken ill – until his death, he exerted every effort, first to cure her and then, when this appeared to be impossible, to surround her with the love and personal attention he felt should be hers. His weekly visits to her in the Maison de Santé near Paris cost him untold nervous force, but as long as he could do so, he kept them up. In the summer of 1940, when it became evident that he would be able to enter Switzerland with his wife, son and grandson, he left no stone unturned to obtain permission for her to join them. This was first granted and then cruelly withdrawn at the last moment. I remember many conversations we had together on the subject during the summer of 1940, when both of us, trapped in a country hotel – fortunately in the 'Free Zone' – were groping for a solution to the problems posed by the defeat of France. I can still hear Joyce's anguished voice when, during the week that preceded my departure, after examining the problem from every angle, he would ask me, 'If she were yours, could you make up your mind to leave her?'

'Who,' says Louis Gillet, his confidant, 'would have recognised in this anxious father, tormented with pity for the distress of a daughter, the famous scoffer, the cynical, satirical author of Ulysses? *Joyce accused only himself. Everything that went wrong in his child's life was to be laid at his door because of the abnormal elements of his genius. He was tortured by this thought, which during the last years of his life remained with him*

constantly; and the spectacle of his sick daughter rent his heart, was almost the only subject of our conversations. Sometimes it seemed to me that I was listening to the lamentations of King Lear carrying Cordelia in his arms.'

Yes, Lear crying –

Howl, howl, howl, howl! – O, you are men of stones: Had I your tongues and eyes I'd use them so That heaven's vault should crack . . .'

There were rumours in Dublin of a strangely oppressed Joyce. In particular one rumour of his going to a certain hotel in the '30's. This story was told by a friend.

A FRIEND: He apparently wasn't too well dressed, because at the reception desk they were somewhat chary about him. However, they proceeded to show him the various rooms in the hotel, and Joyce simply refused room after room, and finally picked, of all places, one of the rooms just under the roof, a sort of attic or box-room or God knows what. Anyway, he spent about an hour inside there, and then tremendous screams were heard – a sort of screaming as though of a person possessed almost. Time passed. Joyce came down, perfectly composed, complete Chesterfield manner as usual. He had a meal, I think, and then went back. After a period, again a repetition of the same business – screams, shouting and all this. Then he came out again – perfectly composed, the last word in suavity – gentle, completely himself.

Joyce, says Gillet, did not write about his agony, he lived it.

MARIA JOLAS: Well, Joyce tried to remain in Paris after the war started: there were certain rather painful complications – family complications – which he tried to meet in Paris. He found the darkness, the black-out in the evenings, extremely painful. Naturally his blindness already isolated him and when there were no guiding points at all in the streets he gave up his Passy home.

Before he left Passy, Budgen went to see him.

BUDGEN: I spent an afternoon with him there. He had a copy of *Finnegans Wake*, hot from the press. He asked me to read the last nine pages – that wonderful, unforgettable death of Anna Livia Plurabelle which is the death of the human body, death of nature if you like, and the death of a single person; and when I'd finished that, there seemed to be nothing more to say, so we just walked out. Both of us had appointments but we were strolling around in a leisurely way. We went over the bridge. Dawdling around Paris leads always to hailing a taxi. We hailed one. I had an appointment at the Dome, and Joyce one with Paul Leon. Joyce set me down at the Dome and I made my way through a traffic jam and I remembered hearing his voice at the back of me saying, 'Lot's of fun.' And it was a catch-phrase he'd invented himself, so I supplied the end of it – 'at Finnegans Wake'.

Joyce, with his family, joined the endless stream of refugees to Unoccupied France. And at length he found shelter in a village near Vichy, St Gérard-le-Puy, in 1940. His friends from Paris gathered round him – the Jolases, the Leons. In the afternoons, Paul Leon would join him in revising Finnegans Wake – *his one root in a rootless existence.*

MARIA JOLAS: He spent a good deal of time listening to the radio; in fact that was practically the only diversion of any kind that was left, during the absolute isolation of those first months after the defeat, and by that time we had all moved up together into the village, in a little hotel called the Hôtel du Commerce, which we had taken, and I had set up a small personal dining-room for the Joyce family, Mrs Joyce and Mr Joyce, and myself, and their son Giorgio, and I was able to give him a certain amount of privacy during that time, to keep him away from the schoolchildren and the various activities and noise.

He was a person who never liked to go to bed early, and being something of a night-owl myself, we often found ourselves, after Mrs Joyce went up to bed, sitting alone listening to the radio, to what he used to call the transatlantic clowns over the National Broadcasting Company.

Joyce had always been a keen listener, and anything about Dublin always had his ear.

MARIA JOLAS: He was perhaps more aware than anyone we knew of what was to be broadcast, and he would call us up. One time he had just heard over the BBC that Yeats was to read some of his poems; well, he called us and said to come to his place immediately; not to listen over our own radio, but to come and listen with him, which we did, with great emotion.

It was typical of the older and mellower Joyce that he denied his youthful riposte to Yeats. 'Even if I had thought it,' he urged, 'it wouldn't have been polite to have said it.'

Life in the French village did not suit Joyce, who longed to get to Switzerland. His friends, the Leons, returned to Paris, where Paul Leon, who rescued most of Joyce's books, was taken by the Nazis. He died at their hands. Mme Leon vividly remembers a visit she had from two civilians –

MME LEON: One wore a brown tweed suit and he turned up the lapel of his collar and said, 'Polizei Gestapo'; the second man was a Frenchman and he produced a card from the Vichy Minister with a red, white and blue band across the corner. I ushered them into the living-room. They came in and one of them sat down at the table. The same table where 'Anna Livia' had been translated into French. The Frenchman was prowling around the room asking questions about various family photographs on the wall. And suddenly the German said to me, 'Who did your husband work for?' I said he didn't work for anyone, he was a professor of philosophy, he was a scholar and he worked for himself. And they said, 'Oh no, he worked for someone. We know it. You must tell us for whom he worked.' I kept denying this, and suddenly he pounced on the large portrait of Joyce we had and said, 'Who is this man? Is this your husband?' I said, 'No, that is James Joyce, an Irish poet and writer. Didn't you know about him?' And he said, 'That is the man your husband worked for; that is why we have come.' I said, 'Why?' I didn't understand what he was driving at. So he said, 'Because we want first editions, and we think you must have some.' So I said, 'Oh, why do you want first editions?' So he answered, 'Weil das wert hat' – because they have value.

FRAU GIEDION: Joyce wanted only one thing: to find a place of peace where work and meditation were still possible. At last he found it. It was on 17 December 1940 that he extricated himself from the confusions of war and reached Switzerland. 'Here we still know where we stand,' he said, as he looked around in a Swiss inn, shortly after his arrival. Even thinner than usual he seemed, when we saw him getting off the train at Zürich, with his superior, rather mocking smile, which partly opened his thin lips, and half-astonished, half-absent eyes which, magnified by glasses, seemed to live a life of their own.

Immediately after first settling down, Joyce set off in search of a flat. I remember, too, he set out for the Librairie Française, to find for his grandson, Stephen, a French edition of the Greek legends. You could see them walking in the snow, his hand in Stephen's, and the excited little boy pulling him forward, enchanted to see for the first time this white carpet, whilst Joyce, dazzled by the snow, seemed to suffer from the too blinding light. Then there was that last Christmas dinner that we shared with his family and himself. The songs, religious and secular, the Irish airs, the Latin canticles in which blended wonderfully the tenor voice of the father and the bass of his son Giorgio. Little Stephen demanded to sing under the table and his request was satisfied. James Joyce wanted to hear again the record he had bought some years earlier. It was 'Ah Moon of My Delight', from the Rubáiyát of Omar Khayyám, sung by the Irish tenor John McCormack, whose voice, at its best, was so like that of Joyce himself.

I shall always remember that last invitation in the setting of an inn not far from the boarding-house where he then lived. The walls of the low little room were wood-panelled. Seated before a carafe of Fondant, Joyce delighted in the astonishing climate of Swiss stability. The old setting of the inn gave a short résumé of the eventful history of the last few months and emphasised the contrast between our peace, which he seemed to consider everlasting, and the storm outside. Nothing was more soothing for us than to hear this from a man accustomed to sounding the mysteries of the future. But the Swiss stability which enchanted him then did not hinder him from railing against the country and its proverbial cleanliness whose effect, according to him, was in some ways sterilising. He even thrived upon this theme and at the moment of goodbye he was talking enthusiastically on dirt, 'You don't know how wonderful dirt is!' he exclaimed. We were then standing outside. The charming background of the old-fashioned inn, softly lit, was replaced by the cruel, cold black-out. His voice reached us in a murmur, through the dark. We said goodbye to him.

On Friday 9 January, Joyce was taken ill.

FRAU GIEDION: Accompanied by his old friend Paul Ruggiero, after a dinner with his favourite Neufchâtel wine, Joyce was overtaken by violent pain. He had been in a happy mood and rebelled humorously, as usual, against the strictly observed hour of closing. A neighbouring doctor, called in the middle of the night, tried a too mild treatment. Forty-eight hours later an operation was decided upon. But it was too late. Joyce began to wander in delirium that evening and insisted again that Nora Joyce, who had not left him, should put her bed by the side of his.

Two days later, at two o'clock in the morning, he died.

FRAU GIEDION: It was the 13th, the date Joyce had always avoided for his journeys and for all decisions which he had to make.

That Joyce should have been taken ill on a Friday and have died on the 13th touched those who knew his feeling.

FRAU GIEDION: I remember the burial, high up on a hill in Zürich, near the zoo. A cold and wintry day hung over the wooded plain and the hillside. A mysterious sun, milky and round like the moon, seemed to hide behind a misty glass.

Hans Gasser remembers it too –

GASSER: It was a ghastly winter day with lots of slush coming down from the sky, and there were no taxis any more, as the petrol rationing was very strict. Therefore I took a tram, and in this tram, going up the hill very slowly, there was assembled almost the whole funeral party. I did not know many people, but they were all talking about James Joyce. There was Lord and Lady Derwent; he was cultural attaché at the British Legation in Berne during the war, and there was his eye-doctor, and the secretary of Paul Klee, the painter.

We arrived at the cemetery and were directed into the chapel. But, as James Joyce did not want to have a priest at his funeral, there was nobody there, and the attendants of the mortician did not know what to do, as usually in Switzerland one has a priest, either Catholic or Protestant. The main speech was given by Lord Derwent, who was usually very brisk but, I think, as he had to perform an official duty, he made a rather formal speech. After this we went into the snow again, and the coffin was carried in front of us, and we walked right to the end of the wall, where the hole for the grave was dug.

Meanwhile in the distance there was the faint roar of the wild animals in the zoo, and we stood round the grave, and again didn't quite know what to do, because again there was no priest, and this time not even an official funeral speech. So we looked at each other in a very embarrassed way until a very, very old man turned up – obviously a man who hovers over the grave, as one sees in almost every church-yard, men who seem to just wait till they are buried themselves. A tiny man who obviously was deaf, because he went to one of those attendants of the mortician, who was holding the rope which went underneath the coffin, as the coffin was not yet sunk into the grave, and he asked, 'Who is buried here?' And the mortician said, 'Mr Joyce.' And again in front of the whole assemblance of mourners he seemed not to have understood it. He again asked, 'Who is it?' 'Mr Joyce,' the mortician shouted, and at that moment the coffin was lowered into the grave.

James Joyce had accomplished his destiny. He had flown past the nets into the silence, exile and anonymity of death.
'His last words,' says Eva, his sister, 'struck me forcibly as the keynote to his whole life.'

EVA JOYCE: His last words were, 'Does nobody understand?' – and I'm afraid that's what none of us did – understand him.

STANISLAUS JOYCE: I confess I have no better explanation to offer of his triumphant struggle to preserve his rectitude as an artist in the midst of illness and disappointment, in abject poverty and disillusionment, than this, that he who has loved God intensely in youth will never love anything less. The definition may change, the service abides.

A FRIEND: But when you sum the whole thing up, when you read all a man has written, you ask yourself the final question, you want to know what exactly was deep down in his mind. To me, anyway, this is a serious theme, to be personal – and may be completely unfounded. However, if you observe that peculiar detachment the man had, in all personal relations and his objective, remote treatment of such things as sex, nationality -- almost everything in fact – I think you can only explain that sort of personality by the fact that deep in his nature there was an incessant and morbid preoccupation with conscience – a despair, a theological despair, as we call it – which he kept at bay by untiring devotion to work and by inordinate artistic ambition. Remember that vocation which he chose for himself – the artifex and so on – the uncreated conscience.

Well, the thing I'd like to know most of all is this: what was the mind of Joyce when he wasn't writing – when he wasn't playing host to the powers – what was his mind in his most desolate hour? And, most of all, what was his mind in his last conscious moments, when the ego faltered? I in charity, and indeed in sympathy, want to believe that beneath the lava of his art, of his life, of the poverty of Trieste, Paris and Zürich, and of his pain – I want to believe that he saw again the very City of God.

GEORGE MOORE

George Augustus Moore was born of Anglo-Irish stock – yet he affected a French bearing and accent. His family had both Catholic and Protestant strains in it – yet he chose to be an agnostic. He belonged to a landowning class with peasant sympathies – and he dwelt only in cities. Out of contradiction and between hammer and anvil, he forged for himself a third man – a writer of character. Yet he had no natural gift for words. Richard Best has a story.

RICHARD BEST: It was curious that George Moore hadn't spoken until he was able to run about. He was a little boy, so his brother, the colonel, told me, after we had buried his ashes on the island in front of Moore Hall. As we were driving away (I had read the oration over his ashes, which AE had written) the colonel pointed out to me a well down by the lakeside in front of the mansion and he said George had never before spoken, then one day they heard a little voice crying out Da-fa-na! Da-fa-na! They went down and little George had fallen into the well and these were the first words.

As a boy, George wanted only to ride a Grand National winner.

CAPT. DICKY BIRD: He took no interest whatever in racing, as far as I could find out. But his father took an enormous interest in racing. In fact, the Moores were the greatest racing people in the West of Ireland next to Sir William Gregory.

Captain Dicky Bird should know. We do know that George was a poor starter. It took him seven years, said Oscar Wilde, to discover grammar, seven adult years. After that he discovered the paragraph. He was fifty-four, and a notable novelist with a score of books to his name, before he discovered the subjunctive.

BEST: I said to him at one time, 'Oh Moore, what you want there is the subjunctive; the subjunctive of that will get you out of the sentence.' 'But what is the subjunctive?' he said .'Oh well,' I said, 'the subjunctive mood is if you say, "If it rains we shall not go." "Qu'il soit" in French, you know.' Moore was delighted with the subjunctive, so I told him there were various subjunctives, for instance there was the jussive subjunctive; – well, I don't think I gave him an instance but one might well have said, 'Jussive subjunctive is like the Ten Commandments – "Thou shalt not commit adultery" would be a jussive subjunctive.' I could imagine Moore saying, 'Oh, but why not? I've been doing it all my life.'

It was at the turn of the century that Moore came to live in Dublin, city of remarkable acoustic properties – to spend the ten most resounding years of his life. In life and in letters it was, says Seamus O'Sullivan –

SEAMUS O'SULLIVAN: It was a time of great happenings, and Moore chose the moment for his entry with considerable dramatic skill. I remember that when he entered a tobacconist's shop near the corner of Ely Place, we, in the excitement of being so near to the great novelist, went in at his heels with the mad idea of buying two cigars of exactly the same brand which we had seen him select.

Lady Hanson recalls his first visit to her parents.

LADY HANSON: I remember Mama had had the drawing-room newly papered, and she was suffering from disappointment at the effect. She had chosen a paper of blue and silver which looked extremely attractive in the piece, but when it went up it looked crude and cold and garish. As a matter of fact she had it changed a fortnight later, but I can vividly recall how it emphasised George Moore's ugliness. His hair was then a dull red, and it fell over his forehead in unbecoming streaks, making a hideous contrast with his lard-like complexion. Later on he became quite a familiar visitor, and we saw a great deal of him. He would ramble up in the evening to see us after dinner; his day's work was over and he was ready to talk.

BEST: He toiled and slaved like a civil servant.

Moore, said Douglas Hyde, taught us all how to work. Only in the evenings did he emerge from his cocoon of canniness, as Gogarty says –

ST JOHN GOGARTY: He was to be seen coming out at five in the evening when, as he said, 'the strain of composition has left my countenance, so I'm going out.'

Brinsley Macnamara had a weather-eye open for these outings.

BRINSLEY MACNAMARA: I had passed up and down Grafton Street

between four and five every afternoon, and he would be taking his customary short walk at that hour, coming from or returning to his house and garden in Ely Place, where, I had been told, he was inventing the story of his life. The one that was later to appear as the work in three volumes entitled *Hail and Farewell.*

The story about the story went that half Dublin was going to be in it as a set of characters. Nobody knew which half. The anxiety of those who felt they were going to be in it for certain was only equalled by the rising jealousy of those who felt he mightn't be going to put them in it at all. Mr Moore walked, therefore, with a slight air of suspense surrounding him as he went. People would see him smiling to himself, and wonder who he might be turning over in his mind for a character just at that moment.

It might, for example, be 'dear' Edward Martyn, Moore's cousin.

FRANK O'CONNOR: Martyn would say, 'Everybody in Dublin except myself seems to be worried about what Moore is saying of them.' Yeats said, 'Ah, yes, Martyn, that is because you don't know what he *is* saying about you.' Martyn said, 'What is he saying about me?' Yeats said, 'He's saying that you started the Pro-Cathedral choir, not because you like choirs, but because you like choirboys.' Martyn said: 'The scoundrel! I'll have the law on him!'

'You wouldn't like it so much,' said Moore's brother, 'when they put you in a book.'

O'CONNOR: Yeats hated both Moore and Martyn. He just felt they were two halves of a writer, and he used to tell endless stories about the pair of them. Moore was rattled about these stories, particularly as Yeats had given it to be understood that they were not to be published until after Moore's death. So Moore sent Yeats a message to say that he had heard he was keeping his stories to be published after his death, but *he* had written down a *lot* of stories against Yeats which wouldn't be published until after Yeats's death. Yeats sent back a message to say, 'Moore is talking nonsense. Moore couldn't leave anything at all to appear after his death.'

No, indeed, says Anna Kelly, his past secretary –

ANNA KELLY: He had no private relations with life, and there's nothing that I would know or a few other people would know about him that the whole world doesn't know about too; because all his conversations, no matter how private, all found their way into print sooner or later.

Moore was too much the storyteller ever to hold back the truth – or the untruth.

LENNOX ROBINSON: One evening, helping him into his handsome coat, fur-lined and astrakhan-collared, I spoke my admiration of it. 'That, Robinson,' he said solemnly, 'is the reward of ten years' adultery.'

I was young enough to believe him, but later on I remembered what Sarah Purser, or some other witty woman in Dublin, said about George Moore: 'Gentlemen kiss and never tell. Cads kiss and tell. George Moore doesn't kiss but he tells.'

What was this third man, George Moore, like?

GOGARTY: Moore had sloping shoulders and pegtop trousers – he always dressed in dark blue. He had a heavy moustache, the top of which looked as if it had been stained with strong tea. He had an underlip that stuck out and a large white forehead and the whole complexion was like porcelain – he had the most wonderful skin. He had white podgy hands – like a gourd or some vegetable divided in two. Yeats described the countenance of Moore as if it were carved out of a turnip, but it was only because Moore had described Yeats, who was addicted to wearing silk ties of the Latin Quarter and dressing in black with poetical inclinations, as an umbrella that somebody had forgotten at a picnic.

So there was great rivalry and Mr Moore walked with a slight air of suspense surrounding him as he went.

MACNAMARA: Always there was his aloof air as if he didn't properly belong to Dublin at all. A curious sort of apparition in our midst, as it were; an exotic creature who had wandered in here out of some other clime. Irish, of course, from top to toe, but he didn't look it somehow, for I had never seen the like of him before. He walked with a self-conscious and graceful stride, a not too obtrusive cane held by the middle in what looked like a soft hand.

No, says Leo O'Neill, he walked in no such way.

O'NEILL: He rather shuffled along. He walked fairly well but . . . he hadn't the walk of an athletic man. He moved in a slow manner.

Perhaps Richard Best can explain this.

BEST: Well, there's a story that Moore said to someone, 'How do you manage to keep up your under-drawers? Mine are always slipping down as I walk along the street.' And the friend said, 'Don't you know there are little loops on the drawers – you put your suspenders under them . . . ' Moore said, 'Here have I been for years suffering tortures in this way, and I never knew what those things were for.'

A willing suspension of disbelief on Moore's part, no doubt.

MACNAMARA: His black, curly-brimmed bowler made a sharp contrast with his yellow hair. He wore the kind of high stiff collar that was known as a 'cut-throat' at the time. It seemed to me to correct his retreating chin, and to some extent to keep more erect the head which had a tendency to turn slightly to the left. His legs, in rather tight-fitting trousers, were neatly carried, and he had small feet that might have been made for a dancing floor.

LADY HANSON: It amuses me to remember an evening at the Gogartys where he was a very intimate and frequent guest. They had a ball one evening and George Moore was among those invited, and he asked me to dance. I was a little surprised, but we attempted it and I discovered to my great pleasure that he waltzed beautifully. That particular winter in Dublin there was revived the old deux temps waltz that he must have waltzed years ago in Paris and he was charmed to find himself at home on a dancing floor. He kept saying, 'But this is delightful . . . this is delightful.' And we both waltzed with great aplomb and enjoyment.

Yet at other times, and in incompatible company, Moore could be quite unbending.

LADY HANSON: On those occasions he would simply sit with a blank stare – he had no civility conversation, and the atmosphere was very trying. I remember after a particularly sticky evening my sister complaining, saying indignantly, 'And George Moore sat, of course, as if he was in the tram.'

'An extraordinary man,' says Anna Kelly, who met him later in a publisher's office where he was looking for somebody who could spell Chekhov.

ANNA KELLY: He was an extraordinary-looking character. In the first place he was the first author I'd ever met who hadn't dandruff on his collar, because in our small publishing office most of the people were – with all due respect to the great – lean and shabby, and they had dandruff on their collars, but he was beautifully tailored. The young men used to pant into the office with their verses, but he wasn't like that at all. He was very sure of himself. He had great dignity and pomposity of manner, and he had an extraordinarily pink and white face and sloping shoulders. The face was soft and melting in outline, as if he had no bones, and he had golden hair and a long silky golden moustache. He looked just like an artful, middle-aged baby. The artfulness was conveyed in his eye, which could be very malicious sometimes, and he was beautifully tailored. I forget now if he had spats, I cannot remember. He was manicured and I'm sure he was pedicured as well, and he never had an unnecessary movement. He sat back in his chair, his hands, pale and boneless, folded across the placid stomach. There was a stomach, but not very much; I suppose it was just a small monument to many good dinners.

Moore's dinners were as intimate outrages as his words. One night, says Gogarty, we were dining at his house and the cook was preparing an omelette, and Moore said –

GOGARTY: 'We'll know exactly what's happening to us when the omelette comes up.' So the omelette came up and Moore took off the cover and then he went out to the hall and blew a police whistle. Presently, a policeman came in and Moore said, 'Go down and arrest that cook.' The policeman went down and said, 'But on what charge, Mr Moore?' 'Well, look at the omelette, she calls that an omelette.' So the policeman stood from one leg to the other, very embarrassed, and he said, 'Well, what should it be?' 'It should be food, but it isn't. She's obtaining money . . . ' 'Oh, yes, on false pretences – that'll be all right, Mr Moore.'

Dint of work and stint of sleep and a mint of food – those were Moore's recipes for living. Monk Gibbon recalls dining with him.

MONK GIBBON: I'd read so much about Moore the epicure, grey mullet and red mullet and all the rest, that I was expecting a meal almost out of the *Arabian Nights*. Actually we sat down to the coldest of cold mutton, garnished with a few potatoes, and I've forgotten what the second course was, but I certainly felt that plain living and high thinking was much more George Moore's line than the sort of meals I'd pictured him having.

And Austin Clarke concurs –

AUSTIN CLARKE: The dinner itself was always simple: soup, perhaps a saddle of mutton excellently cooked, and strange to say, *always* a milk pudding.

Once James Stephens consulted Moore as to how to behave when placed between two strange ladies at a dinner-party.

JAMES STEPHENS: 'Why,' said Moore thoughtfully, 'this is a problem that never struck me before. It is a very real one. If you were an Englishman you could talk a little about the weather, vaguely, you know, a number of Dirty Days and How are You's, and then you could say a few well-chosen words about the soup, and the meat, and subsequently about the pudding, Stephens.'

'Dammit,' said I.

'An Irishman,' Moore said, 'can always find something to say about the cattle, and the crops, the manure – no, not manure – ladies think that is a very strange stuff: they prefer to talk about theatres, actors and hats. I'll tell you; talk to the first woman about how pretty her dress is. Say that you have never seen so lovely a dress in your life. Then turn to the other hussy and say that she is the most beautiful person in the room; admire her rings. Don't ask her where she got them, never ask a woman where or how she got anything whatever – questions like that often lead to divorce proceedings. In short, Stephens, talk to them about themselves, and you are pretty safe.'

He enlarged upon this matter –

'You may talk to them about their hair and their eyes and their noses, but don't say anything whatever about their knees.'

'I will not, Mr Moore,' said I fervently.

'In especial, Stephens, do not touch their knees under any circumstances.'

'I will not, Mr Moore.'

'Restraint at a formal dinner-party, Stephens, is absolutely necessary.'

'I quite understand, sir.'

'Moreover, Stephens, women are strangely gifted creatures in some respects; all women have a sense akin to absolute divination about their knees.'

'Sir?' I queried.

'When a woman's knee is touched, Stephens, however delicately, that lady knows infallibly whether the gentleman is really caressing her or whether he is only wiping his greasy fingers on her stocking. But formal dinner-parties are disgusting entertainments anyhow. Goodbye, Stephens.'

'Psychological problems,' said Moore to Stephens, 'are women and religion and English grammar. They, and all other problems are literary.' For Moore, as for Joyce, the word was life. And, since letters cannot blush, his words were the pallid scandal of women, and the bêtes noires of Dublin tea-tables.

ANNA KELLY: He professed to be fond of women, but he hated their brains, I think he despised women really. He used women like a painter would use them, a decorative piece, a flower for the table of life, and they were very insipid characters. Sometimes he reminds me of Adolphe Menjou. He deserts the sweetest heroines, he gets them into trouble, somewhere or another, and then he just drops them, with half amused pity, pats them good-bye, while fishing in his pockets for the small change of sentimental regret. He loved corsets and little laced-in waists.

'He did,' says Eoin O'Mahoney. 'My grandfather was acquainted with another Mr George Moore, who one day received a parcel at the Irish Land Commission.

EOIN O'MAHONEY: On opening the parcel, Mr Moore was astonished to find a pair of lady's corsets. He had the parcel made up again and delivered immediately, with a covering note in which he apologised for having opened the parcel, to Mr George Moore the novelist who lived up the street at No. 4 Upper Ely Place. By return of post he got a most indignant letter from Mr George Moore, asking him how dared he interfere with other people's property.

ANNA KELLY: Women were the literary complement to his art, he used them like a painter would. You know I think Moore was a painter.

A still-life painter, says Gogarty –

GOGARTY: He was always attitudinising. I sent a young American girl to him on one occasion because she wished to be a budding authoress, and he was delighted. He said, 'Now, won't you sit down? You may keep your back to the window – though you're too young to keep your back to the window. Won't you take off your hat? Well, yes, you have Kathleen eyes.' So she said to me, 'How did he know my name was Kathleen?' She forgot altogether that I'd mentioned it in the letter. 'So Gogarty sent you. Gogarty's a good fellow, but not in the ecclesiastical sense. When I say good, I mean good-natured – I don't mean namby-pamby, you must understand. Now, remember, the whole secret of novel-writing is the story. You must have a story. If you haven't a story to tell there's no novel. Now what is your story? So it emerged, after much hesitation, that the young lady went to a finishing school at Lausanne, and she said, 'And you know, I was seduced.' 'Oh, good gracious, don't use that frightful word! None of us are seduced, we seduce ourselves.' Then finally it ended by his kneeling down and showing her one of his books.

BEST: I remember one night in particular there was a couple standing up against the railings almost opposite Plunkett House – a woman with her head resting upon the shoulder of the man. They stood perfectly silent, not a word spoken. Moore stopped and stared at them. And he said, 'But look at them! They were there when I came past here an hour and a half ago. They said nothing then, they say nothing now. Isn't it an extraordinary thing? I think I'll go up and speak to them.' I said, 'Oh no. You mustn't do that. Don't do that. They're in seventh heaven.' 'But I never could do that – could you?' 'Oh,' I said, 'I suppose I could if I tried.' But it struck me at the time that Moore can never have been really in love, because being in love and loving are not quite the same thing; and love is silent – always.

LADY HANSON: The only thing I can remember in connection with that was on one occasion there was a suitor of mine present and Moore remarked to me that the most becoming background a woman could have was to have a man in love with her, which I think was very sound. It gives you a certain confidence and poise.

Yes, of course, love, like everything else, was a sound *background, never a silent one, for Moore. He loved to pay lip-service and would often talk over these matters with his secretary, Anna Kelly.*

ANNA KELLY: 'Now confess,' he said to me, 'you would rather have two lovers than one?' And with the dew of the Convent and the

Reverend Mother still upon me, and without a lover at all, I used to consider this a very immoral idea. But I had the wit not to say so – after all, he was my meal ticket and a jolly good one.

Every literary skeleton has a human being in the cupboard, and Moore could be the most human and practical of employers.

ANNA KELLY: When he heard that I was living on ten shillings a week, up to the time I met him, he was angry – he had that much social conscience. And he gave me two pounds a week, which was heaven to me at that time. It was the first time I ever had any real money. And it was the first time since I left home that I could afford to buy meat for my dinner – I used to live on black puddings – I hate them since. He made me buy chops, and he used to come round to my room to see me cook them. He was always talking about food, I think he made me food conscious for ever. He said, 'You must always eat well,' and sometimes this alternated with: 'You should read Walter Pater for style,' – either eat well or read Walter Pater.

Style, style, style – all roads and all lame dogs led to literary styles, with Moore. The word was Alpha and Omega to him. 'I used,' says Dr Monk Gibbon, 'to discuss the whole art of writing with him.'

GIBBON: I remember I said to him once, 'It's the *joins* that are the real problem.' And he said, 'Yes, yes, it's the joins.' Actually of course, his own joins are extraordinarily good. That is one of the wonderful things about his narrative prose style. It's like a tapestry, or a river flowing along smoothly. The sentences flow out from one to the other and you build up this accumulative effect in the mind.

A smooth-flowing river, an endless prose tapestry. Or perhaps it might better be called the endless prose tapeworm of literary perfection which greedily absorbed all Moore's working days and all his waking nights to the exclusion of everything else in life. Austin Clarke once sent a verse-play to Moore for comment.

CLARKE: He insisted that the end of the play was wrong; that the demon of gluttony must be, in reality, a tapeworm. So he sent me a long letter which unfortunately got lost some years later, and in it he described in detail how the last act should be written. The tapeworm would suddenly appear, everlasting yards of horrible white, or red tape – and eventually all the characters of the play would be entangled and twisted up and interwound in all this tape as the curtain fell.

The smooth, endless, coiling, serpentine prose of Moore's does not suit the jerky, modern mind.

GIBBON: I can imagine Moore himself saying: 'You must surrender; you must listen to me.' Well, our lives are so busy we haven't time to do that sort of thing.

'Now I know nothing about it,' says Gogarty.

GOGARTY: . . . and far be it from me to set myself up as a judge of literature, but I was talking to an American bookseller in 57th street about George Moore, and he said, 'Even in the days when we used to sell sets of books, and the store was filled with customers, I once went up on a ladder, opened one of Moore's books, and stayed there for half an hour. It was so smooth.'

Yet Moore himself was anything but a bookworm.

BEST: Moore hadn't much of a library. One bookcase was all I remember. He didn't buy books, and he never really read much.

The gaps in his reading would have stabled an army of horses. Larry Morrow has a story –

LARRY MORROW: The story was that Moore as a young man was spending a weekend in a large country house, in England or Ireland. He came down to breakfast on the Sunday morning, turned to his hostess and said, 'Oh, that was a beautifully written book you left at my bedside last night. Exquisite. I sat up until three o'clock reading it.' His hostess was rather bewildered and she said, 'Book? Who was it by?' Moore said, 'The funny thing about it was that I couldn't find any name of the author.' So the hostess was still very perplexed and said, 'Well, what was it called?' 'Oh,' said Moore, 'it was called *The Bibble*.'

JOE HONE: I wonder what he did with all the books he got. I remember his house in Ebury Street, and he only had one shelf.

Well, Sean O'Faolain knows what he did with his book –

SEAN O'FAOLAIN: It was a little embarrassing for me – a young man's first book, like a woman's first baby – nobody has ever done it before – and old Edward Garnett said, 'You must send a copy to George Moore, you know, you've been very much influenced by him.' I was very displeased at this. I didn't feel at all influenced by George Moore. I didn't feel influenced by anybody, naturally – a young man doesn't. However, I sent a copy of the book to Moore with what I thought was a nice little letter saying, 'shove it on your shelves. Just a tribute of a young man to a master . . . ' – or something like that. Whereupon I got back a letter from his secretary saying, 'Mr Moore has received a copy of your book, and wants to know what on earth is he to do with it. He gets so many books.'

So many books, which Moore read by proxy. 'As for reading,' says Austin Clarke –

CLARKE: 'As for reading, our servants will do that for us.' Well, I venture to change a word in that phrase of de Lisle Adam, which was one of Yeats's favourite quotations, for it applies both to Yeats and to Moore in their methods of work. Yeats collected knowledge in the same way as he collected folklore – from other people. Moore was more systematic in his method of collecting, and when I knew him, my friend Ernest Longworth was his principal reader. Colonel Longworth was a brilliant Irish lawyer, classical scholar, and one-time editor of a Dublin newspaper, but he had fallen on evil days, and he was accustomed for a consideration to read for Moore in the British Museum.

I don't know whether he had read up scholastic philosophy for Moore when the latter was writing *Héloïse and Abelard*, but when I knew him, he was certainly copying out in *précis* elaborate accounts of the rival medieval schools of nomination and realism; perhaps it may have been for some corrections, perhaps for a new edition of the book. He told me that Moore knew nothing whatsoever about philosophy or scholasticism because he was quite incapable of abstract thought. But, Longworth said, he had an unerring gift of being able to use with every appearance of accuracy the material that had been summarised for him by Longworth.

Like Yeats, Moore was a magpie for other people's ideas, and feathered his nest with other people's wits. Once he asked young Lennox Robinson to help him with his play Esther Waters – *a dramatisation of his novel.*

ROBINSON: He had the script and he said, 'You, Robinson, can do anything you like with this.' I found it was extraordinary. It was a play that I couldn't understand because it was about horse-racing – I'd never backed a horse in my life; it was a play about pubs – I'd never been in a pub in my life; it was a play about baby-farming, and I hardly knew how a baby was made. But such handicaps did not daunt me and I started to work. Nearly every afternoon during that autumn of 1910 Moore would visit me, inspect my work, grow more and more interested, contribute more and more of his own work to it and, finally, carried away the whole manuscript. When the play was done, years afterwards, by the London Stage Society, my name did not appear on the programme. Perhaps quite rightly, for in the end my only contribution to it was the second act – the baby farm scene, written in my most realistic Cork manner.

Moore must have quite forgotten that I'd anything to do with *Esther Waters*, for it amused me to read, years later, in his preface to the American edition of the play: 'After listening to the second act for two or three minutes, I could not do less than interrupt the rehearsal. "Miss Great," I said – she was the actress – "are you speaking the text or are you making it up?" And when she told me she was speaking the text, I answered, "I only asked because I'd no idea I'd written anything so good." '

Poor George, with all his love and knowledge of the theatre, he never succeeded in writing a good play.

AE, O'Connor says, once told a story to Moore and Yeats –

O'CONNOR: AE told the story of Philip Francis Little to Moore and to Yeats, and he said he noticed the eyes of the pair of them beginning to expand and Moore said in a hushed voice, 'What a wonderful subject for a religious novel.' And Yeats said, 'What a wonderful subject for a poetic tragedy.' Then they proceeded to quarrel about that. First of all they agreed to a collaboration; finally there was a legal action.

The breach was never healed. Years later Gogarty, in London, used to go to see Moore.

GOGARTY: He'd beat about the bush for a good while and he'd say, 'Did you meet anyone of interest, any common friend?' I said, 'Oh, yes, in fact I met Yeats.' So he pointed to a book, Eckermann's *Life of Goethe*. 'Gogarty,' he said, 'that book contains any erudition that Yeats possesses, nothing else; he's never read anything else.' So when I went back to Dublin, Yeats said, 'I suppose you met nobody that I know in London, while you were over there?' I waited awhile and said, 'Oh yes, I met Moore.' 'Oh, you met Moore. You met that fellow. Well, what is he doing?' I said, 'He's going to write a book called *Perfect Poetry*.' 'But he knows nothing whatsoever about poetry. I don't want to tax your memory, but can you tell me what are the perfect poems he's including?' Yeats was waiting in vain for one of his own. 'Well,' I said, 'he put his thumb into his waistcoat; he leaned against his black marble mantelpiece and he recited, "Goldilocks, Goldilocks, over all the wheaten shocks". And that was one of his perfect poems.' 'Now I'll tell you something,' said Yeats. 'When I was down with William Morris at Kelmscott, in came the printer's devil and said, "Excuse me, Mr Morris but there are two blank pages at the end of your book of poems which we'd like filled in." And Morris said, "Excuse me, Yeats!" and with his left hand he scratched in that nonsense about Goldilocks, and that's what Moore gave you as perfect poetry.'

There's a County Mayo saying which goes – 'Scratch a Moore and your own blood will flow.' Charles Duff met Gogarty at Moore's house.

CHARLES DUFF: When I saw Gogarty I said, 'Tell me now, you know George Moore very well. What do you think of him?'
'Do you mean the man or his work?' said he.
'The man,' said I.
'Well,' said he, laughing, 'between you and me, Moore is one of the biggest bores in Christendom.' In due course I was introduced to the Great Man himself. He was very pleasant. 'I saw you,' said he, 'talking to Gogarty a moment ago.'
'Tell me, Mr Moore,' said I, 'what do you think of him?'
'Do you mean his work or the man himself,' said he.
'The man,' I said.
'The man, aha, the man.' And Moore made a priestly gesture, the fingers of one hand pointing heavenwards. 'He's not a bad fellow ... very kind and very well-meaning. But, God save us all, what a bore!'

GOGARTY: Well, I must return to the garden in Ely Place. Once George Moore was leaving Dublin for a prolonged period and he lent me the garden, and I was very grateful. But, to show the cantankerous nature of the fellow, he said to me, 'You mustn't give any garden parties while I'm away, because I hate maids walking on my lawn.' Well, into the garden came, one day, a blackbird. And Moore not alone saw the blackbird, but he saw chapters and chapters of his projected books

with the blackbird in the apple-tree. Now, the trouble about a blackbird
– and about one of these town gardens – is that there are cats, and
blackbirds and cats don't get on very well. There is some sort of
disunion amongst the animal world and I know that blackbirds and
cats are not compatible. And it was conveyed to George Moore, so he
was in a dreadful condition because it meant wiring the garden – which
was of considerable size – and that would interrupt his style; it would
put a penury into the style, which he didn't want to exhibit. So he
thought; he filled his dressing-gown pockets up with stones, and,
during the day, would look into the garden if there was any sign of a
cat, and a blackbird did occasionally sing in the trees. When Yeats, his
rival, heard this he had it conveyed to Moore that cats are nocturnal
animals, and to throw stones in the dark without seeing the target is
really ineffective. So then Moore decided that that was true, though he
reluctantly admitted the source of the truth. So, finally, he consulted
with his cook – not the one that had sent up the bad omelette – but
with a fresh one – and she decided that a trap would eliminate any cats.
So Moore set a trap, and one day Yeats called on me and he was beam-
ing, and I knew he had a story to tell. He said, 'By the way, you heard
about Moore's blackbird?' And I said, 'Oh yes, I used to hear a bird
singing.' 'Well latterly it hadn't sung – it couldn't sing,' he said, 'stuffed
blackbirds don't sing.' I said, 'D'you mean to say he's got it stuffed?'
'Oh no,' he said, 'he hasn't got it stuffed, but he set a trap for the cat
and he caught his blackbird.'

In some ways Moore was slow-witted.

DOSSY WRIGHT: He was known as the 'white slug'. I don't know
whether I should tell you that or not, but it was a fact.

ROBINSON: Yeats had a brilliant mind that went like a greyhound –
and Moore, equally brilliant, was slow, so he couldn't keep up with the
greyhound. It was a most interesting thing; this tick, tick, tick of
Yeats's mind and a perfectly grand mind of Moore, but so slowgoing.
The white slug coming up to the greyhound, you see.

*Slow but sure. All his life Edmund Gosse, his great friend, teased and
pecked at him mercilessly. But Moore, as Roger McHugh reminds us,
had the last word.*

ROGER MCHUGH: A relative of the Somervilles told me that his aunt
had the unpleasant duty of announcing to George Moore that his

friend Violet Martin, the 'Martin Ross' of 'Somerville and Ross' fame, was dead. As she entered Moore's study to break the sad news to him, Moore looked up from his writing. 'I have sad news for you, Mr Moore,' she said. 'I regret to inform you that your friend Martin Ross is dead.' Moore clasped his head. 'How sad,' he said, 'how very sad.' He arose and paced his study agitatedly. 'How sad,' he repeated. 'Here am I in the midst of this,' and he waved his hand dramatically at the books around him, 'alive, and my friend, my dear friend, Edmund Gosse, dead.' The lady interrupted gently, 'I beg your pardon, Mr Moore,' she said, 'it is Martin Ross who is dead, not Edmund Gosse.' Moore drew himself up and looked at her in an indignant fashion: 'My dear woman,' he said, 'surely you don't expect me to go through all that again?'

And yet Anna Kelly says that Moore had no sense of humour –

ANNA KELLY: He had positively no sense of humour. He was very proud of that. He said the only way he could judge a funny story was to tell it to the cook. Then the cook went downstairs and Moore listened at the head of the stairs. If the cook told it to the housemaid, and the housemaid laughed, then he knew it was funny – though I think that the cook and the housemaid were not laughing at the story, they were laughing at poor Mr Moore upstairs.

Yet what about Moore's most malicious and amusing Dublin book, Hail and Farewell. *Was it not pure comedy? Brinsley Macnamara has no doubts about that.*

MACNAMARA: In later years, after I had read *Hail and Farewell* for about the fifth time, each time with fresh delight, I thought of all the plays that Yeats and Lady Gregory must have read without ever finding anything to touch this comic masterpiece, into which he had put them as characters with all the other early figures of the Irish Theatre. He called it a novel, but it is really the best play that the Abbey ever produced. Yet there are still those who'd say that Moore was a failure as a dramatist.

In inventing just one more story of his life he had invented the whole Irish literary movement: a comedy which has had one of the longest runs in history, for, even after fifty years of continuous performance, it is still running well.

Moore had a sense of humour where others were concerned. But a man who takes his craft as seriously as Moore did cannot afford to be humorous about himself, though he may be witty at his own expense. 'I was born,' said Moore, 'I live, I shall die, a peculiar man. I could not be commonplace if I were to try.'

ANNA KELLY: He said, 'Absolutely none of my living contemporaries are worth talking about.' That was his attitude.

Yet, his contemporaries respected him.

O'CONNOR: AE's version of him was exceedingly sympathetic; AE was awfully fond of him. He praised his industry, he praised his courage, and he used to describe him as a man who lived from his own will and centre. The real problem is what made him, up to the day of his death, in spite of his perseverance, only half an artist. I should say that it was this intense devotion to something for which he was not fitted by nature. I always feel that Moore was a misfit. I sometimes think that, like his brother Maurice, he might have been a great soldier. But, somehow, he was all wrong as an artist, and that wrongness went through everything he did. He wanted to be a judge of food, a judge of literature, a judge of clothes and a judge of pictures, and he never had any natural taste.

ANNA KELLY: I liked him. I found him hard to work for but it was good for me to begin hard, because I never got it so hard again in my life. It was my first job, and I had to write shorthand at incredible speed, and I don't know how on earth I ever did it. It was there that I first got to know his ways as a writer, and he was the hardest working writer that I've ever met before or since. I hadn't met many before, but I've met many since. And although he always worked very methodically, he loved it. There was nothing else in life he liked better, than to write and write and write. He used to slave to polish his style. He thought style was a thing in itself. Perhaps he became too obsessed with it in the end. He dictated, corrected and recorrected. He'd spend half a day on one paragraph, and after lunch we'd tackle that paragraph again, and maybe the next morning when I'd come in we had to face the whole thing again. The table was crowded with bits of paper, all scribbled on, crossways, diagonally and everything. He was the despair of editors and printers. If your final page proofs have more than a certain number of corrections, there's a publishers' agreement that you have to pay more – they must have cost him hundreds of pounds. Even a letter to the papers had to be rewritten several times.

Sometimes he must have written at night. He couldn't keep away from it. If he ever took an hour off he felt he had to go back again and do it. And he had to write in company, he didn't like writing by himself. If I felt too lazy he would correct typescripts, but I had to be there all the time – to type, and retype and retype.

CLARKE: The sheer industry and persistence of Moore was shown in his own method of daily work. He advised me to write every day, and always to sit down in the morning and scribble a few thousand words – anything. He assured me that, even though it might be rubbish, nonsense, terrible, in fact, there would always be some phrase, some idea, some little glint in all that which would be of value at some time or another. I tried to follow Moore's advice, but it didn't work in my case.

ANNA KELLY: He had no physical nervous mannerisms at all. All his energies went into his work. I think his entire life went into his work, really. He sat as still as a Buddha, and his hands would be folded across his stomach. Then, after a few sentences, the rhythm would come to him, the hands would unfold, and they'd begin to move, waving to and fro, keeping time to the rhythm. He had a wonderful sense of words. They came just in a regular flowing stream – not a turbulent stream, but a very gentle stream. I think somebody called it the melodic line. Well, his prose, I used to think afterwards, when I did learn to think a little bit, his prose was very like his physique – soft, full of light – and boneless.

CLARKE: He told me once that he had always known that James Stephens would write less and less because Stephens relied completely, according to Moore, on the lyrical impulse; on the sheer inspiration of the moment.

An odd thing happens, said James Stephens, talking about his first meeting with Moore.

STEPHENS: Now an odd thing happens when two writers meet. Without a word being uttered on the subject each knows in thirty seconds whether the other has ever read a line of his work or not. Neither of us had, and we were both instantly aware that life is not perfect, but, while I was full of patience and hope, Moore was scandalised. Still, literature was his subject, and this was so in a deeper sense than in any other writer I've ever met. Moore was dedicated to the craft of writing. He lived for the prose way of thinking: wine, women, and murder. I am sure that when he was asleep he dreamed that he was writing a bigger and better book than any he had yet managed to produce. He loved the art of prose.

In the run of writers, George Moore may have been a poor starter, but he was a stayer, and a sticker for literature.

> *'All, all of a piece throughout,*
> *The chase had a beast in view.'*

When, for good and for all, he left Dublin for Ebury Street he could justly call himself the last great prose stylist of his age. Anna Kelly kept some pages of his manuscripts which were later impounded as illegal matter during the Civil War; they were mercifully rescued from under the feet of soldiery on a barracks floor.

ANNA KELLY: I gathered them together with the few signed copies and sold them, hobnail marks and all, to an American bibliophile who paid me enough to keep me eating well for the next three months. And I had all my time in jail to read Pater of course.

What, Mrs Kelly, of all your memories of Moore, stays with you most?

ANNA KELLY: What stays with me! His devotion to his work. His devotion to his art.

CLARKE: Yet to describe his devotion to his art, his humility, his endless patience over every period, every sentence – well, saintlike seems to be the only word I can think of. It seemed to me also that Moore must have worked out all his exhibitionism and nastiness and faults in those early books of embarrassing self-confessions, and that all that was left was, to use that famous phrase of Arnold's, 'sweetness, and light'.

Moore himself summed it up, sweetly and lightly, in a letter to a cousin who was a Carmelite nun. She had implored him to burn his books and make his peace with the Church he had forsaken. He replied, 'We are the two dreamers of a family little given to dreams; the two who have known how to make sacrifices – you for God, I for art. You tell me that you are perfectly happy, and that there is no greater happiness than to live with God and His Sacraments. I also can say that I am perfectly happy with my art; it fills my life from one end to the other.'

J. M. SYNGE

> And so when all my little work is done
> They'll say I came in eighteen-seventy-one.

In April of that year John Synge was born of respectable and godly parents, near Dublin. He was barely twelve months old when his father died. Years later, Seamus O'Sullivan called to see him at his mother's house in Kingston where he was living.

SEAMUS O'SULLIVAN: I was shown into a large room in which Synge was seated at a table strewn with yellow-covered French books, but the walls of the room in which he sat were covered from floor to ceiling by volumes of theological works. As I looked from these to the paper-covered books, which obviously occupied the dramatist, I remembered suddenly that Synge was the descendant of a long line of Church of Ireland dignatories, amongst them Edward, Bishop of Elphin, who so wisely rejected that gaudily dressed young probationer, Oliver Goldsmith, and by so doing saved the Church from the acquisition of a very half-hearted clergyman – and the world from the loss of a great poet.

Too many books spoil the cloth. But, from the narrow school of family catechists the poet in John Synge escaped, quickly, into the wordless air and bookless wilds of the Dublin hills. As a boy he says,

> I knew the stars, the flowers, and the birds,
> The grey and wintry sides of many glens,
> And did but half remember human words
> In converse with the mountains, moors, and fens.

He was a solitary, silent, meditative lad not greatly given to reading, says Edward Millington Stephens, his nephew –

EDWARD MILLINGTON STEPHENS: He was always a naturalist, greatly taken by books on natural history. As a boy he suffered considerably from colds in the head and rather tended to asthma, so he didn't attend school very regularly. I don't think his mother thought it mattered very much. He did go to school for a while, then he had a tutor, before he entered Trinity College. But he seems to have read, by himself, a lot of things other boys mightn't have done. At about fourteen he read Darwin's *Origin of Species*, and that upset his faith, because he was accustomed to a doctrine which regards the Bible as infallible from cover to cover and the Garden of Eden as just as important as any other part of it.

> If Church and State reply
> Give Church and State the lie.

John Synge would often quote these lines in later years. But as a lad, his shy defection from the faith grieved his mother and troubled himself.

STEPHENS: I always regard his mother as a great influence on his life. She was one of the old school – she brought up all her children very thoroughly instructed in what you might call the evangelical protestant faith – actually her father came from the north, from Antrim, and her mother from Strabane, so she really had a northern tradition. Her father died in the potato famine. He was a clergyman in County Cork.

She was one of that downright, upright, Northern breed which loves a good floury potato and a good flowery sermon. A great expositor of the Bible.

STEPHENS: She certainly was. She had a marvellous gift, and not only did she instruct her own children, but she instructed her grandchildren, so that I know exactly the same teaching as John got as a child. He looked on her really as an example of what a woman ought to be.

So much so, that when he first fell in love it was with a young woman of strong religious conviction.

STEPHENS: She was an early attachment. It was an attachment he referred to as an imaginative devotion, really, to a lady who didn't share his opinions or his ambitions. She was a pleasant girl, who lived in the same terrace as his mother and had once been his mother's guest for a part of the summer holiday in County Wicklow. She liked country life and used to sketch in water-colours and read Wordsworth; and of course she liked John's attentions.

But, though they met often on the road, they had very few opportunities of spending any time together. Her father was a leader among the Plymouth Brethren, and she accepted altogether his evangelical teaching. She would never have thought of marrying a man who, though strict and ascetic in his mode of life, could not agree with her doctrinal beliefs about salvation.

All the same, Synge's puritan upbringing put its mark on him permanently. His frugal way of life, for instance '£40 a year and a new suit when I am too shabby.' His sober reticence. His stubborn single-mindedness. His rigid regard for the truth, for the exact and living phrase.

STEPHENS: I regard him as having been just the same to the end. He was an ascetic person who was very strict in his behaviour in every way, and he hated anything in the way of a lie. I remember one day my brother and I were going out – I was carrying a rook-rifle and my brother was carrying a gun – and he said we mustn't go each with firearms or we'd shoot each other. So I said we wouldn't load them both at the same time. We didn't, until we got to a place where we were stalking a rabbit and the rabbit was sitting up and I loaded my rifle to have a shot at it. I told him about this when I came back, not regarding it as any violation of my promise because I wasn't carrying the rifle loaded, but he gave me a tremendous lecture on speaking the truth.

Out of Synge's sober code of behaviour came the playboy, by reaction.

STEPHENS: In 1902 – it was the year that his plays really came to fruition – my brother and I had a bedroom off his, and he was very pleasant with boys – we could take liberties with him that you mightn't have taken with an older uncle. One morning he hadn't got up and I just opened the door and took a shot at him with a sponge; he jumped out of bed, seized the watering-can that operated as a jug, and turned it upside-down over my head on the floor. It caused some consternation, as it went straight through the floor to the kitchen.

Playboy in more senses than one. He could play the fiddle, the flute, the penny whistle, the piano. Indeed he won a scholarship in harmony and counterpoint at the Royal Academy of Music. Partly it was his inheritance. For the story goes that an ancestor, John Millington, a canon or precentor of the Chapel Royal, sang so sweetly that Henry VIII bade him take the name of Sing. Stephen McKenna told George Roberts that Synge had little respect for the English, but he had great respect for the Synge family and loved to quote from his ancestor, the Archbishop. He hated the idea of the English in Ireland – except for the Synges. He thought the English a heavy and bovine people 'who had achieved a great literature by a mystery.'

Synge had in him that Irish split, that dichotomy, which produced so many fork-tongued/writers – Congreve, Farquhar, Goldsmith, Sheridan, Shaw. He was Anglo-Irish; a Protestant in a Catholic country; a disbeliever reared in a devout environment; a Puritan and a playboy; a University prizeman in Hebrew on the one hand and Gaelic on the other. Between the blades of these scissors he cut the cloth of drama, the many-coloured coat of comedy. Sharpness was all. But to arrive at this sharpness he had first, like many of his countrymen, to leave Ireland. At the age of twenty-one he went to Germany to study music. His mother, who looked askance at the stage and the platform, did not approve.

STEPHENS: But she was always judicious. And when he decided that music ought to be his career she was quite willing to back him up. At the time he did that he hadn't got any money of his own at all.

Two years later Synge gave up his musical career and went to Paris on £40 a year.

STEPHENS: He had about that amount of money as private means and he used to make a few guineas more writing articles. His real home was his mother's house, and he used to stay in Paris, when he wanted to be there, as long as his money lasted, then he'd come home again. His mother was always trying to persuade him to come home because she said he didn't feed himself properly.

'I went to Paris,' said Synge to a friend, 'in order to be quiet, and to wear dirty clothes if I liked.' Stephen McKenna, who met him there, said that Synge told him he had laboured over one article for six weeks and was paid a guinea for it. Said McKenna, 'Oh, he complained about his lack of earning power, but he seemed more concerned at finding two sentences ending with the same cadence when his article was at last published. No, he hadn't a great knowledge of French. I was once about to buy a French encyclopaedia, and Synge said, "Don't buy it. Get the Encyclopaedia Britannica, where the writer won't stop in the middle of an article to tell you how fond he is of his mother."' His family didn't much approve of his writing.

STEPHENS: They thought it was an unprofitable enterprise. Their attitude was, 'Well, if he wants to write, why doesn't he write something that he can sell?'

Synge – so McKenna told George Roberts – had only one room in Paris, meagrely furnished with a truckle bed, a few chairs, a piece of old carpet and a few books and pipes. He did his typewriting with the typewriter on his knees. He had two small bowls for tea and if any more than two friends called to see him one of the company would have to wait till there was an empty bowl.

RICHARD BEST: I remember one morning Stephen McKenna sent me a card, and told me there was a friend of his called Synge going over to Paris. He was a very literary man, he had £40 a year – I remember the sum perfectly well, it seemed to me enormous at the time. Days passed and weeks passed, and I remember one morning awaking in my little flat, looking round my room, which was in perhaps a little disorder, and expressing to myself the hope that this man Synge wouldn't walk in now. I had hardly thought the thought when I heard a knock at my outer door. I thought it was the concierge coming with something, so I went to the door and there I saw a stranger standing before me with a white silk muffler round his neck, and he said to me in French, 'Vous êtes M. Best?' I said, 'Je le suis,' and he said, 'Je suis Synge – pas singe.' So I said, 'Come in, why should we speak French? I'm expecting you.'

We became quite friendly then, and I saw a good deal of Synge. After a time I induced him, as he had only £40 a year, not to be living in a furnished hotel but to set up in a little flat as I myself had. After six months or so I moved out of my flat, taking another one, and I installed him in my old flat, gave him a carpet and went out with him and bought all the necessary things – a bed, some blankets and all that; and I shall never forget I said to him, 'Must have a teapot, Synge.' So we saw some teapots – there was one blue and white; I said, 'Well, now, that would be a nice teapot,' and Synge said, 'Oh, no, I prefer that one – the little humble chocolate-coloured teapot.' So then I inducted him into the way of making tea and all that, and cooking a chop.

Synge, said McKenna, loved Paris. He loved the quiet of it and its tranquil bourgeoisie. He never belonged to the Latin Quarter or to the cabarets. Sometimes he would go to a café and just look on. His favourite walk was from his rooms to the Luxembourg – a long, tree-shaded walk called 'the Poets' Walk'. And he liked, too, the lovely villages on the outskirts of Paris and he loved their names. The boulevards he didn't know or care about. He hated big avenues and chose those which were narrow and winding.

BEST: I remember another curious meeting with Synge in Paris. We were walking down the Avenue de L'Opéra one sunny day and I saw a man coming towards us whom I recognised – a portly man, with a bowler hat and a plain suit. I had just time to say to Synge, 'Mark this man,' because he was on us almost. Synge looked at him, and I looked at him, and this man looked at us very closely, and I said, 'Oscar Wilde,' and Synge said, 'Oh, how interesting, let us go back and meet him again.' I hated this, but Wilde had stopped I remember, and was looking into a big window with Greek vases in it and bronzes. So we turned around and we met him again, a minute afterwards, and Wilde looked at us hard, and I knew Wilde was thinking, 'These two men know who I am.' He was living under the name Sebastian – he had been pointed out to me some months before in the street, that's how I knew him. So I took him in, but I lowered my eyes and I noticed his brick-coloured complexion and his stained teeth which have been described. Well, Synge was immensely impressed by this appearance of Wilde.

He had an immense curiosity about person, place or thing; little escaped him. He would spend hours in the Louvre and he would point out with unerring instinct some little detail of distinction in a picture which others mightn't notice.

'Once,' said McKenna, 'I gave him some reproductions of Burne-Jones and Watts, about whose work I was then enthusiastic. I fancied that I saw in the painting of a hand, the fold of a drapery, an expression of a new sense of mysticism in the world. Synge got furiously angry, stammering and stuttering as he protested that a man who saw such a thing in that work knew nothing about pictures. He took me to the Louvre and going round the galleries he analysed the qualities of the pictures one by one. He wouldn't let me speak until I had soaked them in, and then he said, "Now where's your Burne-Jones and your Watts and all the rest of them?" He thought that no one's criticism of painting was worth listening to if they hadn't a technical knowledge of the subject, and the same with music.'

BEST: I myself was a dilettante – a dabbler in music. I remember I had Beethoven's piano sonatas, and one day Synge opened it at one of the sonatas and pointed out to me the theme and how it developed and varied through the different movements. He played the violin and he had a way of drumming on the table to strengthen his fingers for the violin.

A habit which annoyed his mother. Synge had a wide and wandering interest in the arts, in music, painting, sculpture, writing, coins and medallions, prints and engravings. But it was a choosy, intuitive interest, not an intellectual interest: a 'negative capability'. 'Sometimes,' said McKenna, 'I would read Yeats's poems to Synge in Paris. I read "The Shadowy Waters" with Synge. He thought it obscure but beautiful; one of the most beautiful things that had ever been written. And yet when he was offered the book he refused it. "I might understand it," he said. He preferred diffuseness to definition.'

Because it gave room and rein to imagination. He would have agreed with Coleridge that 'poetry gives most pleasure when only generally and not perfectly understood'. He disliked being pinned down by intellect. He liked to wander, whether in the body or in spirit, in life or in letters. But this wide scattering at last found a narrow gathering. In 1898, on the advice of a friend, Synge packed his bags. 'Give up Paris,' he was told. 'You will never create anything by reading Racine, and Arthur Symons will always be a better critic of French literature. Go to the Aran Islands. Live there as if you were one of the people themselves. Express a life that has never found expression.' He took the advice. And yet, says Seamus O'Sullivan –

O'SULLIVAN: Synge had, to the end of his life, a real love of Paris, that Paris to which he had first gone (as he confided to me one evening as we walked home from the Camden Hall to his lodgings in Rathmines) in order to free himself from the influence – an influence which he felt was becoming too strong – of the Irish poet who at that time, and for many years afterwards, dominated the thought and expression of the younger writers of his day. 'Get away from Dublin,' he said to me as we parted after a memorable walk and talk.

Strange. For it was that same dominating Irish poet, Yeats, who advised Synge to 'get away from Paris', to go to Aran. It was on Aran that Synge found a frame for his living imagination. It was in that bare, primitive, hand-to-mouth place that he, who had such riches of imagination, such endless means and meaningless ends, found peace and purpose.

BEST: I remember Synge telling me that he wanted to do for the Aran Islands something like what Pierre Loti had done for Brittany. I thought it was rather a tall order, and I smiled. But he didn't write then the ordinary English with any distinction. It was when he discovered his Aran Island dialect that Synge found himself.

'Yeats,' said George Moore, 'trained him through dialect: he dunged the roots.' Years earlier, Stephen Crane had roused Synge's interest in islands. And Synge, as Edward Stephens points out, had also a family association with Aran.

STEPHENS: John's uncle, his father's brother, Alec Synge, was the Protestant curate there about 1850. He had a sailing-boat for carrying on his ministrations between the islands and he used it for fishing when he wasn't on religious work and so he got into a pretty serious conflict with the fishermen of Galway. But he wasn't a man to give in; he armed the skipper to the teeth, and so long as he was there he fished.

Dignity, with impudence in the pocket; peace, with violence at its heart. It was this sharp counterpoint of life on Aran that gave Synge, that sober, melancholy man, a heightened sense of drama, and a supreme sense of comedy. He revisited the islands, and particularly the middle island, in five successive autumns. And always, whether sitting on the cliff above or in the kitchen below, he was the shy observer, the silent listener, the stranger. One night, about two years ago, on the middle island I listened to Peadar Coneely telling a story in Gaelic, and this is a translation of it: 'When O'Malley came on the run here long ago he had killed his father by accident. He was working in the field, and his father came and checked him – said that he was spoiling the field. Dispute arose between them, and in anger he lifted the spade over his head; he didn't intend to kill him, but with anger he gave the blow contrarily, and killed the father. After doing it he was attending the father – it hurt himself more than most others – but he didn't intend to leave the place, only an uncle of his told him to go on the run and save himself. The uncle sent a boat into Aran with him ...' It is the story that John Synge heard from old Pandeen Derrane, and out of which he fashioned The Playboy of the Western World.

Richard Best talked once to Synge about his life on Aran.

BEST: He told me how embarrassed he used to be when he went there first. Synge had a little room off the kitchen, where he used to sleep. In the daytime, when he had to obey a call of nature – there were no up-to-date lavatories – he told me rather shyly that he used to go out into a field, overlooking the wild Atlantic, and just when he would be about to perform the major operation he would look round to see if there was anybody nearby; and nearly always, he said, some young woman would put her head over the stone wall. So I said, 'What did you do?' 'Well,' he said, 'I used to postpone that part of my daily routine until night. Then when the inmates of the house were all asleep, I would open my door and steal out over their bunks into the darkness of night.' I often wondered if that wasn't in some way responsible for the illness which eventually carried him off.

'Did you ever think,' said an Aran Islander to me, 'that there was something simple about Synge? There was a wonderment about him that was very fetching.' Synge was not one of those nimble Irishmen who could turn a bicycle on a sixpence or turn a phrase like a corkscrew. He loathed the 'brilliant' talker, and, as Gogarty says, he was a drinker-in and not a giver-out of talk.

OLIVER ST JOHN GOGARTY: The greatest thing I can think about Synge is how he affected the present Poet Laureate, John Masefield. They were fast friends, and the man must have been pretty worthy and Masefield must have been of an affectionate and winning type, or he would not have gained the friendship of that, to me, inscrutable man. In order to summon Synge to your mind's eye, I'd better read a quotation from John Masefield's *Recent Prose*. 'It was a grave dark face, with a good deal in it, the hair was worn neither long nor short; the moustache was rather thick and heavy, the lower jaw, otherwise clean shaven, was made remarkable by a tuft of hair too small to be called a goatee on the lower lip. The head was a good size. There was nothing niggardly, nothing abundant about it. The face was pale, the cheeks were rather drawn; in my memory they were rather seamed and old-looking. The eyes were at once smoky and kindling. The mouth, not well seen below the moustache, had a great play of humour in it.'

He had a face like a blacking-brush, said Bernard Shaw.

GOGARTY: But for this humorous mouth, the kindling in the eyes, and something not robust in his build, he would have been more like a Scotsman than an Irishman. I remember wondering if he were Irish.

His voice, very gutteral and quick with a kind of lively bitterness in it, was of a kind of Irish voice new to me at the time. I've known a good many Irish people but they'd all been vivacious and picturesque, rapid in intellectual argument, and vague about life. There was nothing vivacious, picturesque, rapid or vague about Synge. The rush-bottomed chair next to him was filled by talker after talker, but Synge was not talking. He was answering.

He was always the hole in the conversation. 'Sometimes I thought there was nothing in him,' said a friend, and he spoke of himself as 'existing merely in his perception of the waves and of the crying birds and the smell of seaweed.' He was a silent traveller, as his nephew Edward Stephens says.

STEPHENS: He was never in the least embarrassed by walking in silence. None of his family were. It wasn't a peculiarity of him particularly, the Synges were like that, they were a silent family.

Silent but expressive. 'They speak, but not with their mouths,' says the Psalmist. Synge's hands, for example, spoke for him.

STEPHENS: He'd a peculiar dexterity that was particularly noticeable in the hands of a man as thick-set and powerful as he was. It was a natural gift, perhaps a mode of expression is a better description. As a boy he had made a collection of butterflies, moths and beetles. He had a setting-house full of cork-covered, grooved boards of all sizes, for setting the wings and antennae and legs of specimens. And that required a considerable dexterity. He made a very neat collection. Then his fingers acquired even greater dexterity when he learnt the violin and the piano. He had a personal habit, too, of whirling a small pair of pocket scissors on his finger as he'd saunter about the house chanting 'Holy, Holy, Holy Moses'. I think he always said 'Holy Moses' because his mother wouldn't have liked him to use any stronger terms.

The way his hands moved impressed me very much as a child when I saw him putting his violin carefully into its case, spreading a silk handkerchief gently over it, putting the bow into position, and putting down the lid and fastening the catches. He used to pride himself on his tricks of dexterity. For instance, he used to stand on one foot, put a bunch of keys next to his instep and then, with his arm twisted round his leg, pick up the keys. He was very good at handling fishing tackle, and he used to tie flies when he was a boy. I used to fish with him in the evenings along the river until we couldn't see our tackle, except by holding it against the sky. He could always put on a new fly if one was lost or untangle a cast. He didn't carry much tackle – the cast round his hat and an old wallet with some bluebottle, a hare's ear, an orange spider and a few other flies regularly used on Wicklow rivers. He never wore waders – he used usually to put on a pair of old shoes, and walk in the water just the same as if it was dry land. I have a picture in my mind of him standing nearly ankle-deep in the river, bending slightly, and casting down a dark hole under bushes. I remember the squelch of our feet walking home, and the bats circling round the tops of our heads.

BEST: I remember in those far-off days that Synge wore rather coarse, hand-knitted socks, and he told me that his mother knitted them for him.

'*And I remember,*' *says George Roberts, 'going on an outing with Synge to Lough Bray.*'

GEORGE ROBERTS: We rested by a stream in a little wood about half-way up the glen and one of the party, Maire ni Garvey, leaned back amongst some flowers, which Synge described as 'stretched back until her necklace, in the flowers of the earth', and later on he used the phrase in *The Playboy*. This was an instance of how he noted every event on every occasion. We were lucky that the day was full of change and as we looked at the sunlit lake it reflected the blue of the sky in all its peace and repose. But a change in the atmosphere provoked a gloomy background and I mentioned to Synge that I sensed an evil emanation, to which he agreed. He said he had experienced a sense of the evil when swimming across the lake.

The Shadow of the Glen. Gaiety and gloom, light and dark, freedom and frustration, the play of counterpoint in all Synge's life and works. Was it this incident that Synge had in mind when he called his first play The Shadow of the Glen? *Yeats was deeply impressed with the play and mentioned it to Richard Best.*

BEST: I was sitting on a bench beside him and Yeats said to me in that impressive way – intoning his words – that he had just discovered a man who had all the talent of Aeschylus and Sophocles combined. I said to him, 'How wonderful, who is he?' 'He is a man of the name of Synge.' 'Hang it all,' I said. 'I just tore up his letters the other day – I wish I had known before that.' And Yeats laughed. Well, that was

Synge – I think he had just written *The Wicklow Glen*, but it was Yeats who really discovered a latent talent in Synge, and encouraged him to go on writing.

George Roberts was present when Yeats brought Synge to meet the members of the National Theatre Society.

ROBERTS: He was present at his election and I remember well his genuine look of pleasure as he courteously thanked us. He attended many of the rehearsals of *The Shadow of the Glen*, giving us the rhythm of the speech, but he left the stage management entirely in the hands of W. G. Fay. Although this was his first play he altered practically nothing at rehearsals and was not in the slightest bit fussy or irritable.

The Shadow of the Glen was first performed in the Molesworth Hall on 8 October 1903 and it got a rather mixed reception. There were calls for the author, but when he appeared there were a few hisses. His nervousness at facing an audience even to bow was plain to everybody, but when he heard the hisses a glimpse of defiant pleasure came over his face. I think the hisses pleased him much more than the applause.

The play started a heated newspaper controversy. But Synge took no part in it. He was always averse to defending his work, even to his friends. 'I follow Goethe's rule,' he said, 'to tell no one what one means in one's writing.'

ROBERTS: Although Synge never asserted his belief in his own powers he was quite conscious of his gifts. I remember his being hugely amused by a friend who had heard of the performance of his first play and who sent him a whole library of German plays so that he 'might learn how to write a play'. This reserve passed with many for modesty, but like all great artists he was very far from being self-deprecatory. His lack of self-assertion came rather from quiet confidence that his work was good.

'Good artists,' said Oscar Wilde, 'don't care for each other's work!' 'I never knew,' said Yeats, 'if Synge cared for work of mine, and do not remember that I had from him even a conventional compliment.'

GOGARTY: He was extremely self-possessed, not at all an amiable person, not an offensive person, nor deliberately self-obliterating.

ROBERTS: The next of Synge's plays produced was *Riders to the Sea*, and Synge was very particular that every detail of the properties and costumes should be correct. The petticoats were made under his direction with a broad strip of calico at the top. The pampooties were another difficulty. Synge brought in a pair used in the Aran Islands to show how they were made. The spinning-wheel was another trouble, until Lady Gregory came to the rescue and sent up a large wheel from Galway. Synge himself instructed the girl how to use it. He was exceedingly anxious that the 'caoine' should be as close as possible to the peculiar chant that is used in the Islands and after much searching I found a Galway woman living in one of the Dublin suburbs who consented to show one of the girls how the caoine was given.

She was very nervous about it, though somewhat proud that what she looked on as a country custom should be so eagerly sought after in the city. At the same time, she was very interested in the whole affair, wanting to know what the play was about and saying the caoine was so terrible a thing that she could hardly believe people would want to put it in a play. At first she tried to begin in her little parlour, but she confessed after a few moments she could not do it properly there, so she brought the two girls up to a bedroom and at first it seemed no better, until she conceived the idea that I should act the corpse. She lighted the candles for the wake and then she got that note full of the terror of the dead. I was relieved that she did not take snuff off my belly, but apparently the candles were enough. She was a native Irish speaker and the Irish cadences and rhythm of the words in conjunction with the clapping of her hands and swaying of her body was very terrible and yet very beautiful to look on.

It was George Moore who congratulated Synge on having made great literature out of a barbaric peasant jargon. But many Irishmen, like Gogarty, accuse Synge of inventing a fake peasant language.

GOGARTY: This language I have never heard in the mouth of any countryman in Ireland. It is an ersatz, which has been credited with much simplicity and beauty, but which always offended me by its artificiality.

'Yet,' protested Synge, 'I have used one or two words only that I have not heard among the country people of Ireland.' His nephew explains –

STEPHENS: He used to work in his bedroom, and his bedroom was in a little return where there was only a boarded floor on joists. There was no ceiling and he hammered away upstairs and the door was lying open into the yard. Fellows working on the farm used to pass the door, and the girls used to chat with them as they passed. He naturally heard the conversation upstairs, and he says that he owes lots of that for the phrases he used in the *Shadow of the Glen*.

When he was writing the *Shadow of the Glen* I remember we walked up the old Carrow road. It had stopped raining, but the fog was down on the hills, and it was one of those days when everything appears enlarged by a fog. Bushes up on the ditch looked as if they were trees, and every sheep that jumped across the road looked fabulously large. Of course my brother began to exaggerate and say how extraordinarily large everything was, and Synge jeered at us as he always did, and when we saw a cottage he said, 'Now wouldn't you think that was a cathedral?' So when he got home he put all that into the mouth of the tramp – the tower and church and the city of Dublin is only another version of his joke on us.

He worked with his whole life as his material – and he always thought that an author shouldn't be a phrase-coiner. He loved living phrase. He liked to live among people who used living phrases, and he felt entitled, in fact bound, to make use of the phrases just as he heard them.

ROBERTS: Before he ever started writing a play he had filled many notebooks with phrases he had heard; many of them collected quite near Dublin on cycle rides in County Wicklow. He told me his usual practice was, when he saw anyone coming along with whom he wished to chat, to get off his bicycle and feign that something had gone wrong with it; the curiosity of the passer-by was almost invariably aroused and a conversation would inevitably follow.

Synge has been sometimes accused by his detractors of never having heard many of the speeches they objected to, but anyone who has come into contact with the country people and spoken to them on terms of comradeship knows how their imagination flares into great extravagance of speech. For instance a friend of mine overheard a woman whose child had stolen a piece of sugar cry out at him, 'May the hammers of damnation beat out the soul of you on the anvil of hell.' I told that to Synge and he was delighted.

Was Synge a hard worker, Mr Stephens?

STEPHENS: He wasn't a worker who worked at night. He generally worked in the morning between breakfast and lunch. But you couldn't say for certain. He disposed of his day as he felt. He used to say that a man worked according to his humour; he believed in the effect of moods, and he would fit in his work while he felt like doing it. Once he'd got a thing in his mind he would stick at it till he had it right, and nothing but perfection would satisfy him. He would get a thing as perfect as he could make it. In fact, some people said he had too high a standard, that he delayed himself by his extreme care, even minding about a pause. He used to come up and sit in our garden sometimes, when he was writing *The Playboy*. And I remember him saying a man can't work with the cream of his brain for more than six hours a day.

ROBERTS: He was always a very slow writer, owing to the number of versions he made before he would be satisfied. His method was to work direct on to the typewriter from his first rough notes. He would take his typescript and make alterations in ink until it became covered, then make a fresh copy. Version after version of each play was thus made before it reached its final form. He seldom made alterations once the play was put into rehearsal and this, of course, was of great benefit to the actors. No doubt his constant attendance at rehearsals helped him to avoid the mistakes which other dramatists might be prone to.

It was at rehearsal that Gogarty met Synge.

GOGARTY: The first time I came across him was in a little hall, off Camden Street in Dublin, where a rehearsal of his *Playboy* was about to take place.

James Joyce couldn't be kept away from the theatre any more than moths from a flame. He insisted on coming to the rehearsal, although we were neither of us invited, but he was overcome in the corridor, and he lay down, so I passed on and I said to Synge, 'This play you've written is a satire, surely.' The playboy becomes very famous because he's presumed to have killed his father. Later his father turns up, and the playboy is discredited. I said, 'Surely this is a satire on the want of action in Irish life.' He looked at me very grimly and broke silence, which he rarely did, and said, 'No. It's a work of art.' So he resumed his position, which consisted of sitting down with his two hands folded on the top of a walking-stick, and his chin resting on it.

The reason I wasn't well received was probably that he associated me with Joyce, who was at that moment lying in the fairway and obstructing any of the people who came to see the rehearsal. Joyce afterwards confessed that he didn't mind at all the position, provided the girls stepped over his form. Then Joyce was presumed to have insulted the doorway of Synge's mother's house at Glenageary so that we cannot be said to have been very close friends of Synge.

Seamus O'Sullivan, also, met Synge at rehearsals.

O'SULLIVAN: Others were there who were then making a name in literature, art or music, but even in that distinguished company, Synge was a figure which caught and held the attention. For, apart from the strong and deeply lined features – the features of a man who had suffered much – there was in his appearance something which set him apart from all the rest. He still wore the black cape-coat of his Parisian days, and this combined with the unmistakable perfume of the Caporal tobacco which he smoked continuously in cigarettes which he rolled in the French fashion, without the aid of any machine, gave, to some of us at least, a nostalgic memory of Paris and of the Latin Quarter.

He always, says Dossy Wright, kept to himself at rehearsals.

DOSSY WRIGHT: I always found him very reserved, even in meeting people when a rehearsal was over, or when we had a talking round after rehearsal, when most of the people stayed-behind in the Camden Street Hall, Synge didn't stay very long. He always seemed to be in a hurry to get back to his home.

The Company moved to the new theatre, the Abbey, in 1904, and Synge was made a director. Fred O'Donovan recalls his first meeting there with Synge and remarks on the reticence.

FRED O'DONOVAN: Yes, that was very typical of the man. We had one of our little parties after a matinée, and we came into the Green Room. Synge was there, Lady Gregory and Yeats. Lady Gregory was in one corner of the room, surrounded by her admirers, and Yeats was standing in the centre of the room holding forth very magnificently, surrounded by his worshippers, and then there was this quiet figure, sitting behind the hat-rack in the corner, and I remember distinctly seeing beads of perspiration on his forehead. Nobody taking any notice of him, everybody around Yeats and Lady Gregory – and the man behind the hat-rack was Synge, and I could see on his face he had one great desire, and that was to escape from the room as quickly and unobtrusively as possible.

WRIGHT: He became rather interested in Mollie O'Neill, and then he used to go off afterwards, and Mollie went off with him. I don't think in those days the other directors realised where he was going, or who was meeting him. But Lady Gregory got her suspicions some way or another and found out, and then she was a bit perturbed for a while because at one time she said to me, 'You know, Dossy, it would be very awkward if one of the actresses here became a wife of one of our directors.'

O'DONOVAN: She was very beautiful, in an Irish fashion, very attractive in her personality, and a brilliant actress. Wherever we went she seemed to capture everybody, and I know she was, in Synge's opinion and in the opinion of our audiences, the embodiment of Pegeen Mike in *The Playboy*.

In 1907, as George Roberts recalls it, came the famous first production of The Playboy of the Western World.

ROBERTS: Synge mentioned to W. G. Fay one day in the Green Room that he had started to write a new play about the man who killed his father. 'You will have to play the murderer,' he said to Fay with that peculiar sibilant laugh of his. Well, Synge arranged to publish *The Playboy of the Western World* with me, and in good time I got the MS. It was complete in final form. He brought the MS himself to Maunsel's office and after a hasty reading I expressed my wild enthusiasm for the work to him. I remember the look of pleasure that my excited emotion gave him. His countenance 'put on the light of children praised'. He was excessively sensitive to any appreciation which he knew to be sincere, but just as scornful and quick to detect mere politeness.

The play went into rehearsal at once and the first to demur at some of the speeches were some of the cast. He told me that one speech would have to be cut for the performance and a speech modified, and he said with a twinkle in his eye, 'but *you* must print it as it is *written*,' well knowing that I did not want to cut a word of it.

The next protest came from the printer who begged me to leave out the word 'bloody' (this was before Shaw's memorable use of it). The printer was much shocked at what he called the 'blasphemous' passages. He was on the verge of refusing to print it but was at last persuaded.

Synge himself directed the rehearsals, regardless of J. B. Yeats who was busy sketching him.

ROBERTS: Yet the result was one of Yeats's best efforts and it is undoubtedly the real Synge more than any other portrait. His hat was pushed back from his forehead, from which the sweat was literally pouring, as it always did under any excitement. He was excited under nervous strain at the final rehearsals of his work. When the sketch was being made, Molly O'Neill, who was not on the stage, and was a very interested spectator of the artist's progress, would alternately look over the artist's shoulder at the sketch and at the subject of the sketch. The look she gave Synge as he turned for a moment from watching the rehearsal to look at the sketch amply repaid him for the interruption.

There was not a vacant seat on the night of the first performance of The Playboy.

ROBERTS: The first act was listened to with tense silence and vigorously applauded, although it contained some of the phrases which Synge's enemies subsequently denounced. During the second act there was an uneasy atmosphere in the house and at the end there was a scrappy applause, but there was no outcry until near the end of the act, when Christy Mahon speaks of 'a drift of mountain females standing in their shifts only', at which someone in the pit hissed. A lot of the audience joined in expressing disapproval and a few tried to quell the disturbance. There was a slight lull. Then it broke out again with redoubled fury and feet were stamped and at the same time there was unusually vociferous applause. Between the two groups not a word could be heard, though the players went on till the curtain fell. There were some calls for 'author' but Synge, who was in the back row of the stalls, kept his seat. He was talking to AE as the house emptied, looking defiant and also somewhat concerned at the hostile reception.

The next morning the papers were filled with the vilest abuse I have ever read, masquerading as criticism. The *Freeman's Journal* was rather comic when it sympathised with Miss Allgood at having to say a word that it was sure she would blush to utter even in the privacy of her bedroom. The word was 'shift'.

The next night there were very few people in the stalls, but the pit was full of young men, Gaelic Leaguers and members of Nationalist clubs who, to judge by their faces and scraps of angry conversations overheard before the curtain rose, had come with one intention, to stop the performance. The first act had hardly begun when hisses and booing started. The actors continued to play, but the crowd got more angry and started a continuous stamping of feet to the rhythm of what is known as Kentish fire, so that no words could possibly be heard. But the actors went bravely on. Though their lips could be seen moving, no sound reached the audience. Synge was very much concerned, for fear the audience would begin to throw things at the players, and he insisted on going into the pit, I believe with the intention of preventing anyone who attempted more active violence. I went with him, and presently he was recognised. Damns and curses were heaped on him in language just as strong, and in some instances nearly as picturesque as the words of the play they objected to. In the middle of the commotion I noticed a gleam of humour come into his eye, as he took a mental note of a specially violent curse.

The fact that the players kept on with the script seemed to have an extraordinary effect on the audience and their frustrated fury was getting dangerous, especially as they now fixed their attention on Synge and seemed to ignore the players. They turned round from their seats in the front, yelling, and shook their fists in Synge's face. He sat for a while quite calmly, but with a fixed look of hatred gathering on his face and his jaw set. I began to be afraid he was going to try to clear the pit himself and of course any physical opposition on his part would only give some of his enemies the excuse they longed for. I tried to persuade him to leave but he insisted on staying till the close of the act. We then went to the Green Room of the theatre to encourage the players. As the curtain was about to go up for the third act, Synge was again making his way to the pit. The charwoman of the theatre came to him crying, 'For the love of God, don't go near the pit again. They will kill you.' This amused him so much that he could not resist her appeal and he stayed behind the scenes.

Just as the play was over Yeats arrived. He burst into the Green Room where the company were assembled, with the gleam of battle in his eye. 'This is the best thing that ever happened in my life,' said he. His only fear was that the players would refuse to go on the remaining nights of the week that the play was booked for.

'Synge,' said Yeats, 'came and stood beside me and said, "A young doctor has just told me that he can hardly keep himself from jumping onto a seat, and pointing out in that howling mob those whom he is treating for venereal disease." '

ROBERTS: The rest of the performances turned themselves into a duel between the actors and the audience. The actors made a point of shouting out the speeches the audiences most objected to, and sometimes they made themselves heard above the din.

Poor Synge was laid up after this night and did not come to the theatre till after the week was over. It is hard to say what the real effect was on him. He professed indifference, tinged with amusement. But when the garbled reports appeared in the country papers he said to me he was concerned that some of these might penetrate to the Aran Islands and that this misrepresentation might prejudice the people on whom he looked with affection. He said, 'Perhaps they will not receive me so kindly when I go there again.' I think it was this dread that stopped him from visiting his beloved islands again.

'The Playboy's real name was Synge,' said Bernard Shaw, 'and the famous libel on Ireland (and who is Ireland that she should not be libelled as other countries by her great comedians?) was the truth about the world.' It was Synge's last home-truth, and its reception told sorely on him. Disappointment and sickness turned him in on himself, and his work began to take on a more personal, tragic and poetic tinge in Deirdre of the Sorrows. *One evening George Roberts went to hear him read some poems in his mother's house at Kingstown.*

ROBERTS: He seemed unusually perturbed even before starting to read, and when he began, his voice was so full of nervousness that it was difficult to follow the poems. As he read, however, he became more violently excited than I had ever seen him. He seemed to get back the original motive and mood of the poems he was reading. It was hard to keep one's critical faculties alive under those circumstances. He seemed to be very weary and exhausted with reading them, but he said, 'I will send them to Yeats; I won't read them to him – it's too much expense of spirit.' It was very late when we had finished and as Synge got up to let me out he asked me to go noiselessly lest I should disturb his mother.

In October 1908, Synge's mother died. 'I remember,' says Richard Best, 'the house at Kingstown.'

BEST: I remember the last time I was there with him he took me into the kitchen where he was preparing on the range – his mother was dead – some sour milk tablets, prescribed by Metchnikoff, the great Russian bacteriologist, as a cure for old age. We arranged that I was to go down the next fortnight, and I was told he was in Elpis, the nursing home, so I saw him there. He had grown a beard in the meantime and I remember Synge telling me of his plans, how in a month or so, when he would be out of Elpis, what he was going to do. But he didn't tell me that he was going to be married. And I thought he was searching my countenance, but I felt then that he never would leave . . . that he was a dying man. I said nothing.

One of the hospital staff spoke about Synge to George Roberts, who noted the conversation at the time.

ROBERTS: Just before he died he kept murmuring in his delirium, 'God have mercy on me. God forgive me.' His favourite nurse was a Catholic and used to make him say his prayers each night and morning. She used to pray for him and he thanked God he had someone to pray for such a sinner. He called her his 'tidy nurse' because she was always immaculate when attending him. He liked her and she liked him, and did everything she could to make his last hours happy. Before he lost consciousness she sprinkled holy water over him and he opened his eyes to ask, 'Are you baptising me?' and added, 'perhaps it is best so.' Not being sure of heaven he used to say he'd like to remain as long as he could on earth.

He read portions of the Bible each day, but refused to see a minister or priest. When the matron did bring in a minister a few days before his death Synge chatted to him about the weather and other such-like topics. His 'tidy' nurse was of the opinion that he had much more religion than many who had more pretension to it. His relations called to inquire every day, but never went up to see him. He used to ask, 'Were any of my affectionate relatives here today?'

Edward Stephens, his nephew, went to see him.

STEPHENS: I saw him in Elpis Private Hospital the day before he died. I brought him a bottle of champagne sent by his brother Robert, and a tap corkscrew for drawing out a small quantity. John had been moved two days before from a room overlooking Mount Street, to a sunny room at the back of the house, where there was a view of the mountains.

When I saw him I was shocked by the change in his appearance, but as I was a student of twenty I had very little experience of serious illness, and I did not fully understand how near he was to death. He was too weak to talk at first, but the nurse screwed the tap into the cork of the bottle I'd brought, and gave him some champagne, and then he seemed a little brighter. He asked me whether I had heard any blackbirds singing. And I said, 'Not yet – but I have heard some thrushes.'

And Seamus O'Sullivan also had a kindly thought for John Synge.

O'SULLIVAN: I was told that he had expressed a wish to read again the poems of Robert Herrick, and I sent him by a friend that exquisite little selection which Palgrave published in the Golden Treasury series under the title of 'Chrysomela', and I like to fancy that the little volume was with him in those last days when, as we are told, he had had his bed moved to a position from which he could see, however dimly, the Wicklow Hills. For there may have been a great deal in common between the gay Vicar of Deane Bourne who sang of

> Brooks, of Blossoms, Birds and Bowers:
> Of April, May, of June and July-flowers;
> . . . Of May-poles, Hock-carts, Wassails, Wakes,
> Of Bride-grooms, Brides, and of their Bridal-Cakes

and the poet who walked with no unseeing eye through the hills and glens of Wicklow or lay dreaming on heathery places in Connemara 'and the ways beyond'.

'It is a pity,' said Synge, 'that I should die, for I still have more than one playboy in my belly.'

GEORGE BERNARD SHAW

Some men are born great, and some are more grating than others. In Bernard Shaw, Ireland, the most devoutly conservative of countries, produced the most arrogant iconoclast of his age. He will be remembered for his blaze of wit and his illuminating lack of reverence. The light from that dead star is still travelling. As Sean O'Casey says –

SEAN O'CASEY: He will live in the life that follows us on for his grand plays, for his astounding social wisdom, for his courage, for his fine criticism of music and theatre, for his uncanny knowledge of children, so far exceeding the Peter Panism of Barrie, for his fight for the fame of Ibsen, for his love of argument, for his brilliant leadership of men. In time these will blend together, and Shaw will shine forth in the Cathedral of man's mind, a sage, standing in God's holy fire, as in the golden mosaic of a wall.

St John Ervine, what was his impact on you?

ST JOHN ERVINE: It happened that the first time I heard him was when he spoke on religion – a subject on which he spoke very frequently and about which he felt very deeply, though he was jocular about it. And when I came out of the hall in which he was speaking I felt that the whole of my intellectual life had been strewn on the pavement. It didn't leave me with a sense of loss, it left me with the sense of inquiry, I wanted to find out all the things I'd been told and had taken for granted. And I know now that no man has a right to go about the world with borrowed brains; if he's got brains of his own he should use them, he should think out his belief and know why he holds it, and Shaw was the man who did that more than any other human being that I've ever heard of.

DENIS JOHNSTON: As a good Shavian of the generation whose processes of thought were largely formed by Shaw I rather object now to his being praised for his futilities – and, believe me, he had that side just as everybody else has – while his real virtues are forgotten, or worse still, are sterilised. Shaw himself was the last person to speak respectfully of the dead, simply because they were dead; and I think that we pay his teaching no compliment by standing with bared heads around his cenotaph along with these serried ranks of boxers and ballerinas, of twisters and yucks, of smart operators and warm weather rebels who now claim to have been his closest friends.

I was not one of his closest friends, and for very good reasons. You couldn't live under that upas tree any more than you could sit under the shade of Yeats, if you intended to have any ideas of your own. Now the fact is that Shaw was a much more interesting person, as a person, than either he or the Shavolators would have us believe. If he had his way he would have us regard him as a keen, clear-sighted intellect, always right in what he said, both politically and philosophically, and who never made a slip or did a foolish thing all his life through. And the fact that he has so successfully pushed his view down the throat of the public is, to my mind, at the back of the incredible dullness of nearly everything we know about Shaw's life.

'GBS,' said Shaw, 'is not a real person. He is a legend created by myself: a pose, a posture. The real Shaw is not a bit like him.'

ERVINE: Shaw was the most vital figure in my youth. You'd only got to come into the man's presence and you were stimulated even if he didn't open his mouth. And it's not true that we thought that he could say nothing wrong, or do nothing wrong – we knew perfectly well that he exaggerated almost grossly, but he did it in such a vivid, lively way that we didn't care, and we were able to use our own judgement. In fact we were constantly told by him, 'You're not to think of this idol but think for yourself.' That was Shaw's strongest argument.

JOHNSTON: It's because I learnt from Shaw the same scepticism of greatness, and a profound dislike of anything that savours of magic, that I find it impossible to speak respectfully of him now; not in spite of the fact that he's dead, but because of the fact that he's dead. And if such an attitude requires any justification, I can only quote something that he once said to me. 'Don't bother,' he said, 'about anything they say of you behind your back: the fact that it's behind your back at least proves that they have a regard for you. It's only what they say to your face that need be taken seriously.'

ERVINE: Well, it's very difficult for me to find any failing in him. I loved Shaw – apart from the great service he did me and my generation intellectually; I was under personal debt to Shaw. He was extremely kind to me as he was to many people.

JOHNSTON: But really, you know, when you consider his life, and his example, his knickerbockers and his vegetables, his Fabian pamphlets and his delicate fuss over actresses, it's all so like Ayot St Lawrence, which is just about as undistinguished a villa as is going. And none of it – here's the point – none of it does justice to the Shaw inside – this pastiche of at least six of the seven deadly sins. I think probably we may omit lust but that's about the only one we can omit. His life is a striking example of the peril of success. After a life of contradicting everybody the world suddenly turned round and agreed with him; and as his advice had always been amusing and stimulating, but almost invariably wrong, the world became an intolerable place to live in, and he had nobody to blame but himself. And I'm not saying this after his death: I said it to his face.

Well, as an older disciple of Shaw, what is your feeling, Glenavy?

LORD GLENAVY: Shaw to me was the great liberator. I'd been brought up in the usual middle-class home, public-school life, and conventional ideas. When I first read some Shaw, strangely enough I was started on the *Quintessence of Ibsenism*. I suddenly felt as if many weights had been lifted off me, and I was free to see some of the things and to look at the people round me, especially the social organisation around me, in quite a new light.

I was a young lieutenant in the Sappers, and on some occasion or other in London, I met the daughter of an American millionaire. He, I think, was the head of the firm that first installed the underground tubes in London. She took a great fancy to me, and seemed to think that I had possibilities of becoming intelligent under her care. She was a very devoted adherent to socialism, in fact she was accustomed to lead parades in New York of the diamond-workers, seated on a great white horse. I remember very well that at the time both Marconi and Winston Churchill were in love with her. It was she who shut me up in a room – Princess Gardens, I think it was, in Kensington – and read me the *Quintessence of Ibsenism*. I'm afraid at the time I felt very much more excitement about the *Quintessence of Ibsenism*, and what Shaw had to say, than I did about the lady.

Well, Shaw never allowed a date with a lady to come before an engagement at a Socialist meeting. What was it, Denis, in his past that gave him this 'moral passion' as he called it?

JOHNSTON: It always formed a regular pattern. If you told Shaw that you intended to examine his past, and write about him, he would immediately forbid you to do so; but if you went on and said you were going to do it, whether he helped you or not, he then immediately went to the other extreme, and loaded you down with information about his past. Of course this may just have been natural *bonté* on his part, but on the other hand it seems to me much more likely that he wished you not to dig out the facts for yourself, and that he thought that he could prevent you from doing so by telling you himself.

ERVINE: That I think is true – the astonishing thing about GBS, as I am discovering now that I'm writing his life, is that although he seemed to be telling you a great deal about himself, he told you nothing at all. There are a whole lot of things about GBS – his early life – which are undiscoverable now.

JOHNSTON: To another Dubliner, one of the most fascinating things about Shaw is the fact that only in his old age did he ever reveal what to him appears to have been a terrible secret, the fact that for a short time he attended Marlborough Street schools, in his early youth, and he could never bring himself to mention this perfectly respectable and reputable fact, for a period of seventy years. Now it's true that he did mention it at the end, but only at the end. And what an extraordinary sort of mental block of social and religious prejudice this reveals in his mind, a block that I really think can only be appreciated by an Irish Protestant.

ERVINE: Well, that's understandable enough – you ought to understand it as much as I do. Remember, GBS belonged to the upper classes – he didn't as some people imagine rise up from the proletariat – he belonged to the landed gentry, but an impoverished branch of the landed gentry. And to him, a Protestant and a member of the ascendancy, to be sent to a school mainly populated by Roman Catholics, generally the children of publicans, was a disaster.

JOHNSTON: It's his childhood that we've got to know about, not what he says about himself, and in my belief there were other secrets in his childhood that he has not yet revealed at all.

What was the skeleton in the Shavian cupboard? What was he hiding, and why? Frank O'Connor, you, I think, have a theory about it.

FRANK O'CONNOR: I think he was hiding the fact that he, his sister and his mother had abandoned his father. The old man isn't mentioned at all in his work until very late on – in the preface to *Immaturity*. Suddenly you get the beginning of the man trying to come to grips with the thing that's strangling him. When he begins writing about his father, he writes about him from a funny point of view, but each reference to his father, as he goes on in life, becomes more mature in its realisation of what was really happening. His father was a drunkard – his mother and his sister left his father and went to live in London.

Well, every skeleton has a human being in the cupboard. You, Ervine, must know as much as anybody about the human conditioning of Shaw's boyhood.

ERVINE: You've got to remember he lived in a very queer home. His father was greatly older than his mother. He was a curiously spineless, and yet very impressive, man. He tippled rather a lot. Mrs Shaw didn't love him, never had loved him, and GBS grew up in a loveless home, with a mother who, I think, disliked him because he had a physical resemblance to his father. It was an impoverished home and in some respects an unfortunate home, but he didn't like to talk about that part of his life, he never mentioned it to me. And I knew him so well, that I could ask him questions that it would have been impertinent to ask anybody else. He didn't talk very much about his life until he was about thirty. He had a hatred of poverty so profound that he wouldn't even acknowledge its existence.

'To have been brought up in poverty is to have the chill of it in one's bones all one's life.' That is what Shaw actually said to you, isn't it? That explains the streak of meanness in his old age?

ERVINE: You see, it wasn't only that they were poor, but there was this lack of love in the home. And it's a frightful thing for a child to grow up in a loveless home.

'My mother,' said Shaw, 'never made the least attempt to win my affections.' 'If I were run over by a dray,' he told Lady Gregory, 'she'd say,

"Oh, poor fellow!" but if a beautiful rose were crushed she'd go out of her mind with grief.'

Lady Hanson recalls a long family acquaintanceship with the Shaws in Dublin. It began with a dispute between her mother and Lucy Shaw.

LADY HANSON: The Shaw family lived in Synge Street, which, as all Dubliners know, is round the corner from Harrington Street, then a less noisy and unlovely thoroughfare than it is today. Both families employed the same laundress (it was before the time of public laundries). A table-cloth, missing from the Harrington Street list, was traced to the house in Synge Street, so, directed by the washerwoman, my mother, then about twelve years old, called to claim the missing property. Lucy, who was much the same age, resisted the claim and there ensued a tug-of-war between the two. The ownership must somehow have been decided amicably because the conflict ended and a friendship was formed between the two girls which lasted as long as Lucy lived. She was the master-mind in the group of young people – daring and independent. Her companion, my mother, looked up to her in humble admiration of her brilliance and original opinions.

There was a little boy, George Bernard, who wore a holland tunic and went by the name of 'Sonny'. He was always rather apart from the others and would be seen sitting at the piano, picking out airs with one finger or absorbed in the construction of a toy theatre. My mother remembers him declining to join a party assembled on the front steps, who were engaged in eating sticks of raw rhubarb. As an article of diet, he could not but have approved of it, but he may have disliked the publicity of the proceeding!

He was a shy, self-possessed, serious child who took early and lasting exception to the too familiar names 'Sonny' and 'George'. Bernard, not being a boyhood name, was the one he chose to be known by in later life. He was self-possessed, too, in other ways. 'By the time I was ten years old,' he said, 'my parents had given up the respectable pretence of churchgoing, and I myself had stopped saying my prayers on the ground that I was an atheist. Up to that time I had not experienced the slightest remorse in telling the most incredible lies, but with the coming of the urge for telling the truth for its own sake I found my true vocation.' 'It is the birth of moral passion that turns the child into the man.'

SEAN MACREAMOINN: Mr William Meegan of Dalkey told us his

memories of Shaw at this time. He recalled incidents which seemed to show that moral passion was not yet completely in control.

WILLIAM MEEGAN: We got on all right, only when he'd take my bird we'd fight then. We used to be catching birds and he'd take mine, and then we'd have a scuffle. Sure, he was a good few years older than me, and he'd have the better of it – he was bigger and stronger than I was. He was a strong lump of a fellow with a red face. We used to call him bullock soup, not because he was as red as a bullock, but because he'd been boasting out of the soup the cook used to give him. Och, I remember him well!

Lady Hanson's mother, Mrs Tyrell, remembers 'Sonny' Shaw playing with a cardboard theatre. What age was he then, Mrs Tyrell?

MRS TYRELL: Oh, he was about ten. Mrs Shaw was an accomplished woman. I think it was her brains that Shaw inherited. The father was an old silly. I remember playing bears under the table.

And what was Sonny like?

MRS TYRELL: Oh, he was a very nice-looking boy, he was very dignified.

And a certain Mr Fry, who as a boy ran the streets of Dublin with Shaw, bore out that point –

MR FRY: He was a very correct boy – we got on well together. I played with him, I shot marbles with him, I lashed tops with him, I boxed the fox with him, I robbed the orchard with him. We were never caught – it was a terrible thing being caught robbing an orchard in them days. You'd get five years for taking an apple!

Yes, Shaw was always the dignified playboy. Mr Kerwan recalls his landlady talking about the elderly GBS and her memory of him as a small boy.

MR KERWAN: Well, the first thing she told us was that 'It may have been yesterday or the week before that he passed down the street on the other side and never so much as looked across at the house.' That was rather difficult to believe in itself, because we knew that Shaw very seldom was in Dublin at the time. But we asked her why he should look across. She explained that he had lived there when he was a boy and she was a little girl. And the other thing she had against him was that he'd locked her in a wardrobe and frightened the life out of her!

'My home life,' Shaw said, *'was a torture.' He talked much about this, later in life, to an Irish friend.*

FATHER LEONARD: He told me that his father was a drunkard and he said that when he was a very small child he did not realise about people being drunk, but when he did wake up for the first time to the fact that his father was drunk he said to his mother, 'Father is drunk,' and she said to him, 'Is he ever anything else?'

'I have never believed in anything since,' said Shaw. 'Then the scoffer began.'

LEONARD: I think that incident made a deep impression on him as a child and I think it partly accounted for his attitude towards the family.

'My family, though kindly, might be called loveless,' said Shaw. 'But what did that matter to a child who could sing A te O cara *and* Suone la tromba intrepida *before he was perfect in the church catechism.'*

LEONARD: Music was really one of the great passions of his life at that time. His love for music was one of the deepest things in his whole character. I remember him saying that he thought some of the most beautiful religious music that was ever written was the music in the tempest scenes in *The Magic Flute*. And there was one thing that amused me very much when he told me that in the funeral march in the second movement of the 'Eroica', the English critics couldn't understand at all why that gay little tune comes on towards the end of the second movement: he said it was perfectly clear to him because when he was a boy his Uncle George was superintendent of Mount Jerome cemetery, and Shaw used to attend quite a number of funerals, and when they got as far as Harold Cross – up to that the funeral procession had been proceeding very sombrely – the jarveys whipped up the horses and they went off at a gay trot. Then, when they came near the cemetery, they relapsed into the funeral march; so it was perfectly clear to him, he said, the meaning of that movement – it was probably the same at funerals in Vienna.

'My father,' said Shaw, 'found something in a funeral which tickled his sense of humour, and this characteristic I have inherited. The gift of ridicule which I inherited is my most precious possession.'

LADY HANSON: I think GBS wrote heartlessly about the father and I think he owes a great deal more than he admitted or perhaps realised.

But it was to his mother that Shaw owed his interest in music. Dublin, says Lady Hanson, was at that time a centre of musical activity.

LADY HANSON: Mrs Shaw was a highly trained musician who sometimes, as an amateur, sang the leading role in grand opera and composed and published songs, forgotten now, which had a success. There was a fine living to be made by orchestra conductors and teachers of singing. The most popular and successful was Vandeleur Lee, whose special method for producing and preserving the voice GBS often recalled and believed to be unique.

Mrs Shaw became Lee's devoted pupil and admirer.

LADY HANSON: Lee comes into the picture when the family left Synge Street to take up their abode in Hatch Street. There, it seems, Vandeleur formed part of the household. A large room was allotted to him in which he gave instruction to numerous pupils. Encouraged by his success in Dublin, he decided to move upon London. He took up his quarters in Park Lane and soon acquired a name among the rich and titled as a teacher of singing and again he made an immense success. Shortly after his position was established, Lucy and her mother migrated to London and the Dublin dwelling knew them no more. Lucy was about twenty when she left Dublin; she had a lovely soprano voice, exquisitely fresh in quality; it had, of course, been well trained by the family friend who, by degrees, became a suitor, but Lucy would have none of him. Lucy was the star and heroine of our childhood and her coming was wildly welcomed by us young ones. We delighted in her ribald talk and her often Rabelaisian humour.

ERVINE: Mind you, Lucy was a pretty hard woman herself. She treated GBS very badly when he came to London, and implored her mother to turn him out of the house. But she was a very able woman, she had great vivacity. Oscar Wilde and his brother Willie were both in love with her. And she might have married what's called well, but for some reason or another she married a second-rate actor who was no earthly use to anybody.

LADY HANSON: I retain in my memory the picture when Lucy and he swayed to and fro, his arm round her waist, to the waltz tune which recurred through the opera:

> 'I swear to be good and true
> To the maid whom I fondly adore.'

But it turned out otherwise, for he proved to be incapable of fidelity and the marriage came to an end; she sternly divorced him and no more was heard of him until, in the closing years of her life when she was dying of a deadly consumption, he, alone and forlorn, was permitted to spend each Sunday afternoon at her house with an assignment to wind all her clocks!

ERVINE: The odd thing about it was that that man's family were very fond of her; a curious woman – Shaw never liked her.

LADY HANSON: Her last years were made serene because her brother, then rich and famous, surrounded her with comfort and secured her from financial stress.

ERVINE: She, of course, when he became famous, was, as all relatives are, ready to sponge on him hard. But it wasn't a happy beginning of life.

LADY HANSON: I possess many of her letters – brilliant, witty and oh so cynical – all written in an easy and finished style. I quote a passage from a letter written to her friend, Constance Shaw, warning her against the danger of allowing human affection to gain control. 'Love, my dear Con, is dead sea fruit, whether parental, fraternal, or marital, and anyone who sacrifices their all on its altar plays a game that is lost before it is begun.'

A loveless household. But life has its compensations. When love flies out the window, sharpness of wit comes in at the door, on the heels of poverty.

LADY HANSON: I think there was very little family affection between them. None of the family went to the father's funeral in Dublin. I think Lucy happened to be in Dublin at the time, perhaps with her touring company, but it meant nothing to her. I can't remember ever having heard her make a reference to her father. He was abandoned by them all.

'For the very solid reason,' said Shaw, 'that he could not support them. In leaving him they took off his shoulders a burden he was unable to bear

and glad to discard. I believe it was the happiest time of his life.' Peace, perfect peace, with loved ones far away.

O'CONNOR: What the biographers all overlook is that Shaw did not leave him and go to London. Shaw stayed on with him and worked in a lawyer's office. And that went on for about a year and then Shaw did leave him and finally the old man died in a house in Leeson Street. I've forgotten the name of the people in whose house he died.

'And was gathered to his fathers in Mount Jerome Cemetery in the fullest Shavian gentility,' said Shaw. Home life in Dublin may have been a torture, school a prison, and office-life a cul-de-sac. But to the intuitive Irishman, and Shaw was an intuitive if ever there was one, every fixed place, person, job, belief, thing, is a prison. He spends his life and uses his wits trying to get out of it, and he seldom takes a return ticket. 'I had one moment of ecstatic happiness in my childhood,' said Shaw, 'when my mother told me that we were going to live in Dalkey. I had only to open my eyes there to see such pictures as no painter could make for me.' Ireland has indeed her beauty spots but, to the mercurial Irishman, beauty is in the eye of the beholder. 'I left Ireland,' said Shaw, 'because I realised there was no future for me there . . . Dublin was a desert.' Unlike Joyce, he had no afterthoughts. More than thirty years passed before he set foot in the city again.

ERVINE: He hated Dublin. There's no doubt about that and he made that perfectly plain in one of his letters to Mrs Patrick Campbell, written comparatively late in his life when he was staying with Sir Horace Plunkett; he described himself driving into Dublin and hating every house he saw on the way. He loathed the place. And I think myself it is a loathsome city.

For the Irishman, too far east is best. 'No man prefers the city that conquered him to the city he conquered,' said Shaw. All the same he carried much of Dublin with him: its scepticism and an accent which, as Dr Bodkin says, was unmistakably Dublin.

DR BODKIN: Someone brought him into the Athenaeum and I was sitting there with Max Beerbohm, whom I'd only met for the first time on that particular afternoon, and D. S. McCall, who was a dear and old friend of mine. The two of them, before Shaw arrived, had commented on the fact that my speaking voice and accent were very like his. 'Oh,' I said, 'well, why not? We've both had the same sort of middle-class Dublin upbringing and he was born in South Frederick Street, or somewhere of the sort, and I was born in North Great Denmark Street. They mentioned this to Shaw, who was quite obviously hurt that anyone could suppose he spoke with such a patently Dublin brogue as I did.

He carried, too, memories of the National Gallery, which as a boy he frequented and which he revisited long afterwards with Bodkin when both were staying at the Plunketts.

BODKIN: Thirty years later I had a postcard from Shaw. At the time I'd been living in Birmingham for over ten years and I don't suppose I'd met him twice, and he wrote to me – I have the postcard still – saying, 'Do you remember the meeting at Plunketts years ago, if so may I ask you a question? I'm making a will leaving my Irish property for certain public purposes which may prove impracticable. In that case it is to go to the National Gallery (your old shop), to which I owe much of the only real education I ever got as a boy in Eire.'

Picture gallery, concert hall, and theatre had been his boyhood's enlargements. When Shelah Richards was producing his St Joan *at a Dublin theatre she received a telegram from Shaw.*

SHELAH RICHARDS: This theatre, the Olympia Theatre, has been called the Olympia for as long as I can remember, but way back, I suppose, in Shaw's boyhood, it was called Dan Lowry's Palace of Variety; it had not been called this for at least sixty years –

Yet Shaw sent the telegram to Dan Lowry's. Austin Clarke, too, recalls a faint far Irish bell which was struck by GBS during a public debate in London.

AUSTIN CLARKE: Bernard Shaw, as is well known, was expert in the use of topical phrases, and when Lady Rhondda rose up to speak he called out, 'Go in, Lady Rhondda, and win!' The entire audience cheered that gallant sentiment to the echo, and seemed to delight in it. I suppose they thought it was a perfect sally of Irish wit. I use the word 'sally' deliberately, for when Shaw himself was speaking he varied that old phrase, which we all know, 'Tom, Dick or Harry'. No doubt he found it inadequate, for it doesn't include the other sex, and must have sprung up in those days when man was master. So Shaw said instead, 'Tom, Dick or Sally Noggan'. And that phrase, spoken in the cultured

Dublin accent which Shaw never lost, startled and thrilled me. For Sallynoggin was not the name of a dashing young lady, but the name of a small village in Co. Dublin, near which I had lived. Moreover, it's not very far from Dalkey where Shaw himself had spent a good number of his earlier years. Was it some local expression remembered from the past by him? Had that place-name come suddenly from his subconscious mind that afternoon? Well, this tiny and perhaps trivial question has often teased me, and indeed now I shall never know the answer.

JOHNSTON: Now these sort of things in a man's background may seem trivial and unimportant, but they do give clues to the assumptions and snobbism of the formative years of his life, and they're far more important in his subsequent work than the veneer and intellectual superficiality which he acquired in middle age.

Well, it would be interesting, Denis, if you could give us examples of unconscious assumptions or snobbish prejudices on Shaw's part, based on his early years.

JOHNSTON: He was prejudiced, for instance, about education, and about the medical profession, for personal reasons. He was prejudiced, I believe, about people like Oscar Wilde – not that he didn't stand up for Wilde after the disaster, but he used to depreciate Wilde as a writer in spite of, or maybe indeed because of, all that he owed to Wilde himself. To the end he never could bring himself to admit that *The Importance of Being Earnest* was a good play.

I suggest it was the prejudice of Synge Street against Merrion Square; he never got over it. Compare his attitude towards O'Casey, who was not Merrion Square, and who was proud of that fact. He always spoke very highly of O'Casey; in fact, I remember him once saying that the second act of *The Silver Tassie* – that's the war act – was the finest thing that had ever been written for the stage. Well, it is a good act, but to describe it with a generalisation of that kind can hardly be a considered judgement. It was an expression of regard based on, shall we say, the opposite of prejudice. And it shows that Shaw, in fact, was not innocent of emotional judgements; and thank goodness for it, because the picture he liked to paint of himself as a bright 'smarty' who always knew the answer and said it just before anybody else, is a boring picture, like one of these terrible children who always know the answer to a riddle and say it with a nasty laugh. It's one that he doesn't deserve.

What do you think, Sean O'Casey?

O'CASEY: Shaw's one of those men, mentioned by Yeats, who will be remembered for ever, remembered for his rare and surprising gifts and for the gallant way he used them. Some critics have said that Shaw's no poet, and a man almost incapable of emotion, opinions that can only provoke in me a grand guffaw. There is poetry in a lot of his plays, emotion in most of them, and of course, talk and laughter in all of them.

Yes, in talkative Dublin the poetry is in the pithy and pat remark, and, in that sense, Shaw was a poet. But not in Yeats's sense. Yeats was not a bit enamoured of Shaw's laughing, sceptical, rational outlook. 'A smiling sewing-machine', he called him. You see, with Shaw ideas led to words – which is the way of prose. But with Yeats words led to ideas – which is the poet's way. Someone once asked Yeats in a Dublin street how he was feeling. 'Not very well, not very well,' said Yeats. 'I can only write prose today.' I think it was you, O'Connor.

O'CONNOR: The great problem for me is why was Shaw such an extrovert? Because the early Shaw was a poet. He wasn't an extrovert at all, and he wasn't a social reformer – he's the young man in *Candida*.

'The secret in the poet's heart,' said Shaw of Candida, 'is that the domestic life is not the poet's destiny. The starry night and not the cosy room is the place for him.' That 'something', O'Connor – which you say turned the shy poet Shaw into a sociable, brassy extrovert and prose-writer – was due, in your opinion, to an emotional twist brought about by abandoning his father in Dublin.

O'CONNOR: Now it's quite possible for a cold-hearted man or a cold-hearted woman to abandon a parent in that way and not to suffer for it. But for a warm-hearted man like Shaw – the Shaw we've been discussing – that's entirely impossible. A man cannot commit what he knows is a crime against nature, without having that coming against him all the time, and I'm certain that Shaw's extroversion was an attempt at running away from this secret reality which he dreaded.

Exile, I suppose, is a sort of extroversion. 'There is no favouring wind under heaven for the Irishman,' says the proverb, 'except the wind that blows his ship away from Ireland.'

LADY HANSON: Mrs Shaw took a house in Fitzroy Square where mother and daughter were soon joined by George Bernard. They lived in an artistic set, associating with musicians, painters and theatre people.

'In London,' said Shaw, 'my shyness and sense of inferiority were a hindrance and I managed by sheer perseverance to overcome my natural disinclination to make a laughing stock of myself.' Long afterwards he talked to Father Leonard about this period.

LEONARD: He told me about the various adventures that he had, and as he said himself, living on his mother, and writing for eight or nine years without any return whatever, then gradually getting, at last, one of his early novels inserted in a Socialist paper. They used to give very little to him, but when they hadn't much news he said he used to get near two or three sheets.

'I don't think she read a single one of them,' said Shaw, talking about his mother. 'When my MSS were returned she wasn't in the least interested. She accepted me as a burdensome good-for-nothing, just what she would expect from the son of my father. My father at least had satisfaction in seeing my work in print.'
L. A. G. Strong says that his mother remembered Shaw at this time.

L. A. G. STRONG: She remembers her aunt Caroline rating Shaw in his mother's presence for not going out to work, as a man should, and bringing in the money. Yet we know from Mr St John Ervine's researches that, as a matter of fact, Shaw was contributing to the household, but he didn't deny her accusations. My mother said he sat there stroking his red beard, his eyes twinkling, and nodding agreement with these tirades – they were very good-humoured tirades, because they were the best of friends. She just went for him; what came into her head she poured out, this aunt Caroline. And several times this happened. He certainly had the laugh on her presently, but he obviously bore her no malice, for they remained friends up to her death in 1906. And years afterwards, I remember going to see *Heartbreak House*, and being absolutely staggered to hear my great-aunt Caroline's accents, rhythm of speech, and phrases, in the person of his Mrs Hushabye.

LADY HANSON: Grandmamma had immense belief in George Bernard Shaw. I quite well remember his mother saying to her, complaining, 'George will be thirty next month and he's never made a shilling.' Grandmamma would reply, 'Wait.'

Lady Hanson recalls, later on, going with her mother to visit the Shaws in Fitzroy Square.

LADY HANSON: I remember he sat on the floor at mamma's feet and he ate ripe cherries the whole time. He was very pleasant and nice to her, and she was asking him if he remembered this person and that person, and what became of so and so, and he would put her off in some cynical fashion, because he hated to be reminded of his Dublin days. That was obvious.

It is difficult for the Irishman to detach himself from his native place. Emotionally he is very involved in it. But being an intuitive, shifting, mercurial character he cannot stand the sticky mess and morass of emotion. To him it's a prison; and he at once takes flight to the starry sky, or to the coal-hole. He becomes a poet or a satirist. 'I have in an extreme degree the mercurial mind,' said Shaw. A cold, unconcerned mind, seemingly. 'Whether it is a missed train, or a death among my nearest and dearest, I show this inhuman self-possession,' said Shaw.

ERVINE: He wasn't cold, he was emotional, but he was afraid of his emotions. He affected hardness.

Lady Thomson, you felt that Shaw was rather callous in the matter of his mother's death.

LADY THOMSON: He was most ribald about her cremation. He told us that it was interesting in as much as when his mother was burnt, the heat was absolutely white heat; when his sister during the first war was burnt, the flames leaped up and were yellow; nothing like the heat that his mother had, which was gruesome but interesting.

'Shaw, you certainly are a merry soul,' said Granville Barker, who accompanied him to the cremation. St John Ervine, what do you say?

ERVINE: It was a form of grief. Shaw was a very emotional man, which was a fact that very few people realised, and so ashamed of being emotional and so eager to get rid of the reputation of being emotional, that he pretended to a callousness that wasn't true about him. When GBS was staying once with Lady Gregory and Yeats was there, Yeats told me afterwards they were talking about death one day, and GBS said that death to him was comic, and greatly shocked both of them. My explanation of it was that that was an attempt to disguise his hate and horror of it.

Necessity was the mother of circumvention. 'What bereaved people need,' said Shaw, 'is a little comic relief.' Faced with a serious and incendiary problem he would at once withdraw from it and tackle it safely with the cold tongs of wit. 'I realise,' he said, 'the full significance of the singular fact which has led me to play with all the serious things of life and to deal seriously with its plays.' Indeed he confessed once to Kingsley Martin that he had never reached the heights he should have because of the clown inside him who tripped him up. He could never resist cutting a public caper. So he became, for a generation of Englishmen, the supreme dealer in shocks and stares. Father Leonard recalls Shaw's first public speech in Ireland.

LEONARD: Shaw began by making very exaggerated statements. I thought that he was using the technique that he used in England to startle and upset people; when he made these outrageous statements in Dublin, where they were used to them, they all began to laugh. He got quite annoyed and he said, 'This is no laughing matter, I'm perfectly serious.' They all laughed twice as much. I think he recognised his mistake, for from then on he spoke very seriously, and he was listened to very attentively.

The faculty of standing words or ideas on their heads – by means of pun, epigram, bull, or what-have-you – is a singularly Irish one. But it is never, to a creative mind, a matter of mere verbal juggling: it is a serious pursuit of truth, an imaginative attempt to break up the too-too-solid ground of accepted belief. Truth lives in the cracks – and the wise-cracks – of speech. 'Not "in vino veritas",' said Joyce, 'but "in risu veritas" – in laughter, truth.' And Shaw, the teetotaller, had no need to stimulate or simulate gaiety. Lord Glenavy recalls taking him on car rides in Ireland.

GLENAVY: He liked to lean far out and throw a musical yell down the steep side into the valley, causing Mrs Shaw in the front seat to show concern. Sitting happily on the high back seat, with flowing hair and beard, and arms folded across his chest, he was trolling out in a skilful tenor as we passed through a village. No wonder the country people turned to stare.

What kind of thing did he sing?

> De Valera had a cat
> It sat upon the fender,
> And every time it heard a shout
> It shouted 'no surrender'.

GLENAVY: I remember him silent and depressed on only one drive, when we took him to Puck Fair in Killorglin. The tethering of a he-goat, for the days of the fair, on a platform at the top of the high wooden tower struck him as barbaric. He could see no inspiration from it, for the crowd on the street and in the pubs. He soon asked to be taken away. Arrived at Carra late for tea, he sat in gloom, refusing everything but a glass of water.

He was a highly conscious person and what he called his 'artist nature' was disturbed by the raw unconscious gaiety of Puck Fair with its hum of excitement, its thousands of peasants, its whiskey galore, its tinkers and showmen. Yet he might have turned a pretty enough penny at any Irish fair. Dr Bodkin once saw him manipulating an immensely heavy German musket.

BODKIN: It was on the ground; Shaw took it by the end of the barrel and pivoted it into a perpendicular position by his wrists. We were all amazed at his strength and then after lunch he took an apple from the compote in the middle of the table and cracked it with his fingers.

But Shaw the intellectual showman, the king of debaters, who had held many a platform, could not bear to see King Puck, the goat, enthroned on a popular platform. It offended all his values. In his childhood he disliked the lower orders of the Dublin slums and in his maturity he distrusted the democratic mob, the beggars on horseback. 'The overthrow of the aristocrat,' he said, 'has created the necessity for the Superman.'

ERVINE: All Irishmen are natural lovers of dictators. The Irish are believers – believers in aristocracy – they are the most devout lovers of royalty in the world.

True; and Shaw, like Yeats, belonged to the Ascendancy in Ireland, to the aloof, fastidious and tidy aristocracy; at least to what he called a 'downstart' branch of it.

ERVINE: He was a very tidy man. It was an extraordinary thing about GBS when you saw him, you expected – if you had never met him –

to find him rather dishevelled, but he wasn't, he was extremely neat, he took a great pride in his tidiness. Somebody once told me that they thought he was frightfully conceited because he carried a comb about with him, and a little brush with which he brushed his eyebrows. I don't think there's anything conceited about that, it's a natural sense of order.

'You don't know how wonderful dirt is,' said Joyce, who belonged to a lower Dublin order. 'I have read several fragments of Ulysses,' *wrote Shaw.* 'It is a revolting record of a disgusting phase of civilisation; but it is a truthful one . . . To me it is all hideously real: I have walked those streets, and known those shops and heard and taken part in those conversations.' *Pearse Beasley, one of the playboy rioters, recalls the opening night of Shaw's censored play* Blanco Posnet, *in the Abbey Theatre.*

PEARSE BEASLEY: The play was produced on 25 August 1909, on the Wednesday of Horseshow Week. A number of English and foreign critics were present on the first night. James Joyce came from Trieste, where he was working on the *Piccolo de la Sera*, and here I first met him. I was introduced to him by a fellow journalist as a man who had come all the way from Trieste to see *Blanco Posnet*. I found him gentle, modest and courteous.

Alas, years later when Shaw was asked by the Stage Society to read Joyce's play Exiles, *he censored it.* 'I reported,' *he wrote to me,* 'that three unmentionable passages must be blue-pencilled. It was necessary to combat the current notion that the Stage Society existed for the performance of indecent plays.'

ERVINE: I knew Shaw for about forty years and knew him pretty intimately – I lived next door to him for quite a while – I never once heard GBS use an expression that could bring a blush to the cheek of a deaconess. I can't remember having heard him say 'damn'. He was a very fastidious man – his language was fastidious. He was a very courteous man – I only knew one man who was as courteous as he was and that was Thomas Hardy. But GBS was what I would call a roundhead with curls – he was a strange mixture of Puritan and cavalier. He was very fond of women – far fonder of women than he was of men.

But never passionately in love? 'Intellect is a passion,' he said.

ERVINE: People forget that between his twentieth and his twenty-ninth year he led a very impoverished life. He was a very poor man and he couldn't indulge in any of the – what shall I say? – 'sins' that other young men could; he hadn't the money and, moreover, he was a very fastidious man – he wouldn't pick a woman off the pavement – that wasn't his nature at all. But when in his twenty-ninth year, actually on his birthday, he was seduced by a woman at least fifteen years older than himself – a very ardent and very entertaining widow – then all the years of abstinence and starvation were suddenly swamped. After that a great many women came into his life. He was very attractive to women – extraordinarily attractive to women and very intelligent women too. It was a staggering sight to watch Shaw at any kind of meeting – the way the women cluttered round him like infatuated hens. He wasn't a monk, not by any manner of means, he was ardent right up to the end.

A fire burning in a mirror. His marriage – a happy one – was in some ways a remarkable one, don't you think? It rather bears out the idea of his cold, dispassionate nature.

ERVINE: But the fact is that Charlotte, who was a very remarkable woman, a woman of highly individualised character totally different in every respect from GBS, loathed the whole thought of sex, and she would not marry anybody unless there was an agreement that the marriage should not be consummated, and Charlotte died a virgin. You know, she was on the point of becoming engaged to the Swedish writer Axel Munthe.

There's a general impression that Charlotte was a sort of door-mat – she wasn't – very far from it. She had a will of iron that woman, she was a very likeable woman, I was devoted to her and so was everybody that knew her, but she was far more cranky than GBS. GBS wasn't cranky at all, many of his what are called cranks were the result of economic circumstances when he was young. He became a vegetarian, in my belief, largely because vegetarian meals were cheaper than carnivorous meals. But Charlotte had ideas about food, though she wasn't a vegetarian, which were far more cranky than GBS's. The extraordinary thing about these two very dissimilar people was they were devoted to each other. GBS loved her dearly and she was devoted to him. He once said to me, 'If Charlotte were dying I know an infallible way of bringing her back to life.' And I said, 'What's that, GB?'

And he replied, 'I should take to my bed and say *I* was dying.' And Charlotte would have come out of the grave to help GBS.

O'Connor, you had a story about her funeral.

O'CONNOR: Gabriel Pascal told me on one occasion that when he heard that Mrs Shaw was dying he came back by plane – the plane was delayed so he didn't arrive in time for the funeral. He came to Ayot St Lawrence and met Shaw and Shaw was full of high spirits. Shaw began to do dance steps in front of the house and Pascal said to him, 'Really, really, it's rather surprising after your wife's death.' And Shaw said, 'You don't know what it's been like, Pascal. It's as though all your life you've been carrying a beautiful silver casket on your shoulders and it was too heavy for you to bear and at last you leave it down and you just want to dance and sing the whole day, that's how I feel after it.'

'I never grieve,' said Shaw, 'but I never forget.'

ERVINE: He certainly loved her very dearly; in fact, he was so desolate after her death that the poor old man was lost.

JOHNSTON: It's a lamentable thing that she didn't survive him. It would have saved his latter years from some situations which can hardly be spoken about, but which I hope are being described privately for posterity, because it makes a fantastic ending to the life of a very great man that is almost as sardonic as the last days of Swift.

ERVINE: She was an extraordinarily interesting woman but she loathed publicity. She hated the crowds that were always running after GBS and she hated the people who came to see them – partly because, as always happens in these circumstances, they take no notice of the wife and devote all their attention to the husband, and make the wife feel that she's no right to be there.

'She disliked me for some reason or other,' said Sean O'Casey.

O'CASEY: I remember once we were at a lunch, and Shaw never commented upon what she used to say to me, he'd sit silent and listen; leave it to me and her. One day at lunch I had had a difference with Agate in the press, and she was very sociable to me. Then when we were half-way through the meal she began about this propensity to quarrel, and I sat silent, it's rather embarrassing, you know, if you're attacked

and criticised, and she said, 'Oh, you quarrelled with Yeats some time.'
I said, 'I didn't quarrel with Yeats. I had an argument with him over a
play of mine, a difference of opinion, I wouldn't call that a quarrel in
any sense of the word. I still think I was right.' And then she said,
'You're not content with that, you've quarrelled with Agate. You'll
never get anywhere if you go on doing these things. You mustn't be
quarrelling with everybody. Why do you do it? It's senseless, man.'
'I can't think,' I said, 'there's something in me that forces me to do it.
I suppose it's the Holy Ghost.' 'What do you mean – the Holy Ghost?'
she said. 'Define your terms before you use them. What do you mean?'
Shaw intervened, 'He means,' said Shaw, 'that *he* has got something,
and *I* have got something, that you haven't got.' Mrs Shaw shut up.
Shaw had great power over her.

ERVINE: Anybody who thinks that Charlotte was a door-mat is making
the profoundest mistake any human being could make.

LEONARD: She took great care of him in every way, and at the same
time one may say that she managed him.

*It was Mrs Shaw who, when Shaw was at a loss for a subject, suggested
Joan of Arc as a subject for a play. Lord Glenavy recalls a certain night
in Ireland when he and his wife and Shelah Richards were invited to the
Shaws' sitting-room.*

GLENAVY: When Mrs Shaw had seated us she said, 'Mr Shaw thought
he would like you to come tonight as he has just finished the last page
of his new play.' 'What is it about, Mr Shaw?' we asked, very much
flattered. 'Joan of Arc,' he said. Then he gave us a long and fascinating
talk, explaining how he had interpreted her acts and her life. In high
spirits, now that he had his composition completed, he made his
sketch of it for us humorous and quizzical, inviting comment but
not really expecting it. When he was finished we sat in a hush. Then
I heard my wife break out in a tone of bewilderment. 'But Mr Shaw,
there's a lot that matters about Joan of Arc that you haven't put in!'
Mrs Shaw gasped, but he burst into laughter. 'That's interesting,' he
said. 'What is your case? What do you know of Joan?' My wife struggled with her argument, that she had always been greatly attracted to
Joan of Arc, had read all she could about her, was able to imagine her,
and to understand the feelings which had led her on, feelings Mr Shaw
seemed to have left out. He listened with twinkling eyes, as my wife

mentioned instances of what she meant, until she suddenly gave up. 'You see,' said Mrs Shaw, summing up the discussion amiably, 'you have mainly felt about Joan. Mr Shaw has mainly thought about her.'

Shaw's great gift to the theatre was the play of ideas. In his plays, too, as in his life, there was that detachment from feeling, that figure-of-eight movement of the mind, which enabled him freely to take both sides of a question, to comprehend both saint and sinner. Perhaps it was his bi-partisan Irish background; but just as Joyce could sit on both sides of the sense, just as in Gaelic there are no words for 'yes' or 'no', so in Shaw's plays there is no plain white or black, no villains. All men are variations in search of a theme. And the music is in the counterpoint.

LEONARD: One time he said to me that the first thing he thought of in casting players were the voices. He liked to cast the play according to the type of voices, soprano, alto, tenor and bass.

He was as benevolent and many-sided in life as in letters. You remember, O'Connor, once in Ireland.

O'CONNOR: That was at AE's – one night I was there with Sir Arnold Bax, and Bax and myself were agreeing that Shaw's prose was rather dowdy. Then I glanced at AE and saw that agonised expression on his face which came on it whenever you were blaspheming from the literary point of view, and he said very slowly in a low voice, 'Well, all I know is, if ever an angel of God walked this earth in the form of a man, his name was Bernard Shaw.' After that he began to tell a few stories about Shaw's kindness. First of all when James Connolly, the Irish Labour leader, was executed in 1916 he left the care of his children to AE who had no money of his own – and AE wrote around to a few friends of his to ask for money to keep the children and Shaw cabled him sixty pounds and 'as much more as you want'.

I knew once an instance of a young man who was concerned in the 1916 Rebellion, and his wife was known to Shaw, and he wrote her not to have any worries at all about money matters; that as long as her husband was in prison he'd look after her and the family. Mrs Shaw told me after that she never knew anything about it.

And you, Ervine, must have instances from England.

ERVINE: Let me tell you a story about him. When G. K. Chesterton died, GBS, knowing Chesterton very well and having a great affection for him, wrote to Mrs Chesterton and this roughly is what he said: 'I know that G.K. was careless about money, that he never bargained as he ought to have bargained for price – he always got less than he ought to have, and if you are in any financial trouble as a result of his death will you please draw on me up to four figures.' The amount of kindness he did to people throughout his life was incalculable.

Was it that he hated poverty more than he loved the poor?

LEONARD: I don't think that he had the same passion for law as he had for justice.

Mr Dooley, the member for Tipperary, on one occasion made an impassioned plea in parliament. 'All I ask for my beloved country is justice,' he exclaimed. 'Justice be damned,' said Balfour. 'There isn't enough to go round.' Shaw, when told this story, remarked huffily, 'Balfour could never have said anything so good as that.'

JOHNSTON: In his old age he used to repudiate most of the rude remarks about other people that had been attributed to him, but here again I don't think that he does himself justice. He could be exceedingly unkind, particularly to other writers.

'My wife,' says Glenavy, 'once asked Shaw why he didn't stay in Dublin.'

GLENAVY: 'What would there be for me now in Dublin?' he asked. 'Well,' she said, 'isn't there the famous conversation?' 'Whose?' he inquired. She suggested Oliver Gogarty, reputed for wit among other talents. 'Silly Dublin persiflage!' he commented severely.

And Gogarty recalls an occasion –

OLIVER GOGARTY: I, being of a gossipy nature, once at lunch said, sententiously enough – I was a younger man – that all great men knew they were great. I was going to follow up by quoting Milton's 'Who in no middle flight intends to soar above the Aeolian mount.' Anyhow, I said all great men were aware of their greatness. And Shaw shut me up immediately by saying, 'So was Marie Corelli.'

Was Shaw unhappily reminded of his boyhood days in a Dublin office? One day, he said, an apprentice there remarked 'that every boy thinks he is going to be a great man'. 'The shock that this gave me,' says Shaw, 'made me suddenly aware that this was my own predicament.'

GOGARTY: I met him two or three times, and I met him in a house near Pinner, which was near his cottage, and I didn't like him, to be candid, because he absorbed the conversation. He waited until there was silence round the table, then he thrust out his red beard and he dictated to the public, such as there were.

LEONARD: Oh no, quite the opposite. He was a most attentive listener to anybody, no matter how foolish their remarks might be. He was deferential and very, very courteous, and in ordinary conversation with a group of people he was always amusing, always gay. He'd listen carefully – if you wanted to talk, he'd listen; if you didn't want to talk, he'd talk.

GOGARTY: He married late in life, and he married a woman whom he turned at once into material. He said, 'I married her because she had plenty of money and she was an old woman.'

LEONARD: He told me one time that he did not marry her until his income was on a level with her own.

GOGARTY: But she happened to be a lady and in her will she left money to teach the Irish manners. That money was left to teach her husband manners, in my opinion, and he was the most perspicacious man, in his own opinion, that ever existed, and he didn't see the satire. She left her money to teach him manners.

Would you agree, Ervine?

ERVINE: Well, Charlotte was a far more ardent lover of Ireland than GBS. GBS was not particularly in love with Ireland at all. But Charlotte was, and her love was entirely sentimental. I used to argue with her about it. And there was no intellectual basis in it whatever. But she was very conscious of the fact that GBS, through those lonely years of very acute hardship, had become extremely shy. He was a shy man. And the only way he could overcome his embarrassment at being in company was by showing off. And she got it into her head that that was true of a great many Irish people – which a lot of circumstances account for. And therefore what should be done was to leave all her money, about £150,000 I think it was, to some sort of organisation which would enable young people to come together and rub their edges off, just exactly as they do at Oxford and Cambridge.

GOGARTY: He was essentially a shy man and then when he got the ground under his feet, when his mother ceased to support him, he became arrogant.

JOHNSTON: Now, what those real facts were about his background I don't profess to know; but I don't believe that his definitive biography has been written yet, in this particular connection.

The debate continues. The shy showman, the idolised iconoclast, serious and gay, kind and cold, courteous and rude – what were the early roots that nourished this dichotomy, this equivocal character?

ERVINE: I don't know. When he went to a school in Dublin, the last school he attended, he met there a boy called McNulty, who was regarded as the pet lamb of the school, the high writer and all the rest of it, and of course, Shaw just went over him like a steam-roller. Now this man McNulty was a great friend of GBS's. I think he was the only man that his sister Lucy really loved. He never came to anything but he had a considerable opinion of himself in his young manhood. He got a job in the Bank of Ireland at Newry, and he and GBS constantly wrote to each other. And later in life GBS implored McNulty to destroy the letters, and McNulty, like a fool, did. I hope that that man is suffering torments in the next world for that infinite folly, because probably in those letters we'd have got a light on Shaw that we shall never get now.

'Shaw,' said Yeats, 'is haunted by the mystery that he flouts.' 'Well,' said Shaw, 'if you can't get rid of the family skeleton you can at least make it dance.' How happy Shaw would have been had he lived to hear of the American who offered the crematorium attendant £10 for a spoonful of GBS's ashes. As he himself remarked once, 'Life, happy or unhappy, successful or unsuccessful, is extraordinarily interesting.'

OLIVER ST JOHN GOGARTY

Poet, wit, playwright, athlete, surgeon, senator – the epitome of his time and place, the Ireland of Yeats, Joyce, and Synge. In a Dublin where every word was feathered for flight and barbed for repetition his tongue was the sharpest, his wit the readiest, his friends, and enemies, the most illustrious. Of Gogarty, the poet laureate William Watson wrote:

> Three Olivers before your time
> Were not unknown in prose and rhyme;
> One was the paladin or pal
> Of him who fought at Roncesvalles,
> And one brought Drogheda to pillage,
> And one wrote 'The Deserted Village';
> But sorra an Oliver ever seen
> Compares with him of Stephen's Green.

Dudley Walsh recalls him.

DUDLEY WALSH: The first time I met Gogarty was with my father in the Stephen's Green Club and I thought I'd never seen such an impatient man. He rushed down the corridor of the Club in the hall, produced a half-crown from his pocket and said, 'I owe this to McCann or somebody,' and he thrust it in my father's hand and rushed out of the door. I said, 'Who is that?' and my father said, 'That was Dr Gogarty.'

'The fact is,' said Gogarty, 'that no Irishman can endure being himself for long.' Always on the go, Gogarty was the most mercurial of men. As Kevin O'Shiel says,

KEVIN O'SHIEL: You'd be going along and he'd be talking to you about his opinion of the opponents of the Treaty and suddenly the next minute he'd be telling you something in the Greek classics, or quoting a great friend of his, Hugh McDiarmid. And then the next time he'd be telling you some rather salacious story about a lady.

Glancing quickly from one thing to another, like a bird, very mercurial, very quick. The only place I could never see Gogarty happy would be in prison, I think nearly every place else in life you put him he'd find something to interest him.

All gateways were getaways to Gogarty. He loved outings, as Lord Glenavy recalls.

LORD GLENAVY: He was the first person in Ireland to have a Rolls-Royce car.

LADY GLENAVY: The first butter-coloured Rolls-Royce in Ireland.

LORD GLENAVY: One of his great pleasures was to take friends up the mountains driving at speed in the Rolls-Royce. The experience of speed was something, but the great experience was to hear Gogarty on any occasion – it might be a passing cart, or children running out of a house, or cattle in a field – describing one's exact sensation in some extract from poetry, not a cliché, lines probably one had never heard before, but when he had said them and you had listened inwardly to them you felt, here is an amazing gift. That was the best part of Gogarty. We passed a country wedding party, and it was an instance of one of those analogies at which he was very prompt. On seeing this procession he turned to us and said, 'The desire of the cow for the bull, of the mare for the stallion, the ache of the maid-of-all-work for the private of any battalion.' Gogarty was a young man, no inhibitions, no restrictions, no great cares, and I think then was at his very best.

ROBERT O'DOHERTY: He just was twenty-five years younger than anyone should be at his age at any particular time – in outlook, in physique and in everything about him.

O'SHIEL: My happiest memory of Gogarty is as a charming companion, a perpetual boy. I always thought he had the Greek qualities – first of all the love of beauty, then curiously enough, I suppose some people wouldn't agree with me in that, a love of sense of proportion.

PADRAIC COLUM: It would be possible to see Gogarty in another way. To see him as the Roman, the man who spoke the language in order and command, and I think his little verse on the Petronius is very revealing,

> Proconsul of Bithynia,
> Who loved to turn the night to day,

Yet for your ease had more to show
Than others for their push and go.
Teach us to save the Spirit's expense,
And win to Fame through indolence.

I knew him as this man who had such a tremendous fund of poetry. For instance, we would go out for walks in the Dublin hills and all along the way he could declaim poetry. What impressed me most, being unscholarly myself, is the way that he could take hold of, say, a strophe of Pindar's, recite it, bring before you the whole performance of what would have been the performance of one of the great odes. It was magnificent. And then there were lots of people in Dublin at the time who had a tremendous verbal feeling for poetry, but Gogarty was distinguished by the fact that it was not only in English that he had this fund of poetry, but in Latin, in Greek – I never heard him use French. Latin, Greek, English of course, and Lowland Scots which he was very fond of, not only Burns but minor poets around Burns whom he could repeat with great gusto.

'*I owe him a vast amount,*' *said Monsignor Patrick Browne, translator of* The Divine Comedy *into the Irish.*

MGR PATRICK BROWNE: It was he that introduced me and made me a continual reader of Dante, whom he loved himself, and from whom he could quote most of the great passages by heart, and of which he was a wonderful interpreter, as he was of the classics, also.

What about the early Gogarty who figures as Buck Mulligan in Joyce's Ulysses*? 'Stately, plump Buck Mulligan,' the book begins.*

PEARSE BEASLEY: There's one thing I used to wonder; why Joyce called him plump Buck Mulligan, because in his later years he had a trim figure, no elderly spread or anything like that. It didn't seem an appropriate phrase at all.

DENIS JOHNSTON: The only thing that would dry him up was any suspicion that he was being courted as Malachi Mulligan rather than as Oliver Gogarty. If he thought that this was the reason for your interest in him he would dry up at once and no mention of Joyce would pass his lips. There was some justification for this – he was a wit and a poet in his own right and to be treated as a character in a book by a man whom he rather looked down on was more than could be expected of Gogarty.

What do you think, Padraic Colum?

COLUM: I think that here is a very extraordinary thing. You discover that you are more living in the pages of a book than you are in your personal life – that is a queer happening, isn't it? And Gogarty must have discovered that, because Buck Mulligan is so much more alive than Oliver Gogarty in his later years. It must have been a very strange thing to waken up and wonder whether you are Buck Mulligan or Oliver Gogarty. What would have happened if Dr Johnson had survived and read Boswell, and found that he was much more alive in Boswell's pages than he was in his actual life.

AUSTIN CLARKE: I admire Joyce's long struggle against hypocrisy and his courageous fight for frankness and freedom of expression, but I couldn't help sympathising with Dr Gogarty at the time. I suppose like most medicos he'd been a little wild in his youth and sown some wild oats in the best Victorian tradition – but not too many, since he was an athlete and a champion who won a lot of prizes in cycle races. But the melancholy Joyce had portrayed him as a sort of eighteenth-century buck and also a romantic Byron and quoted a lot of his priapic verses. Joyce and other famous Irish writers in exile portrayed themselves always as martyrs and misunderstood men, victims of Dublin, but the real martyrs have been those, I think, who've stayed in Dublin working for the literary revival, keeping it going, while they were being exploited by their fellow-Irishmen abroad.

WALSH: There was probably a social barrier, because Gogarty had been born in Rutland Square and his father was a very eminent surgeon, while Joyce's father hadn't been a great success, had been a rate-collector, and Joyce probably hadn't really very much money for drinking around pubs.

Martha McCulloch – did Gogarty mention Joyce to you?

MARTHA MCCULLOCH: Oliver Gogarty had more money in the Dublin days than Joyce, and he indicated that financial help which he gave to Joyce was not returned – I can't say returned, that would be bad, but he lacked gratitude of any kind. And that often he'd been malicious towards Gogarty in a way that he need not have been.

I think Gogarty was an easily wounded person.

MARTHA McCULLOCH: He had terrific pride, and more than a modicum of conceit.

'Joyce wasn't a gentleman,' said Gogarty. Brinsley Macnamara, you knew Gogarty long and intimately.

BRINSLEY MACNAMARA: It began to dawn on me that he was not really a Dubliner at all but a Meath man and with the Meath manner of making comedy. His father had come from Nobber in North Meath and the name of Gogarty was a highly respected one all over the royal county. I have always felt it was this touch of provincial difference that was in Gogarty which set him eventually at odds with James Joyce, his contemporary and close literary companion for a while. It was the clash of the Dublin jackeen, which Joyce really was, in his efforts to show off his learning which was actually only his cleverness before the other, who was so securely based in solid country character and safe acquaintance with the classics of Greece and Rome. One of Gogarty's finest acts was his refusal of offers, financially most attractive, to write a book on Joyce at a time when his former friend had become the literary rage of America. The reason he gave me for this showed the difference between the two men better than any other explanation that I know of. 'I just couldn't do it,' he said. 'The man was too sad. Joyce was the very saddest man I ever knew.'

Celtic gloom had clashed with Attic gaiety.

JOHN CHICHESTER: I met Oliver Gogarty about thirty years ago in the old Palace Bar – that Dublin hostelry where one met primarily for talk, with drink a very minor consideration. He struck me as being an incredibly ebullient individual, he was hopping around all over the place. His talk was wonderful – epigram and repartee fairly scintillated from him.

COLUM: It's hard to take a piece of wit out of its period, and out of its context, but I will honestly say that he was the most quick-witted person I ever met in my life.

O'SHIEL: He had an extraordinarily quick mind – if you could imagine a magnificent intelligence put into a quick bird's brain.

MONK GIBBON: Gogarty's great rival at one time, in the field of the nose and throat, was another specialist called Keogh, and Gogarty said, 'When a patient comes to me in a really bad way, I have a look at the left nostril, and I say "Oh", and I have a look at the right nostril, and then I say "Keogh".' Well, that is a typical Gogarty story.

JOHN COLBERT: There was a solicitor that he hated because he thought he had deprived him of his heritage and one evening he opened the evening paper and saw that this man had been taken to hospital from an accident, and it was a Rolls-Royce car that had knocked him down. Oliver instantly said, 'At last, struck off the Rolls.'

Robert O'Doherty, you were Gogarty's trusted solicitor and friend. How did you find him, as a companion?

O'DOHERTY: His humour was always tinged with malice of a delightful nature; sometimes plenty of it, always a little of it. I often drank with him into the late hours of night, and in the morning we never failed to meet for a swim to recover from the effects, if any, of the previous night. Some dairies were open in the early morning where you could get a pint of buttermilk, and then you were perfect to start the day.

When would Gogarty's drinking day start?

O'DOHERTY: It began at one o'clock, or before one, with three or four people and it generally ended at six or seven o'clock with ten or eleven people – lesser beings that were there to hear the words of wisdom fall from his mouth.

I never knew such a city for writers to be found loitering with intent to work. If you want to avoid them you have to dive into a pub. If you want to meet them you still have to go into a pub. 'If God had been any good,' cried a desperate Dubliner, 'he'd have put a nip of whiskey in the air.'

WALSH: But Gogarty, you know, didn't drink very much, he only drank lager beer, vast quantities of lager, but I think that's probably due to the fact that he was rather vain about his figure.

CLARKE: He told me that he was threatened with hardening of the arteries.

O'SHIEL: His trouble he told me was that he could never get drunk, he considered that a bad sign.

Noll Gogarty, as your father's son, you can resolve this question for us.

NOLL GOGARTY: He gave up whiskey in 1917 and as far as I know never drank any whiskey subsequently. When he took to a literary life he had almost of necessity to drink something. When he was consorting with the people that he met in Dublin pubs to give him – what shall I say – colour to his writings, he drank beer.

Cathal O'Shannon met him in later years in a bar in Galway.

CATHAL O'SHANNON: We talked for about an hour and a half and he said his doctor's orders were that he couldn't take any spirits or anything like that, and he drank mineral waters. Now how the devil he kept on drinking gassy mineral waters for an hour and a half I don't know.

Brinsley Macnamara remembers the Gogarty parody on Yeats's poem 'The Old Men Admiring Themselves in the Water'.

> I heard the old, old man say
> Mineral waters – the doctor ordered me Liffier.
> His face was like the face one sees
> In Galway county families,
> By the halters of flapper meetings led astray,
> Where tide is low and bookies pay, mainly faulters,
> I heard the old, old man say
> What do you think will win today
> By the waters?

'I wish,' said Lewey, the waiter in the Bailey Tavern, 'I wish I had the shoes Dr Gogarty wore out on me bringing whiskeys to his friends.' You, Dr Bodkin, were once at a Gogarty picnic in the Dublin Hills, and Augustus John was there.

DR BODKIN: I thought Gogarty was giving him far too much drink, he was drinking without any regard; so at one stage we were sitting on the sill of a cottage window, Gogarty handed John a huge tumbler of whiskey, John put it down for a moment and when he wasn't looking, I spilt it on the ground. Gogarty was furious with me, I've never seen him so angry before. He had a curious queer streak, in that he liked to get people shaky on their perches. I've seen him take Seamus O'Sullivan and fill him with drink at the bar counter in Suffolk Street. Gogarty would perch Seamus on the bar stool, and Seamus in the end had no way of getting off the stool, except by falling, so he had to remain there, until he'd sobered down a bit. Gogarty enjoyed this thoroughly, bade him good-bye, and went and left him there. It's borne out in Joyce –

when he leads the rout from Hollow Street, into the Red Lamp Quarter, they're all soaking in drink, but Gogarty is sober and observing.

The truth is that Gogarty, lucky man, was born 'above-par' as Padraic Colum points out.

COLUM: Joyce had a physical weakness that needed it, whereas Gogarty was a hundred per cent fit, he didn't need drink, and he was rather contemptuous of the way that Joyce took his liquor. I remember him saying to me about the two of them going home together after a night out, 'Joyce curled up in the cab like a tobacco spit.' It was very contemptuous.

'Joyce was not a gentleman.' Austin Clarke recalls an evening spent with Gogarty, revisiting the shades of Nighttown.

CLARKE: The last evening, perhaps I should say the last morning, I spent with Oliver Gogarty in Dublin is for me a memorable one. I'd met him at some party and in his generous way he offered to drive me home. It was about half past one in the morning, and he drove – as he always did – at a terrific speed, all the more so as the streets at that time were completely deserted. Suddenly he said 'Let's go down to Monto,' that being the local name for the brothel district, at one time notorious as one of the worst brothel districts of all European cities, perhaps Eastern ones too, and of course known from that lugubrious Victorian chapter in *Ulysses* known as 'Nighttown'. I must hasten to add that Nighttown was no longer there. So we came to that strange, silent district in the moonlight and drove slowly past empty slum houses with boarded-up windows and my senior talked to me of those days he'd known long ago, evoking memories of almost legendary figures – a veritable dream of fair but frail women; May Oblong, Mrs Mac the Bawd, Fresh Nelly, Liverpool Kate, Piano Mary and that well-known shebeen keeper, the incomparable Mrs Becky Cooper. The poet had celebrated them all in his ballads, but I like best that lyric which he recited to me in the moonlight there in a desolate lane, the engine of a sports car faintly running. Most people in Dublin know it by heart:

> I will live in Ringsend
> With a red-headed whore,
> And the fanlight gone in
> Where it lights the hall-door;

And listen each night
For her querulous shout,
As at last she streels in
And the pubs empty out.

I could hardly get a word in, there in the deserted Monto, Gogarty
talked so much of the past, but at last I did succeed in capping one of
his stories. I told him how, one night, during the Black and Tan
terror I had been out with Padraic O'Conaire. He was a Gaelic writer
to whom a most respectable statue has been erected in Galway city.
We were caught out after curfew and to save our lives, no doubt, we
took refuge in one of the shebeens in Nighttown. The pub kitchen
was comfortable; it was winter-time, big fire roaring in the open range.
Well, it was long before the Guinness book of poetry had even been
thought of by Lord Moyne but Guinness was the drink of Nighttown
after hours and I can tell you it was expensive, a shilling a glass, and
you'd to stand a complete round to everyone there. Suddenly, a young
lady who had probably had too much Guinness started a wild dance;
quicker, quicker she whirled to the tune of what is known as 'gob
music', and suddenly, as her skirts flew up, we saw with astonishment
the flag of the Irish Republic; for that ingenious and patriotic daring
young lady had chosen for her petticoat, knickers and so on, the
colours of our forbidden flag, the green, the white and the yellow.

*Sir Compton Mackenzie, your old friend Gogarty invited you to attend
the Tailteann Games in Dublin, the time he won the Gold Medal for
Poetry.*

SIR COMPTON MACKENZIE: That was in 1924. There was a great
gathering. Gogarty thought, well, I'm going to have the people who
amuse me and I like, and who have spoken out for Ireland at the time
of the troubles, and said for God's sake is this going on any longer, as I
did later on over Cyprus, let's say. And so he had G. K. Chesterton,
Augustus John, Edwin Lutyens and myself; Willie Yeats in tremendous
form as a Senator, going about with a terrific top-hat everywhere, and
that of course amused Gogarty enormously.

Where did he put you up?

MACKENZIE: G.K. and I were at the old Viceregal Lodge, with the
Governor General. Augustus John put up with Dunsany, and there
was a typical practical joke by Gogarty. He told Dunsany that Augustus

John was a passionate teetotaller and couldn't bear the thought of liquor in any form. He also told Augustus John, now for God's sake, Augustus, don't ask for a drink, because it upsets Dunsany; you'll only be there for two or three nights, then you'll be staying with me in Ely Place. Well, Augustus stood it until Dunsany tried to teach him how to play the great Irish harp. This was too much for John, without even mentioning a drink, so he climbed over the wall at Dunsany Park and walked, about fourteen miles, I suppose, to Dublin.

In Dublin if you have to go anywhere you never run; it's unlucky. And, besides, it uses up the valuable breath which could be spent on talking. Gogarty was a very talkative companion.

MACKENZIE: He was an absolutely first-class companion. He was one of the greatest raconteurs I have known. People accused him of monopolising. I think towards the end he did monopolise a bit, but not at his peak – he was perfectly glad to hear other people doing it. But all older people, probably, who are good raconteurs, will monopolise the conversation towards the end. I probably do, I don't know, still it's pretty difficult not to, you know, when you get older.

JOHNSTON: In his later days, as an old man, his verbal exhibitionism got a lot more mellow and, to my ear, he became much more entertaining. After all, he had known everyone in the literary world of his day and, although it seemed wise to treat many of his yarns about Yeats, George Moore, and Max Beerbohm and Kipling with a grain of salt, you had to admit that they were vastly entertaining, and I suppose this was really the secret of his charm in his latter days. For all his amusing malice was principally conditioned by a desire to please his listeners, not just to talk for his own satisfaction, which of course is the real distinction between a good companion and a bore. Wilde, I am sure, had the same generous quality of liking, in his conversation, to give pleasure to others.

O'SHIEL: He was a great host, he'd never monopolise. I was always affected by his inherent good nature, his generosity, his kindness. If there was a shy fellow in the room he'd never be ignored, he'd pull him out. The fellow would whisper some little joke and Gogarty would make a tremendous thing of it, you see, so the fellow would be all delighted with himself. But he disliked intensely the monologist, if that is the right word.

Dr Bodkin, a friend once consulted you about asking Gogarty to his party.

BODKIN: I said, well, you take your life in your hands, but you'll be entertained. So he asked Gogarty to a dinner-party, and I was privileged to be at it. There were a lot of intelligent people there, Tim Healey, and various people of the sort, and Gogarty conducted a monologue during part of the dinner, but anything more brilliant I haven't heard. He'd obviously planned it, and he fished for a cue, got on some current topic, and someone then made the obvious remark, and the obvious remark was Gogarty's cue and he built up a great structure of wit and badinage. The surprising thing was I heard him somewhere else, a few months later, when the performance was repeated almost verbatim. It was a stage performance, but when you heard it the first time its effect was of sheer spontaneity.

MAJOR FREYER: Well, I maintain that I would rather hear a good story, one of Gogarty's good stories, ten times over than a less good one the first time; for instance, one friend of Gogarty's had a glass eye, and one evening at dinner at Jammet's, Oliver, at the end of the dinner, lifted his glass and said, 'Drink to me with thine only eye.' Well, I think that's perfect. Oliver was one of those people who, if he could think of a witty thing to say, would say it at my expense, at the expense of his greatest friends, because the wit would forgive it.

BRIAN AHERNE: I have heard him on occasions say unkind things about somebody whom we both knew, and then to go the following day to visit him and to bring him some money if necessary and give it to him without question.

He never allowed a kind act to get in the way of a good crack.

MACNAMARA: He seemed impelled by some devilish thing that was in him to say some harsh or bitter thing. But he really never meant it. There was no malice in them, none whatsoever.

BODKIN: But he'd say them to their faces, I'll do him that justice.

LADY HANSON: I didn't dislike it; he encouraged a reciprocal tongue, you see.

Let's have an example. Lady Glenavy's story about the painter, Orpen.

LADY GLENAVY: It was just after Orpen died. At one time Orpen and Gogarty were practically inseparable, everywhere one went the other went, and they were full of funny stories about each other. I was lunching in Ely Place with some people who lived almost opposite Gogarty's house. After lunch, we were talking, and I could see Gogarty in the window of his house, peeping first out of one window and then out of another; he saw there was a lunch party going on and he wanted to find out who was there. We came out on the steps after the lunch and Gogarty's hall door suddenly opened and he shot across the street. I saw he had a funny story, he had something to say, and he began gasping to me, 'Our painter, our painter,' he knew that I had been as great a friend of Orpen's as he had, 'our painter never got under the surface until he got under the ground.' I was so furious I just said, 'I hate you, Gogarty,' and he turned and ran giggling back into his house and shut the hall door.

'But don't you know,' said a Dubliner to Mrs Yeats who was defending Gogarty, 'don't you know that the man is sitting somewhere at this minute saying the most scandalous things about you?' 'And don't you know,' said Mrs Yeats, 'that a man may do that and still be the most loyal friend you ever had?'

O'SHIEL: If you were Gogarty's friend, you could do no wrong. Amongst the little circle of close friends you were the subject of his butt, but if anything happened to you outside, from some other fellow, down the doctor would come in the most formidable way he could – he was a good man with his fists in his younger days – but generally in the Irish way of attacking, the scribe would write some caustic thing about your enemy, which satisfied you.

WILLIAM COSGRAVE: If you were a friend of the man it mattered little how fortune smiled on you, you were still his friend. Generous, open-hearted, at times inclined to be expressive about men and things; but you could understand that with him.

He was a friend of Arthur Griffith, the founder and conscience of Sinn Fein.

COSGRAVE: He was a very close friend of Griffith; I've never known a man to idolise another as much as Gogarty idolised Griffith. He was almost mortally wounded when Griffith died, he was so very, very much attached to him.

Mr O'Shiel, you remember the night of Arthur Griffith's death.

O'SHIEL: Griffith died in the morning, of a stroke – he bent down to lace his boot and died, and Gogarty was called in. Well, that evening I was up with the crowd, and Gogarty was there, hard, cynical as ever, laughing; he was ten times more bitter against Griffith's enemies and opponents than ever, but that was about the only difference. And many people said, 'Extraordinary that man, a man like that was so close, he does seem to be quite unmoved.'

But you knew the true story of what had happened that morning in the nursing-home.

O'SHIEL: What happened was this. Gogarty came in and I came in and we examined Griffith. When he was absolutely certain he was dead, Gogarty burst into tears and he walked to the window saying, 'My poor Arthur, my poor Arthur.' That night he had pulled the whole thing round to cynicism, which I called his mask, his armour.

Yet Griffith and Gogarty were completely opposed in temperament, Mr Cosgrave?

COSGRAVE: Oh, yes. That was a peculiarity of Gogarty's – he could accommodate himself to almost any type of person. He had certain affinities and affections, a certain number of people whom he respected one way or another, and nothing that he could do was considered too much for them. He was a very remarkable man. He was a fast friend, you know, of Collins.

And at a time when Michael Collins was on the run, with a price on his ead, Gogarty bravely gave him shelter?

COSGRAVE: He did. He never considered that a matter of courage; it was a matter of friendship.

Shelagh O'Mahoney has a story about a surgical operation which Dr Gogarty performed in his own home in Ely Place.

SHELAGH O'MAHONEY: Gogarty had arranged to do an operation on Sir Neville Macready, who was then the newly appointed commander-in-chief of the British Forces. This was the morning scheduled for the operation; Gogarty was wakened by machine-gun fire and rifle fire. About ten minutes later a frightfully persistent banging at his back-door worried him to the extent that he couldn't stand the noise, and he got up and investigated. As he opened the door a tall figure of a woman in a shawl lurched breathlessly past him into the passage.

Gogarty cautiously put on the light, saw this figure tear off the shawl and discard a very palpable female wig. Then the figure suddenly seemed, like something out of *Alice in Wonderland*, to shoot up, and a brawny, root-like arm was cast affectionately on Oliver Gogarty's shoulder and a buttery West Cork voice said, 'Begob, Oliver, they nearly had me that time, boy.' Who was it but Michael Collins, Gogarty's friend, the rebel leader, who was once again on the run from the Crown Forces. Meanwhile, up at the Castle, Sir Neville, who was a very punctual man, was just setting out for Gogarty's house for the operation, and at nine o'clock precisely he arrived complete with armoured cars and bristling with all sorts of panoply of war. The maid opened the door and the bodyguard of about six or seven officers, all trench-coated and hands on holsters, swept past the poor maid and followed the receptionist and Sir Neville right into the improvised operating theatre. Here they were met by Gogarty who was calm, but very affable, and in the corner of the operating theatre was the rather burly figure of a dark young man with a white overall and a surgical mask. Very calmly and suavely Gogarty said, 'Excuse me, gentlemen, I haven't introduced you to my new anaesthetist, Dr Collins.'

Gogarty, says Michael Noyk, was an extraordinary mixture.

MICHAEL NOYK: Shortly after he became attached to the Meath hospital as a doctor, he threw a garden-party in Ely Place at which he had the Chief Justice, a gentleman called Peter the Packer, and other loyal people. The moment that was finished in the evening he went off to a man who had a little tobacco shop and who was a bit of a comic and a story-teller, and then he met all the men in the early Sinn Fein and the Gaelic League – an extraordinary contrast.

O'SHIEL: I think I'm right in saying that any man of the old movement, IRA or whoever he was, would go up to the doctor's door and knock at it, and come away the richer for a fiver.

CHICHESTER: He was very kindly to the poor. On one occasion a poor old woman came to him; she'd some slight eye trouble and a monstrous wen, which literally hung over one shoulder. Well, Oliver treated her and then, diverting her attention for a moment, he snipped the wen off. The old woman, instead of being grateful, was furious; it was her chief means of livelihood; it excited pity everywhere. It was a perfect goldmine.

MGR BROWNE: But he never showed his loving generous heart so much as when he treated children in the hospital; his speech would turn into indignation when he thought of what they were suffering in this city, at the time, through its lack of sanitation, and especially in housing; slum landlords, and all that kind of thing. You would feel there that there was a real charitable heart beating in Gogarty which balanced all the very cynical speeches which are reported of him, and which were quite true.

Of all cities, Dublin has the lowest flashpoint of wit. And Gogarty was a past-master in the unpremeditated art of epigram and riposte. He was also a poet. It didn't help him in his profession.

CLARKE: Well, I suppose in any country a doctor who published poems, even if they were highly moral, would soon be distrusted by his patients and his colleagues.

And in Dublin, Dr Bodkin?

BODKIN: They don't trust you in anything, as you ought to know; if you're a poet, it's about the worst reputation you could have. How could a man be a serious businessman, if he writes verse!

MRS WILLIAMS: He's quite right. I would mistrust a surgeon that painted portraits better than he took out tonsils. I'm sure I would.

Was he happy in his profession, Mrs Williams? You, as his daughter, should know.

MRS WILLIAMS: He was a very good surgeon, and up to the time that he got restless and felt that time was running out for him, and that he wanted to go out into the world more, and meet people and write, he was quite happy with his surgery.

Dr Bodkin agrees.

BODKIN: I remember he operated on Stephen McKenna, the translator of Plotinus. McKenna broke down with an abscess in the inner ear, and Gogarty operated on him at a moment's notice. McKenna told me that years afterwards, when he was in Switzerland, he went to the greatest specialist on the subject, who asked him who did this operation, and said, 'I didn't think there were two men in Europe who could do that operation; it's a great feat.'

But his versatility – he was even the first amateur airman in Ireland – went against him, as a surgeon.

BODKIN: Oh, yes, I'm sure it did. And then his colleagues were a bit frightened of him.

CLARKE: Gogarty's outrageous Rabelaisian parodies and Victorian jokes about religion were unprintable at that time and went round orally in the same way as limericks among businessmen.

Monk Gibbon, you used to meet Gogarty at Yeats's house.

GIBBON: Gogarty was one of the people that you were fairly certain to see; he breezed into the room, I won't say breathing affability. Several people have said to me that Yeats was afraid of Gogarty. Gogarty could be distinctly malicious, and it's possible that Yeats was. Gogarty would come in with his latest funny story, or his latest piece of gossip, and straightaway I felt myself in the presence of a fundamental insincerity. Just as certain aspects of Yeats alienated me, in the same way I was alienated by Gogarty straightaway. I suppose I was a prim young man, and Gogarty's conversations and his anecdotes were amongst the coarsest things to be encountered in Dublin.

But Yeats invited the coarseness, the dirty stories. Yeats was a rather lofty, cut-off person but, in principle, he believed that a poet should come down from his ivory tower, should know all the dirt; and Gogarty's stories were a sort of roughage for the poetic gizzard.

GIBBON: Well, you're a very good devil's advocate, or angel's advocate. You put the case extremely well for the defence. As a matter of fact I believe Gogarty's poetry may be the key to the mystery of the whole man. As you know yourself, as a poet, nothing else counts; if you are a poet, poetry comes first and before all. If you have several other professions your second string can never compensate for your first. Gogarty was not devoting his whole life to the thing that probably mattered most to him, and that was poetry.

MRS WILLIAMS: He was a natural born poet and it came absolutely naturally to him. He said to me, 'It's a knack with which you're born, this ability to write poetry; some people can paint, I can write poetry.' He might write between an antrum and a tonsil.

And he wrote a poem about you, I believe.

MRS WILLIAMS: That happened a long time ago. He very often used to take my mother and myself, when I was quite small, up the Dublin mountains in the summer evenings. We were up at Ticknock one evening – he liked to go up and see the sunlight on the granite and get the view of Dublin Bay from the Dublin Mountains. I was wearing a pair of white sand-shoes, and I was running in the long grass and when I came back to my parents, my shoes were completely yellow, which upset me a little. My father explained to me how it was the pollen off the buttercups that had covered my shoes. My mother said, 'you can brush it off,' and it was that that started the poem 'Golden stockings you had on, in the meadow where you ran'.

> Golden stockings you had on
> In the meadow where you ran;
> And your little knees together
> Bobbed like pippins in the weather,
> When the breezes rush and fight
> For those dimples of delight,
> And they dance from the pursuit
> And the leaf looks like the fruit.
>
> I have many a sight in mind
> That would last if I were blind,
> Many verses I could write
> That would bring me many a sight.
> Now I only see but one,
> See you running in the sun,
> And the gold-dust coming up
> From the trampled buttercup.

I never confirmed it with my father, but I think that must have been me; it's too great a likeness to the incident for the poem to have been anything else.

And politics. Where did your father's politics spring from?

MRS WILLIAMS: I don't know the answer to that one. It was long before I had any feeling for that; I remember all the leaders in the house; Michael Collins, Griffith, Joe McGrath and all these people. My father suffered directly through the Civil War. He felt that De Valera was responsible for the Civil War in Ireland; I don't think he could ever forgive him for that.

BODKIN: And that explains in great part his abiding hatred of Mr De Valera.

BEASLEY: He had a very great dislike of Mr De Valera. But one time, when he heard that one of Mr De Valera's sons had been killed by a fall from a horse, he was suddenly sympathetic and sorry. He said, 'I'm a father myself. I can feel for Dev.'

MGR BROWNE: I think that his fidelity to Griffith led him into a kind of hysteria against the Republican party. I think that was a most regrettable thing. It led him to all lengths of bitter speech and for me it is the greatest misfortune that that kind of parting deprived me of Gogarty's fairly constant company for the rest of his life. I met him at times, and I found him always gay and always friendly with me as in the old times; but I felt also that there was something then between us that had never been between us before.

BEASLEY: Gogarty was placed on the first Senate by the Cosgrave Government on account of his literary attainments.

Mr Cosgrave, President of the Executive Council of the Irish Free State.

COSGRAVE: I don't think he dealt with politics in a serious manner at all. He wasn't a politician in the sense in which people are continually on the platform and so on. I remember him on a platform but once.

O'DOHERTY: He wasn't cunning enough. He was too genuine for politics. He said what he meant and what he thought, and that sort of person does not as a rule succeed in politics. He spared nobody.

Nor was he spared. On a bitter winter's night, during the Civil War, Gogarty was kidnapped from his home in Ely Place and taken to a boathouse on the Liffey. 'Isn't it a fine thing to die to a flash?' said one of his captors. But Gogarty escaped and swam the river to safety. And Dublin celebrated his exploit in 'The Ballad of Oliver Gogarty'.

> Come all ye bould Free Staters now and listen to my lay,
> And pay a close attention, please, to what I've got to say,
> For 'tis the Tale of a Winter's Night last January year,
> When Oliver St John Gogarty swam down the Salmon Weir.
>
> As Oliver St John Gogarty one night sat in his home,
> A-writin' of prescriptions or composin' of a poem,

Up rolled a gorgeous Rolls-Royce car and out a lady jumped,
And at Oliver St John Gogarty's hall-door she loudly thumped.

'Oh, Oliver St John Gogarty,' said she, 'now please come quick,
For in a house some miles away a man lies mighty sick.'
But Oliver St John Gogarty to her made no reply,
As with a dexterous facial twist he gently closed one eye.

'Oh, Oliver St John Gogarty, come let yourself be led,'
Cried a couple of masked ruff-i-ans, puttin' guns up to his head.
'I'm with you, boys,' cried he, 'but first, give me my big fur coat,
And also let me have a scarf – my special care's the throat.'

They shoved him in the Rolls-Royce car and swiftly sped away,
What route they followed Oliver St John Gogarty can't say.
But they reached a house at Island Bridge and locked him in a room,
And said, 'Oliver St John Gogarty, prepare to meet yer doom.'

Said he, 'Give me some minutes first to settle my affairs,
And let me have some moments' grace to say my last night prayers.'
To this appeal his brutal guard was unable to say nay,
He was so amazed that Oliver St John Gogarty could pray.

Said Oliver St John Gogarty, 'My coat I beg you hold.'
The half-bemoidered ruff-i-an then did as he was told.
Before he twigged what game was up the coat was round his head,
And Oliver St John Gogarty into the night had fled.

The rain came down like bullets, and the bullets came down like
     rain,
As Oliver St John Gogarty the river bank did gain;
He plunged into the ragin' tide and swam with courage bold,
Like brave Horatius long ago in the fabled days of old.

Then Oliver St John Gogarty a mighty oath he swore
That if the gods decreed that he should safely reach the shore,
By the blessed martyr Oliver and by the two St Johns,
He'd present the River Liffey with a pair of bloomin' swans.

He landed and proceeded through the famous Phaynix Park;
The night was bitter cold, and what was worse, extremely dark;
But Oliver St John Gogarty to this paid no regard,
Till he found himself a target for our gallant Civic Guard.

Cried Oliver St John Gogarty, 'A Senator am I!
The rebels I've tricked, the river I've swum, and sorra the word's
    a lie.'
As they clad and fed the hero bold, said the sergeant with a wink:
'Faith, thin, Oliver St John Gogarty, ye've too much bounce to
    sink.'

The sting of course is in the tail of the ballad – 'too much bounce to sink'.

BODKIN: It was a very clever comment on the whole thing, and, of
course, riddled with the suggestion that Gogarty never swam any river.

Did he swim the Liffey, Dudley Walsh?

WALSH: There's a lot of doubt cast by the malicious people of Dublin.

MACNAMARA: He never mentioned that feat at all to me, because I
wouldn't have believed him.

FREYER: I told him, 'Well, I was very amused, Oliver, about that stunt
of yours.' 'Oh,' he said, 'stunt? No stunt at all, I can assure you.'

*A very modest man. What in fact did happen on the night of 12 January
1923? Brendan Considine speaks on behalf of the Republican Forces who
captured Gogarty.*

BRENDAN CONSIDINE: During the course of the Civil War a situation
had arisen whereby prisoners held by the then Free State Government
were being executed by way of reprisals for certain military activity
pursued by the Republicans. With a view to counteracting this policy
of reprisals it was decided by Headquarters Staff of the Republican
Forces to apprehend certain personages of influence and power who
were known to be strong supporters of Government policy and who
publicly condoned those acts of reprisal. Among those listed appeared
the name of Dr St John Gogarty, who was duly taken into custody.
To the credit of his captors the operation was carried out under very
great risk since his home was situated in the shadow of Government
Buildings. Those in charge, in accordance with instructions, treated
their prisoner with every respect. As to the prisoner, he behaved with
great courage and with the utmost confidence and discussed with his
captors many subjects of mutual interest, interspersed with wit and
humour which were part of his make-up. The manner of his escape was
in keeping with his general conduct during his detention, confident and
courageous.

Mrs Butler, you were living in a house by the Liffey-side and you remember a certain freezing night in 1923 when the river was in flood.

MRS BUTLER: It was on a January night, might have been a little past ten, when a knock came to the door and I opened it. There was a person standing just in his trousers, waistcoat and shirt-sleeves. He was like as if he was shaving, the cream was on his face and it made him terribly ghostly, and the water was in little bubbles, dropping, running off his face. I first thought really it was a ghost, and I screamed. My father was sitting there and he ran to the door and grabbed him and put him down on a couch outside in the hall. He said it was all right, he wasn't in for any harm, or for robbery of any kind. He took out his gold watch and said, 'Here, you can take my watch and chain.' So then my father got him up and gave him a coat and he went out, wet as he was, and he says to father, 'Take me across to the Depot.' So Father took him across to the Depot gates.

Mrs Ellis, you remember that night at the Police Depot in Phoenix Park?

MRS ELLIS: Oh yes, I remember it as if it was only yesterday. We had just moved into residence in the Civic Guard Depot, my late husband, Dr Ellis, having been appointed surgeon to the Guarda. It was a bitterly cold night, and there was a call from the guardroom to say that there was a man there who had just staggered in, having swum the Liffey after capture by the Irregulars. So my husband went over to the guardroom and he saw this man, rolled up in a blanket in front of the guardroom fire. My husband was mystified and said, 'To whom am I talking?' and he said, 'Gogarty, Oliver St John Gogarty.' Everything possible was done for him, he was in an extreme state of collapse, and before he left that night he gave my husband as a memento a very valuable gold cigarette case. My husband contacted the Government Buildings, and spoke to Mr Cosgrave, and after some time an escort arrived and Dr Gogarty's sojourn with us was over.

You, Mr Cosgrave, were Prime Minister at the time.

COSGRAVE: It wasn't a nice dip to get in the winter, but I met him that night afterwards and he was just a little bit excited. I suppose he had taken some stimulants, you see, but otherwise all right and not bitter. If there was any bitterness at all, I should say that it was that numbers should be engaged on what was only a one- or two-man job. Oh, he had courage and it showed at that time.

CONSIDINE: It is sad that a man of such high qualities should entertain emotions which do him little credit. In his last book he takes pleasure in describing the murder of the officer responsible for his capture and records the possession of a keepsake – a bullet dug out of the body of the victim.

It was during his perilous swim that Gogarty vowed that if he got away he would give two swans to the Liffey. Noll Gogarty, his son, was there when the vow was kept.

NOLL GOGARTY: I remember Yeats being there. In fact, there's a very fine photograph of them going up to the Trinity Boat Club where the swans were liberated on to the Liffey. I know he had a great deal of trouble getting the swans and now of course the Liffey is full of swans.

MACNAMARA: The swans were presented, but that was in tune with his Latin poetry mood of the time; the sort of Catullus mood.

And with the swans, Gogarty gave a poem to the river, Joyce's river, Anna Livia, 'To the Liffey with the Swans':

> Keep you these calm and lovely things,
> And float them on your clearest water;
> For one would not disgrace a King's
> Transformed, beloved and buoyant daughter.

> And with her goes this sprightly swan,
> A bird of more than royal feather,
> With alban beauty clothed upon:
> O keep them fair and well together!

> As fair as was that doubled Bird,
> By love of Leda so besotten,
> That she was all with wonder stirred,
> And the Twin Sportsmen were begotten!

MRS WILLIAMS: He had a tremendous love of swans, in fact he used to claim nearly every swan on the Liffey, he'd look at them and say, 'They must be the offspring of my two.'

CLARKE: My admiration for Oliver grew in later years and I no longer regarded him as just another amateur writer of verse, for in his fifties he abandoned his medical profession and became a professional author. No doubt he was compelled by literary ambition, long repressed.

MRS WILLIAMS: It was always within him that he wanted to write. He was a poet since he was practically a child.

CLARKE: As a free-lance writer he was foolish to expect that he could live by his pen as he had lived as a specialist, used to large fees slipped into the hand. And then there was Gogarty's great mistake as a European in settling down in the United States. His last years there, when the novelty was over, were spent in comparative poverty, a sad end.

And why, Mrs Williams, did your father go to America?

MRS WILLIAMS: He wanted to see the world. Before he left for New York he told me, 'I'm getting on, and I want to see far more of the world before I die, than I have been seeing in either Dublin or London.' He was a man who liked to be at the centre of things and for a while London was the centre and then New York took the place of London and he went there. He liked stimulating company always round him.

Yes, he had always his wits about him. David Flaherty recalls him in New York.

DAVID FLAHERTY: He was always the centre of attraction. He preferred the pubs, like Tim Costello's, a favourite hangout of writers and newspapermen.

JOHNSTON: I doubt very much if he greatly enjoyed the last years of his life in America. America is not really a country for conversation.

AHERNE: On one occasion in New York, in a bar on Third Avenue, there were five or six of us sitting in a booth, and Gogarty was telling many of his wonderful stories. We were about to move off but he said, 'Now I want to tell you this.' So he proceeded to tell another story and when he was about to come to the point, a young man, sitting by the bar, went over and placed a coin in a jukebox. All hell broke loose. The expression on Gogarty's face changed; he became very sad, a combination of sadness and anger, and he said, 'Oh dear God in Heaven, that I should find myself thousands of miles from home, an old man at the mercy of every retarded son of a bitch who has a nickel to drop in that bloody illuminated coal-scuttle.'

FLAHERTY: Gogarty's life in America wasn't an easy one; but I never found him downcast or feeling sorry for himself. He was always well-groomed, alert, amusing, and excited about something or other. He looked many years younger than his age. But he was always a generous friend. I remember him pawning his watch to help a friend who couldn't pay the rent.

'You never,' said Gogarty, 'see a clock in a well-regulated tavern.'

JOHNSTON: He always preferred a free-for-all and sooner or later he would give way to a wisecrack that was not always appreciated, like the moment when he made the comment on the sale of St Nicholas Church in Fifth Avenue to a business concern – a little poem which goes:

> To set mankind a clean example,
> Christ scourged the cashiers from the fane,
> But the revenge was sly and simple,
> The money changers bought the temple,
> The hard bright eyes are back again.

But America did provide him with a living during his last days, once he had given up his medical practice. And, after all, it is only an overnight journey from Shannon, nowadays.

O'SHIEL: I think he knew he'd made a mistake, but being so proud he never liked to recognise that he had. One of the last times he was over in Ireland I was lunching him in the Bailey, and he said he hoped to be over soon again, and I said, 'Do you ever think of coming back?' Well, of course, he had the Greek illusion about life going on for ever and you're always young, and he'd say, 'Oh, yes, I'm coming back, definitely.'

Noll Gogarty, you felt your father was happy in America?

NOLL GOGARTY: He was happy in the sense that he felt that he was perfectly free. I also know that he was happy because he felt he could write and talk as he liked without criticism. But towards the end of his life he would have liked to have come back to Ireland and he was unlucky in that, had he lived a little longer, he would have been back. As far as I know, and as far as my sister was able to tell me, I believe he did see a priest some time before he died.

CLARKE: In Ireland, as in other countries where there's a strongly organised and aggressive religion, scepticism is, of course, secretive and subtle; one has to rely on an old-fashioned Voltairian subterfuge.

Of course it has its pleasures – that of living dangerously. Gogarty was a complete sceptic, though he had to conform outwardly. But his last gesture was, I fancy, one of bitterly jocose conformity, far away in New York.

'I knew a phoenix in my youth.' There was an unforgettable occasion when, as a Senator of the Irish Free State, Gogarty almost succeeded in getting the Phoenix put into the Wild Birds' Protection Act. To David Flaherty in New York he gave his poem on the Phoenix.

FLAHERTY: I take the liberty of repeating it, for I believe it sheds a new light on a man regarded by many as a cynic.

> The Phoenix and the Unicorn
> Are in the hills again,
> Two messengers of God to warn
> Our scientific men
> That, though they scale and scan it,
> With 'Thus far and no more',
> There's things upon our planet
> There's no accounting for.
>
> So urgent is each image,
> I feel I must go soon,
> To seek in lonely pilgrimage
> The Mountains of the Moon,
> Because these faithful eyes of mine
> Would see, ere I expire,
> The Unicorn's anfractuous tine,
> The Phoenix fledged with fire.

For all his caustic wit, Oliver Gogarty was at heart a believer with a child's sense of wonder.

Oliver St John Gogarty was buried in a remote graveyard in the West of Ireland. Professor Liam O'Briain was present.

LIAM O'BRIAIN: I and the President of my college, Monsignor Padraic de Brun, decided to go to the funeral. Both of us were very old acquaintances and friends of Gogarty, so we drove down one beautiful day in winter, through the heart of Connemara. This was one of the most charming funerals I was ever at. We Irish are very strong on funerals, and I've always been strong on funerals myself, and this funeral is one I recall with particular pleasure. Everything went exactly as Oliver would have liked it.

MGR BROWNE: It was one of the things that he would have loved, a very good country choir to sing over him. There was nothing of gorgeous Palestrina or harmonies or anything of that kind, it was the plain chant mass, and it was most fitted to the simplicity of Gogarty's character.

O'BRIAIN: When we came outside, it was fine, but cold, and there was a journey of seven or eight miles to the graveyard. So we all got into cars and drove after the hearse to the cemetery. I thought I knew every inch of Connemara, but this particular district I was not acquainted with at all. We had a long drive along a narrow winding road, along the side of a mountain which sloped down to the sea, and formed below there a sort of very small fjord.

MGR BROWNE: The cemetery is sloping, a rather steep slope, and Gogarty's grave was at the very lowest corner of it beside the lake. Over his grave there was a willow tree that grew from one end and was bent down and reached to earth again on the other side. Then, when the grave was filled, Father Hanrahan, the parish priest, the celebrant of the mass, came and poured the Holy Water on Gogarty's grave.

O'BRIAIN: And here, I really had to chortle. Because the bottle which contained the Holy Water was a whiskey bottle. And I said to myself, how Oliver would enjoy this. I seemed to feel a shake in the coffin which had gone down. Just as the ceremonies were begun by the priest, a swan appeared below in the water – in this little fjord. And this swan turned round and looked up, and all through the funeral that swan stayed there without a stir, looking up at us the whole time.

MGR BROWNE: Oh, it was a wonderful sight, that was. The swan came out from among reeds, drew himself up beside the bank and was still for two or three minutes, and then, like the swan at the end of *Lohengrin*, as if he were bearing the soul and not the body of Oliver with him, turned, and went out in the lake between another set of reeds, and was lost. And we felt then that the spirit of Gogarty had gone away.

The last word is Gogarty's:

> Our friends go with us as we go
> Down the long path where Beauty wends,

Where all we love forgathers, so
Why should we fear to join our friends?

Who would survive them to outlast
His children; to outwear his fame –
Left when the Triumph has gone past –
To win from Age, not Time, a name?

Then do not shudder at the knife
That Death's indifferent hand drives home,
But with the Strivers leave the Strife,
Nor, after Caesar, skulk in Rome.

F. R. HIGGINS

'After Yeats,' said Frank O'Connor to me, years ago, 'Higgins was incomparably the ablest man we had in the Abbey Theatre.' Now, Frank?

FRANK O'CONNOR: No, I remember him best as a comic character. And that's the unjust part of anything I have to say about him. Do you want me to tell you what he was like? He was a big fat handsome man. I'm very Irish in this – I like handsome men. He had a huge Falstaffian body and a dark love-lock that was always tumbling over his eyes. And he had tiny feet like the feet of a Chinese woman, as though they'd been tied up when he was young and they couldn't possibly support this colossal frame of his. As well as that, I think more than anybody I've ever met, he had what I call Irish charm. I detest Irish charm, but I'm always a sucker for it. I fell for Higgins's charm every time, and it was a very real thing. After you'd spent the first evening with Fred you felt you'd made a friend for life. He was so amiable, so kind. Then, when you went away, within an hour he was doing a wonderful parody of you for your worst enemy. And when you met him again guilt was building up inside him and he gave you a queer look under his eyebrows, and you knew perfectly well that he was wondering when you were going to hit him.

Let's see what others thought of Fred Higgins.

JOHN CHICHESTER: A most gentle, kind and very good man. Extremely modest.

ALEC NEWMAN: I pretty well loved him, he was the greatest big lump of a boy and merry person that you ever came across. Anything could make him burst into laughter. He was a grand person.

SEAN O'SULLIVAN: It was impossible not to like him, he was completely devoid of the frightful qualities so many of us have – the quality of cuteness and cunning – he just didn't know what it was. He didn't know how to use people to his own advantage.

ROBERT O'DOHERTY: I just never could like him. I can't give the reasons because I never really had a reason, but he struck me as a very selfish type and inclined to be aggressive if he could get away with it.

DR LEVENTHAL: I have heard rumours of fisticuffs and things in Dublin taverns. Of course, like all poets in Dublin he quarrelled with his fellow poets, but that is to be expected.

O'CONNOR: He was always getting hit by somebody in a pub, and it was usually in an argument about what he used to call 'pouettry'. I remember once getting a letter from a friend of mine which contained the news that Christopher Marlow had been stabbed to death on Tuesday night in the Palace Bar. And, of course, Christopher Marlow was Higgins again. Whenever it came to poetry it was always liable to come to blows. There was another poet who wrote him a long letter of protest all about poetry, and Higgins used it as toilet paper and carefully sent it back. He had that sort of delicate touch in controversy.

Donagh MacDonagh recalls the famous row in the Palace Bar when Louis MacNeice, an admirer of Higgins's verse, was present.

DONAGH MACDONAGH: Well, Louis MacNeice had just had a book published by the Cuala Press called *The Last Ditch.* Tempers were frayed because various other people hadn't been published. Into the Palace Bar came various bespectacled characters, including Higgins, Austin Clarke, Paddy Fallon and Brinsley Macnamara. And one word, as I say, borrowed another. Higgins, who had had a few drinks, made a rush at Paddy Fallon saying, 'Fallon, I've been waiting a long time for this,' on which they all removed their glasses, and Fallon knocked Higgins down and Austin Clarke attempted to intervene with his umbrella saying, 'Children, children,' to the delight of the audience. But in the middle of it, also trying to make peace, was Alec Newman, then Assistant Editor of the *Irish Times*, with a camera hanging round his neck. When it was all over he went across the road to the *Irish Times* and told the startling news to Bertie Smyllie, the Editor. Smyllie, who had a marvellous news sense, instead of asking for details, looked at the camera round Alec's neck and said, 'Where are the pictures?' And he said, 'My God, I never thought of it.'

NEWMAN: I always think of Smyllie and Fred Higgins and Brinsley Macnamara as a sort of curious triumvirate. And what a triumvirate! Don't talk about the three Musketeers, these are the three Porthoses.

I think they averaged twenty stone, conjoined they were sixty stone, and to watch those three going out for a walk up the Boyne was something wonderful!

Sean O'Sullivan painted a portrait of Higgins.

O'SULLIVAN: I like to paint somebody looking at me because it gives more force to the portrait and I'm able to talk and paint at the same time. If you talk to a sitter they forget they're sitting, otherwise they look as if they're just sitting, instead of sitting and thinking. But after only a few minutes Fred Higgins said to me, 'Sean, I cannot sit here looking you in the eye. I'll have to look away.' That's why the portrait in the Abbey shows him almost in profile, not quite. He was very sensitive – you wouldn't think so to look at the big bulky fellow that he was.

'Beef-bellied, pea-eyed men of Meath,' as Higgins described himself and his clan.

O'SULLIVAN: I could tell by looking at an Irishman, nine times out of ten, if he were a Protestant or if he were Catholic, and curiously enough the only mistake I made was with Higgins. I had known him for some years – and accidentally I discovered he was not a Catholic. He had the beefy look of an honest-to-God Irish Catholic peasant – but he was a Protestant.

At the root of all writing there is conflict, a clash, a split of some kind. Higgins, like all Irish writers, was a deeply split person. Born in County Mayo, in the Catholic and Gaelic-speaking West, he was brought up in the English Pale. His father, a County Meath engineer, was a strict Unionist of the Protestant ascendancy tradition. But his father's son was not. Fred Higgins was a rebel with nationalist sympathies; a poet, passionately interested in Irish folk tradition.

O'CONNOR: I used to call him a Protestant with all the vices of a Catholic, if you know what *that* means.

MONK GIBBON: He liked to be thought a real native product. You see, your Irish Protestant is always in danger of feeling himself the white blackbird. He realises that native character is almost as much identified with Catholicism as his own religion is with the Ascendancy. Higgins knew what the real taste of Ireland was and he wanted to feel himself part of it; it's men smelling of tar and lobster pots and stable dung, and the fields, and the sand-dunes, and that was the kind of Ireland that Higgins felt, and that he's translated into his poetry with extraordinary success.

It was a poem by Padraic Colum, about a cattle drover, that changed Higgins's whole outlook. It came, he said, as 'a revelation', 'a joyful shock'. 'I saw that the raw thoughts and dull occupations of peasants were, as by magic, etherealised. Poetry produced that magic, and loveliness became possible in daily surroundings . . . Rocks became emotional, and poetry welled in my own nature.'

PADRAIC COLUM: I had been in the United States and knew only tantalising bits of the poets who had succeeded the insurrectionary poets of 1916. Austin Clarke and Fred Higgins were names that I just knew. I remember meeting Higgins in coffee-shops where we had discussions of verse technique and themes for poetry. His contemporary – a little younger contemporary, I think – was substituting the Gaelic vowel rhymes – assonances – for the conventional rhymes: this was Austin Clarke. It was an innovation that affected the verse of Fred Higgins. One of the poems of his that I very much admired got its delicacy of rhythm from his use of vowel sounds. It is an invocation of a sanctuary of one of the early saints:

> Fresh in wild holiness over
> Each glittering mile,
> And green with the blessings of Cellach,
> There lies an isle,
> Foundered on its own shadow
> Of brambles and grass –
> Its salvage of brambler still bending
> Where saints sang the Mass;
> Yet healing of sleep and the quiet
> Of wells still are there,
> With cold rushes telling their beads
> On stones of dumb prayer.

O'CONNOR: A little too lovely for me. It's all very well but when I see vowels being handled with all that caution, I just long for somebody who is going to blather it all out like Paddy Kavanagh or Emily Dickinson, somebody who'll just toss it off. He is watching every vowel as he states it. When I began writing, Fred and I were in different camps. His school I used to call the painters and decorators, they were always so anxious to be Irish when they were writing. They couldn't begin to write at all unless they got themselves up in their war-paint. And I always had the feeling, whenever I read their work, that they were coming along and saying, 'Me big terrible wild Irishman.'

GIBBON: You could say that his attitude was that of the wild Irish boy. Yet the self that we project is generally the anti-self, and actually in Higgins's case it had to contend with an air of almost nonconformist gravity. He was very staid to look at. He moved deliberately, he was stoutish. Of course, he was playing a dual role. And he was big enough not to be in the least ashamed of the fact that he was playing that dual role. I respected him for it. He was a poet and he was in the paint department at Brooks Thomas holding down a job and supporting a wife. Well, that was one side of his existence. But probably the very fact that he was doing that made him all the more anxious to escape to his anti-self, which as I say was the wild Irish boy. The last thing that you could ever have called him would have been a literateur.

Cecil Salkeld recalls meeting him in Dublin, at Brooks Thomas.

CECIL SALKELD: That was the first time I'd found out Fred's real job, which was editing about six papers. He worked only one day a month on Fridays and published six trades journals – the *Oil and Colour Paint Review, Our Feathered Chums, The Furniture Man's Gazetteer*, and other similar things.

AUSTIN CLARKE: Higgins was not only a poet, he was also really a pioneer of the Labour Movement. Soon after I knew him he founded a Clerical Workers Union and was instantly dismissed from his employment.

CATHAL O'SHANNON: And then Fred started a little paper, *The Irish Clerk* I think it was, and in that way I became associated with him.

CLARKE: He showed amazing practicality, ingenuity and cheerfulness. He was for instance the first to found a women's magazine in Ireland.

A Dublin lady gave Higgins a little money to start a small magazine. The fist number he called Welfare. *The second number – and the last – he called* Farewell. *Then, in 1932, tired of city life, he said farewell to Dublin.*

CLARKE: In his early thirties Higgins was a stout genial figure in the Dublin literary circles, but he still had this dream of living far off in the

West and I think he wanted to catch the last of the disappearing traditional life. And strangely enough he did achieve his dream. He'd no interest in money and his wife shared his courage. So they moved furniture, books, everything, to a cottage on the shores of Loch Conn, opposite Mount Nephin, the mountain mentioned in so many of the Gaelic love poems of the past.

MRS HIGGINS: We had a courtship of about a year and five months, and then we got married and he thought that we should move to the West for one year, but eventually that period stretched out to three. We went to live in a very beautiful spot on a promontory between two lakes, Loch Cullin and Loch Conn, seven miles from the town he was born in, Foxford, County Mayo.

CLARKE: Beyond were the wilds of Erris where Synge had set *The Playboy of the Western World*, and the districts where the last of the Gaelic poets, Raftery, had wandered.

Here Higgins was in his element among the dark men of the West, as he says in this poem which he called The Dark Breed.

> With those bawneen men I'm one,
> In the grey dusk-fall,
> Watching the Galway land
> Sink down in distress –
> With dark men, talking of grass,
> By a loose stone wall,
> In murmurs drifting and drifting
> To loneliness.

O'CONNOR: Well, that's the point I was making to you. Here the County Meath Protestant had to dress himself up as a wild Irish Celt before he could begin to write at all, and he had to write things about the bards of whom he knew nothing and about Irish prosody.

GIBBON: He liked to dramatise life. When he went down to Mayo he liked to think of the men that he saw at the country dances there as very devils of fellows.

Perhaps he wasn't so far wrong, as Austin Clarke found when he went to visit Higgins in Connaught.

CLARKE: At that time there was a new craze in the United States

known as petting parties, and it seemed to have reached the remote
parts of Connaught. I don't know how, perhaps through the post;
but nearby was the cottage and the party almost every night to which
we adjourned – dancing, melodeon playing, mouth organ, and long
after midnight when the turf fire was almost out, out went the paraffin
lamp, and hugs, kisses, pinches, smacks, cuddling, on and on and on,
and often at dawn we saw the first light glimmering on the sloe
blossoms, as we went home. But after about twenty-five of these
petting parties the joy and the continual strain of so much continence
was too much for me. As a town mouse, I said, 'Fred, if this is country
life, I'm going back to the city.' And so I fled back into the simple
Bohemian life of Chelsea.

*One notable man of the West whom Higgins delighted in above all others
was Padraic O'Conaire the poet. Higgins wrote a very fine poem on the
death and wake of 'Padraic O'Conaire, Gaelic Storyteller'.*

O'SULLIVAN: My favourite poem, and I think perhaps one of his best.

> They've paid the last respects in sad tobacco
> And silent is this wakehouse in its haze;
> They've paid the last respects; and now their whiskey
> Flings laughing words on mouths of prayer and praise;
> And so young couples huddle by the gables,
> O let them grope home through the hedgy night –
> Alone I'll mourn my old friend, while the cold dawn
> Thins out the holy candlelight.
>
> Respects are paid to one loved by the people;
> Ah, was he not – among our mighty poor –
> The sudden wealth cast on those pools of darkness,
> Those bearing, just, a star's faint signature;
> And so he was to me, close friend, near brother,
> Dear Padraic of the wide and sea-cold eyes –
> So lovable, so courteous and noble,
> The very West was in his soft replies.
>
> They'll miss his heavy stick and stride in Wicklow –
> His story-talking down Winetavern Street,
> Where old men sitting in the wizen daylight
> Have kept an edge upon his gentle wit;

While women on the grassy streets of Galway,
Who hearken for his passing – but in vain,
Shall hardly tell his step as shadows vanish
Through archways of forgotten Spain.

Ah, they'll say: Padraic's gone again exploring;
But now down glens of brightness, O he'll find
An ale-house overflowing with wise Gaelic
That's braced in vigour by the bardic mind,
And there his thoughts shall find their own forefathers –
In minds to whom our heights of race belong,
In crafty men, who ribbed a ship or turned
The secret joinery of song.

Alas, death mars the parchment of his forehead;
And yet for him, I know, the earth is mild –
The windy fidgets of September grasses
Can never tease a mind that loved the wild;
So drink his peace – this grey juice of the barley
Runs with a light that ever pleased his eye –
While old flames nod and gossip on the hearthstone
And only the young winds cry.

Yes, Higgins could *slow his step at a funeral,* could *discipline his poetic line. But more often his Pegasus took off in a glorious gallop and beating of wings, with neither bridle nor bit on it, while the poet would carefully lock the stable door in case the horse might come back again. Poetry in a hurry, breathless, exuberant, overloaded with rich phrasing, devil-may-care, very Irish.*

GIBBON: But it is all part of this gallant display of 'banner and pennant' as Yeats would have called it. I think that's partly why they got on so well together later on.

To the English ear, which likes understatement, it is all rather excessive and therefore not quite in good taste. But to the Irish mind which likes gesture, bravado, gallivanting, and rhetoric, it is an acceptable tradition. Padraic Colum recognises this side in Higgins.

COLUM: Out of this side of himself he developed the ballad with the refrain. He did a grand piece of extravagance combined with good humour in his 'Ballad of Captain O'Bruadir' ·

When Captain O'Bruadir shook a sword across the sea,
    Rolling glory on the water,
I had a mind O'Bruadir would make an earl of me,
    Rolling glory on the water;
So I shut my eyes on women, forgot their sturdy hips,
And yet I stuffed my 'kerchief by playing on their lips,
While skirting by the brambles, I quickly took to ships,
    Rolling glory on the water.

In Ireland, words fly to a tune as a woman flies to a mirror.

CLARKE: Curiously enough Higgins composed, even in his early poems, to the rhythm of Irish airs and of ballad tunes.

It might be a folk-tune, or a dance-tune, or a popular song like 'Hello, Patsy Fagin', or maybe a hymn tune. Alec Newman remembers being baffled once by the source tune of a Higgins poem.

NEWMAN: I remember meeting Fred and telling him we'd failed to fit a tune to his poem. Shortly afterwards I met him again and told him that at last it had occurred to me, the title of the tune was that once very popular hymn 'Safe In The Arms of Jesus'. I shall never forget Fred on that occasion. He went completely hysterical with delight, the great fellow.

MRS HIGGINS: His father used to bring him to church, and on Sunday evenings would hold a community hymn singing amongst the family. I remember being in on one before Fred and I married, and I learned then that that was usual on a Sunday evening. His father was also a great lover of Irish music.

Hence the early interest which Higgins had in tunes. The trouble about writing words to tunes is that the tune tends to take over and to run away with the words, as so many Irish poems show. But Higgins was very wise. When he had finished a poem and shaped it to a tune, he threw away the tune and kept the lyric. Successfully. And that, no doubt, was why W. B. Yeats, when he wanted to become a popular poet and to write songs for the people, called for Higgins's help.

COLUM: Yeats, who was always ready to make new departures in his writing, found a fresh inspiration in the very illiteracy of the ballads that Higgins was so ready to deliver. This was at a time when Yeats was getting weary of theatre management. He was declaring then,

> My curse on plays,
> That have to be set up in fifty ways,
> Theatre business, management of men.

And so he made Fred Higgins his lieutenant in the theatre.

'We used,' said Higgins, 'to work together, welding his words to Gaelic tunes.' Not that Yeats was much of a collaborator for, as Sean O'Sullivan says, he was completely tone-deaf.

O'SULLIVAN: He told me that if God Save the King were played he wouldn't recognise it.

Except, of course, when the audience stood up. Anyhow, the result of the welding was deplorable.

O'CONNOR: There was something extraordinarily funny about the picture of this man who was tone-deaf writing songs, and another man who was a public-house singer setting them to Irish airs of a sort, and then a third man writing them down in staff notations.

'The music of the poet has nothing at all in common with that of the musician,' said José-María de Hérédia, the French poet.

GIBBON: But, of course, the great advent in Higgins's life was his friendship in later years with Yeats. In my mind I have to draw a distinction between the earlier and the later Higgins. Basically, he remained, I'm sure, the same man, but in certain minor and chiefly external ways his friendship with Yeats produced a sort of revolution. I don't think the first advances were made by Higgins at all. They came from Yeats.

Mrs Higgins recalls a late afternoon in Dublin after her husband's return from the West of Ireland.

MRS HIGGINS: I was there on my own when this knock came to the door, and when I opened the door there was the notable W. B. Yeats. He asked, 'Is it here where F. R. Higgins lives?' and I said, 'Yes, I'm May Higgins, F. R.'s wife, would you please come in.' He came in and we made an appointment for Fred to call to see W.B. at his home in Riversdale some three-quarters of a mile perhaps distant from that little house of ours. From then on visits were many between W.B. and Fred.

GIBBON: Higgins leaped at the opportunity. Some of his friends thought, 'Huh, he's being bought,' but I think that's unfair to everybody concerned. By that time Higgins had been recognised as a fine and individual poet.

MRS HIGGINS: Fred had arrived before Yeats took any recognition of his work. Fred's work had drawn very good reviews from the English critics, and I honestly think that it was because Fred had arrived that W.B. did take notice. But then I do think that Fred must have benefited from the master.

GIBBON: Little by little Yeats's influence upon Higgins did show enormously in Higgins's personal mannerisms. It became laughable the way Fred put on what was almost a duplicate of the Yeats manner. But running concurrently with that was a definite opposition complex upon Higgins's part.

COLUM: But the elder poet and himself must have hit it off very well. They even began to resemble each other. They were both dark of face, and as Yeats was increasing in girth, Higgins's burliness did not contrast greatly with him.

LEVENTHAL: He used to have his hands clasped behind his back in much the same way as W.B. clasped his in walking.

COLUM: Then Yeats's authority gave a self-assurance to the younger poet. There was a distinct transference as between the two.

MACDONAGH: Yeats was a little obsessed with Higgins. Higgins to him really represented a kind of warty lad that he liked to write about in his old age. And he wanted to relive his life in terms of Higgins. Higgins wrote heavily sensuous or heavily sexual poetry, which was largely in his head, but to Yeats it was very compelling, so that he adopted Higgins to a great extent. He took him into the Abbey, he made him manager, he took him into the Cuala Press, he insisted on him writing a very unsuccessful play called *The Deuce of Jacks*, a kind of Dublin verse play, and he sent him off on the fatal Abbey tour which helped to kill Higgins.

LEVENTHAL: 'I suppose Higgins was something like Yeats's wild oats,' I once heard somebody say. He would come and amuse the master with the everyday doings in the world outside the castle, so to speak.

O'CONNOR: For the last years of Yeats's life Higgins was his greatest friend in Ireland. Sometime somebody will have to do a book about that friendship, it was an extraordinary one. Yeats was a very shy man, he was one of the shyest men I've ever met in my life. The only intimate friends he could possibly make were people like Gogarty and Higgins who were complete extroverts and didn't mind butting into his drawing-room and telling him indecent stories in the first couple of minutes. Once Yeats made a sad little confession to me. I had said to him that night, 'I know I've been frightfully unjust to Higgins's poetry, merely because he belonged to a different party.' Yeats looked at me and he said sadly, 'You don't realise, O'Connor, that at my age there's one thing a man can't do without, and that's another man who will talk about women to him. Higgins talks to me about women.'

'We poets,' said Yeats to Ethel Mannin, 'would die of loneliness but for women, and we choose our men friends that we may have somebody to talk about women with.'

O'CONNOR: That was all very well but what Yeats didn't realise was that every harmless little remark he made to Fred Higgins was repeated within twenty-four hours in a vastly improved and extended form in a Dublin pub. I'm as big a gossip as anybody, but I found some of Higgins's stories about Yeats very embarrassing. Once he embarrassed me so much that I got up in the middle of a story and walked to the other end of the room and just said, 'But Fred, I never leave that house without feeling like a million dollars.' And a very queer thing happened because the tears suddenly came into Higgins's eyes, he broke down and said, 'I feel exactly the same, Frank.' And he did, you know. That was the remarkable thing about him. He was far too sensitive a man not to be inspired by the Yeats household, just as I was. But he couldn't resist the opportunity of a good joke.

NEWMAN: I see no harm in the relationship with Yeats at all. In fact, I think it did a great deal for the modelling of Fred Higgins as a poet.

MACDONAGH: I think it was very bad for Higgins. It may have been good for Yeats. Yeats's poetry towards the end of his life, the last ten or so years of his life, took on a great richness and kind of folk quality which he deliberately, or unconsciously – I think probably deliberately – took from Higgins. And at the end of the period Yeats had acquired this racy ballad quality and Higgins had nothing left.

GIBBON: Each of them gave to the other's muse something that it stood in need of. I don't think Higgins's own poetry can be said to show a perceptible influence from Yeats at all. The influence passed into Fred's mannerisms and that was about all. There was an extraordinary, an amazing, love-hate relationship between these two men. I think what they shared in common was that they were not men of action either of them. When I first knew Higgins, I already had three years as a soldier behind me, and I was interested in peaceful things – the lyrical, the simple and everything like that: I'd seen plenty of violence without wishing to introduce it into my work. But in Yeats and Higgins, both of them not men of action, there was this extraordinary delight in the vigorous and the active.

MRS HIGGINS: The last meeting between Fred and Yeats was in Riversdale. I remember that night when Fred returned home, how elated he was over this wonderful poem that Yeats had just finished. He had memorised some of the lines, and he walked up and down the dining-room repeating these in a great voice, trying to imitate the dignified, haughty, proud Yeats, with his right hand up, as he recited the lines.

> Irish poets, learn your trade,
> Sing whatever is well made,
> Scorn the sort now growing up
> All out of shape from toe to top,
> Their unremembering hearts and heads,
> Base-born products of base beds.
> Sing the peasantry, and then
> Hard riding country gentlemen,
> The holiness of monks, and after
> Porter-drinkers' randy laughter;
> Sing the lords and ladies gay
> That were beaten into the clay
> Through seven heroic centuries;
> Cast your mind on other days
> That we in coming days may be
> Still the indomitable Irishry.

Higgins, like Yeats, scorned the poets of the thirties. 'In our Irish poetry,'
he told MacNeice, 'you will find an exaltation, a riotousness of imagination
and action, a fiery magnificence of speech that distinguishes it from the

pale, bloodless, defeatist verse written today in England. Verse that, in Yeats's words, cannot cry to "the great race that is to come".' As a young man, Higgins had walked the streets of Dublin, talking endlessly about modern poetry to Austin Clarke.

CLARKE: We were both 18. Fred had revolted into the Nationalist Literary Movement and shortly after we met, his father turned him out because he refused to join up and fight for King and Country, so he went off to live in lodgings. One of his finest poems, 'Father and Son', which was written long years afterwards, must have come slowly and eventually from that terrific conflict of emotion.

Long years afterwards, another young poet walked the same streets of Dublin with Higgins, talking poetry – Padraic Fallon.

PADRAIC FALLON: I have only just simple impressions – of the huge hat he always wore, and myopic eyes with a sort of shrewd glance in them, and he would generally be standing in a crowd and he'd jog at my pocket and say: 'Have you anything there for me to read?' which was just a preliminary to his showing me some of his own. And then we might wander out upon the streets or the quays, communing and philosophising. It was out of such a day that he produced that lovely poem of his, the elegy to his father. I was in this city and I just strolled around for a chatter with him, and he said he'd got something to show me, but he hadn't altogether done it. So he started to alter it, and was charmed because he thought he had discovered a new kind of easy poetry movement.

Father and Son

Only last week, walking the hushed fields
Of our most lovely Meath, now thinned by November,
I came to where the road from Laracor leads
To the Boyne river – that seemed more lake than river,
Stretched in uneasy light and stripped of reeds.

And walking longside an old weir
Of my people's, where nothing stirs – only the shadowed
Leaden flight of a heron up the lean air –
I went unmanly with grief, knowing how my father,
Happy though captive in years, walked last with me there.

Yes, happy in Meath with me for a day
He walked, taking stock of herds hid in their own breathing;

And naming colts, gusty as wind, once steered by his hand,
Lightnings winked in the eyes that were half shy in greeting
Old friends – the wild blades, when he gallivanted the land.

For that proud, wayward man now my heart breaks –
Breaks for that man whose mind was a secret eyrie,
Whose kind hand was sole signet of his race,
Who curbed me, scorned my green ways, yet increasingly loved me
Till Death drew its grey blind down his face.

And yet I am pleased that even my reckless ways
Are living shades of his rich calms and passions –
Witnesses for him and for those faint namesakes
With whom now he is one, under yew branches,
Yes, one in a graven silence no bird breaks.

GIBBON: Actually his phrases are quite wonderful and have remained – you can begin to form some kind of a final verdict on a poet after thirty years. I come back to Higgins now and I'm simply enormously impressed by his achievement.

In a letter to Higgins about his second book of poems – The Dark Breed – *J. B. Priestley wrote in 1927, 'I cannot help feeling you are entitled to more consideration and praise than you are receiving either in London or in Dublin.' Why didn't he receive it? Donagh MacDonagh.*

MACDONAGH: Well, that's difficult to say because he was very unlucky. His best book, *The Gap of Brightness*, was published just at the beginning of the war at a period when people weren't reading very much and certainly weren't buying books. In consequence it didn't get the reception it should have, and it's been neglected since. I think very few people know even of its existence today.

Desmond McCarthy reviewed Higgins's last book, The Gap of Brightness, *in 1940. 'This slender volume,' he said, 'has impressed me more than any recent verse that I have come across. His pencraft – I must repeat this – is a joy to those who love words that fit the thing.' The news of this fine review and late recognition was splashed all over Dublin on the posters of* The Irish Times *by Smyllie, the Editor. What other city would celebrate a dying poet like that! For Higgins was gravely ill. His wife placed a copy of the poster at the foot of his bed where he might see it when he wakened. He saw it, and at once rose up, put on his clothes, and went into Dublin for a last reunion with his friends. His bent body – in a phrase from one of his own poems – his*

> *'bent body seemed as an old crane's*
> *Lost in a great overcoat of wings.'*

His thoughts now ran home to the County Meath of his forefathers. 'Mac,' he said to Brinsley Macnamara, 'when you go down to Laracor again, put your arms round the land for me.' A few days later he died. Sean O'Sullivan went to his funeral service in the Protestant Church.

O'SULLIVAN: I was sitting next to Smyllie of the *Irish Times*. Smyllie was in tears, he was crying unashamedly. They played a very unsuitable hymn, anthem, whatever you call it, something from Tennyson, for Fred Higgins's demise. 'There'll be no moaning at the bar when we put out to sea.' I can tell you in every bar in Dublin frequented by Higgins there was moaning, he was so well liked, so well loved.

Higgins was buried in the graveyard at Laracor, beside the church of which Jonathan Swift was once Vicar. A Dublin poet who was present, Donagh MacDonagh, spoke for everyone when he wrote these lines:

> 'as the coffin sank beneath the green
> Level of our world I mourned the child
> Lost in the leaden body.'

AE (GEORGE RUSSELL)

Poet, painter, playwright, philosopher, mystic and visionary; politician, rural economist, editor, memorable talker – AE was the Socrates of Dublin, the one writer in that irreverent city who was always spoken of with respect and affection.

MONK GIBBON: Yeats and AE, they provided the most marvellous antithesis. Even in appearance they did that; Yeats a clean-shaven, Roman pro-consular senator, Pontius Pilate perhaps, AE a bearded Greek. The Greeks got tired of hearing Aristides called 'the just', but I don't think the Irish ever minded AE being called 'good'. To them he was just a big, lumbering man who preached co-operation and believed in fairies. You can't condemn a man for riding round Ireland on a bicycle and starting creameries, and if he likes to believe in fairies, well that's his business. If AE had claimed to be a good poet or a good painter, that would have been a different matter, they'd have very quickly put him in his place, but he didn't, and so they were content to let him just go on being a good man.

What was he like?

LADY GLENAVY: Well, there was the beard and the hair and the glasses and the brown, large clothes we all know. He was very large, he had a sort of wild look but it wasn't wild with fury, he was wild with warmth and vitality and terrible interest in everything. You met him in the street, he was in the middle of something he was going to say to you before you almost recognised he was there and it was enormously exciting and a great pleasure to meet him. With Yeats one had no – at least I had no – point of contact whatever. I couldn't say anything to Yeats, he'd say things to me.

GIBBON: You must never forget that both men, when they were very young, had expected some kind of a spiritual revelation. In a sense AE was an initiate, his personality was an achieved personality and Yeats, who was an incomparably greater artist, in some obscure way felt that and resented it. Mrs Yeats put her finger right on the spot – 'AE is the nearest you and I will ever know to a saint, you are a better poet, but you aren't a saint,' she said to her husband.

LADY GLENAVY: The quality of sainthood. You couldn't imagine him being mean, vicious, malicious, any of the things that everybody is in Dublin. There was none of that in him, a sort of radiance came out of him.

JAMES O'REILLY: I think he had no enemies. If you knew AE it would be very hard to fall out with him, or have anything more than a momentary hard word, which would go in a moment. You could disagree perhaps violently with him but you never left him without being friendly with him, or he would never leave you, I think, except on terms of friendship.

LADY GLENAVY: He was a great friend of everybody. I remember going to his house once with James Stephens. We drove up to the door and waited outside and James was a tiny little figure on the top of the steps. Then the door opened and suddenly there was the figure of AE with his arms out, and in a second James Stephens seemed to disappear into the beard, into the brown suit, into the other man, just enveloped in affection and warmth and conversation right away.

FRANK O'CONNOR: He was that sort of man. Within half an hour he'd enveloped you in the sort of universal curiosity and affection in which you forgot all your shyness; it was like an old fur coat, a little bit smelly, and definitely designed for somebody of much nobler stature than yourself, but though it might threaten to suffocate you it never left you feeling cold. Russell would cheerfully get you a new doctor, a new wife, a new flat or a new job, and, if you were ill, he'd come along and cook for you and nurse you. I knew this because one evening when he came to my flat, and found I'd been ill for the preceding week, the tears came into his eyes and he said, 'You should have sent for me, you know. I could have cooked for you, I'm quite a good cook – I can cook chops, you know.'

GIBBON: AE pushing open the door on a Sunday evening to admit you to Rathgar Avenue looked something between a Russian moujik and Jupiter on Olympus, except that one hardly expected to find Jupiter puffing at a pipe. It was a delight to find oneself in the company of a mind as clear, lucid, tolerant and beauty-loving as the Greek mind. Remember, the Greeks were mystics as well as humanists. A Greek could well have said what AE said in one of his casual weekly articles, 'The highest virtue is wisdom, and wisdom is the right relation of our own being to that in which we live and move and have our being.' I would say that AE is the nearest thing Ireland has ever had to a prophet, I don't mean a political prophet, they've always been six a penny, I mean a prophet of what a man could and ought to be. Now George Moore, who was a fairly critical individual, said that AE's one fault was that he had no faults. Remarks like that embarrassed AE. He begged Moore to include his faults, but the only fault that Moore could discover was that AE couldn't distinguish between turbot and halibut.

Dublin in those days had its literary at-homes. There was W. B. Yeats's on Monday night, very select, George Moore's on Saturday night, select, and, most popular, AE's on Sunday night.

AUSTIN CLARKE: AE was extremely courteous and patient. The hall door at number 70 Rathgar Avenue was left ajar on every Sunday night, but when he heard the sound of the heavy hinges as someone pushed it open AE immediately left his room, crowded with guests though it was, and hurried out into the hall to greet the newcomer, friend or stranger from overseas; his burly figure bent, he beamed short-sightedly through his spectacles. Poets and writers gathered every Sunday evening at number seventy and visitors, well-known or otherwise, found their way into the house from eight o'clock onwards. The talk was incessant and only stopped at about ten o'clock when tea was served by Mrs Russell.

LADY GLENAVY: Mrs Russell was splendid. There again, there was a story that George Russell got married and he hadn't time for a honeymoon, so he sent Mrs Russell to Maryborough alone and she had her honeymoon there and then she came back and took over the housework.

CLARKE: Sometimes the poet's two sons came in and brought around the cups of tea, while AE drifted rather helplessly around with a plate of homemade scones. After tea, by prearrangement, Mrs Russell would raise her voice and say, 'George, you were telling me yesterday about Mr Asquith's speech in the House of Commons.' Or 'George, you mentioned that particular question about Partition to me during the week.' A remark of this kind was the signal for a general hush, and AE started a discourse for a full hour without interruption except when friend or visitor ventured to ask him a question. Sometimes American women visitors were present, and inevitably they asked him about fairies. He spoke to them at length about the ancient and invisible race of Ireland, while we, who knew it all by heart, talked quietly in corners. In these frequent disquisitions AE showed the same patience as Yeats. AE had a wonderful memory, and many poems and passages by younger poets were stored in it. To the young, his praise and enthusiasm were a constant incitement. Frequently he would quote a poem of ours to one or more visitors, much to our delight and embarrassment. 'I am an extinct volcano,' he would say, and by implication we felt we were full of imaginative fire and rumblings within.

GIBBON: His kindness to young poets irritated Yeats who, by the way, could be kind to young poets himself. You see, AE felt that poets really mattered. They were, he said, the soul of the nation; the first letter I ever had from him – and I was a complete stranger to him then – was a long one encouraging me to take the craft of poetry seriously. I never heard AE make any public utterance, he was brilliant as a private conversationalist.

DR MICHAEL TIERNEY: He didn't monopolise the conversation. He was a charming conversationalist and could keep on for hours. He had a beautiful voice, and you could listen to him for a very long time.

O'CONNOR: He was a creature of habit and his conversation, like his life, ran in patterns, well-formed phrases, ideas, quotations, and anecdotes, that he repeated year after year without altering an inflection. He wasn't skilful in the way he introduced them into the conversation, and they were usually so general that they had a tendency to obliterate conversation. 'Leonardo advised young painters to study the stains in old marble in order to discover compositions for their own paintings.' That was a standard phrase, and it was very difficult to relate it to any subject you happened to be discussing. And after a time you began to see the subject coming at you from a mile off, and found yourself hitting out at it as if it were a wasp. That repetition got him the name of being an old bungler among my friends, and I understood the criticism, even though I disagreed with it. In fact, Russell was a man of intense intellectual vitality – ideas came to him almost too rapidly, and his experience, whenever he chose to draw on it, was profound and varied, particularly when he remembered it casually as a result of something somebody had just said, and it came to him with the freshness of a theme he had just discovered.

ARTHUR POWER: Marvellous talker. I think he was the best talker I ever heard in my life; a continual flow. In contrast to Yeats, who was a staccato talker, he had a continual build-up of imagery and he would talk the whole evening on his ideas.

CECIL SALKELD: When I was visiting him he usually had an exhibition on Sundays, that is the Sunday evenings, when all the people were there. There would be three or four three-legged easels stuck up in the corner where the tea-things were, and on these would be medium-sized canvasses, say about 20 by 24, of cherubim and seraphim, enormous wings surrounded by rainbow-coloured, very violently coloured, aura, and perhaps a volcanic peak or two in the background, and sometimes a red sky or a black sky with very large, five-pointed stars. And the interesting thing was that, though I regarded these pictures as very remarkable, they reminded me very much of Blake's drawings, except that they weren't as well drawn. The conversation moved about them as if they had been pictures of actual facts. AE would simply say, 'This cherub visited me at about half past three this morning.' And then would ensue a discussion as to whether cherubim had exactly those kind of wings, whether they were long enough, big enough, or bright enough, and the general question of auras would be discussed as if this was something that everybody saw. I frequently wondered whether it could possibly be the same rainbow that I frequently saw around street lanterns in the Dublin fog. But I was genuinely puzzled at the sincere and practical way in which these pictures were discussed. As works of art they had no meaning for me at all and I don't suppose many of them have survived.

And yet at one time every member of Mr Asquith's Cabinet owned specimens of AE's work. 'I believe him,' said the late Dr Bodkin, 'to have had a streak of genius as a painter.' Lady Glenavy recalls an exhibition in Leinster Hall.

LADY GLENAVY: Mr Russell had forty-nine pictures in the show; he painted a picture very quickly. The story in Dublin was that he hurried home from his office, having worked very hard on his paper all the morning, and in the afternoon he sat down to have his tea and he painted a picture with a teaspoon while he was having his tea, and then dashed off again to something else. He sold his pictures very cheaply for four or five pounds but they sold, everybody loved them, and he never really settled down to learning anything about drawing or painting, he hadn't time, he had to be painting the thing that was in his head.

Cecil Salkeld recalls a visit of AE to his first exhibition of paintings.

SALKELD: I was just under seventeen when I gave my first exhibition at No. 7 Stephen's Green, which had been in the past old John B. Yeats's studio. This was my first in my native city. There were a very large number of pictures and, of course, I watched out for various reviewers. I didn't know most of the newspaper reviewers, and very few of them gave me more than a line or two, but I did know AE, and when he came in I watched him with interest. He paid for his catalogue, went round the room very carefully and solemnly, and when he reached the end he went round the second time. I was surprised at his silence, because AE was not a silent man. When he reached the door I went over to him to thank him for coming and I expected him to make some comment, instead of which he put on his hat, folded his arms, took a deep sigh and said, 'Young man, I used to be a painter once,' and with that he departed down the flight of stairs, and his co-operative boots clumped down the stone passage to Stephen's Green. Almost immediately, I heard the door open and another series of steps come up, and to my great surprise it was Willie Yeats. He turned to me immediately and said, 'Was that George I saw going out?' I said, 'Yes.' 'Ah,' he said, 'he's probably going to cut you up in the *Irish Statesman.*' So I told him what George had said, and Yeats marched round the exhibition and bought two pictures, which I presume was intended as a potential gesture of disapproval of George.

Once, at AE's house in Rathgar Avenue, it was argued that the object of a work of art must itself be beautiful, if the work was to be beautiful. Salkeld objected and put the case for a picture of a pair of old boots. AE was scornful.

SALKELD: I told this to Yeats later on and he said, 'Did he say that? Well, you know, George is a dear, kind, just and generous man, but he's a cowardly old spinster.'

Why this antagonism between two life-long friends, Yeats and AE, old schoolfellows?

CLARKE: Yeats, who never visited 70 Rathgar Avenue, raged against the rascals who spoke there against him, but I never heard him being spoken about without respect. Often AE told me of their early years together; how Yeats in his adolescent years had described to him his dream play *The Shadowy Waters*, and quoted passages of it for him. He told me, too, how Yeats had gone out with Sligo fishermen to hear at dawn the different cries of seabirds. But each year the play seemed to lose something of that early imaginative glow and magic. About his own youth AE never spoke. He seemed to find in the youth of his friend a constant imaginative inspiration which fascinated him even in his middle years. In only one way did AE criticise Yeats: he held that he was not truly a mystic, but only interested in the subject.

POWER: Yeats was a man of the passions, he believed in them, while AE remained the mystic who walked the roads of Armagh. That was the great difference between them, and I believe that at the end there was a certain coolness between them, because of a difference of philosophy.

GIBBON: I remember Lennox Robinson telling how he used to see Yeats and AE hobnobbing like two old cronies over the fire until a stranger arrived. Immediately, Lennox said, Yeats's attitude to his old friend would become subtly inimical. I am inclined to say that Yeats was unconscious of his resentment. If I visited Yeats in Merrion Square on his Monday evenings and AE was there, Yeats was delighted to see his old friend and it was terribly interesting to listen to them both talking because, to give them their due, they were both great talkers, but they both gave the other man an occasional innings.

'I am a good Christian,' said AE. *'I pray not only for my enemies but to have enemies to keep me alive. It is our friends we should guard against.' And in a letter to his publishers he asks them to put this dedication in his next book, 'To W. B. Yeats, my oldest friend and enemy'.*

GIBBON: Oh, that's rather amusing, because I've heard AE talk a tremendous lot about Willie, he was always talking about Willie and he could criticise Willie's later prose very frankly but I've never heard the faintest suggestion of hostility on AE's part. Willie was such a great poet that he had always been a hero to AE and he remained a hero to the very end. I think that deep down the friendship had created both men. Their whole work grew out of the days when Yeats used to ride in on Katherine Tynan's father's dairy-cart to Dublin, and when Russell was an art student. Lily Yeats has described to me how those two boys used to sit down, after the rest of the Yeats family had gone to bed, in the practically underground Victorian kitchen, discussing the mystic forces that made the mushrooms grow.

'He bores me terribly now and he was once so interesting,' wrote AE of Yeats, thirty years later. 'Why can't he be natural? Such a delightful creature he was when young! And at rare moments when he forgets himself he is still as interesting as ever – almost!'

O'CONNOR: Yeats and AE had a very peculiar relationship, which, toward the end of their lives, was largely hostile on the part of Yeats, and hurt on the part of Russell. Though as I got to know both of them better I noticed more and more in Russell that oscillation between love and hatred for Yeats. I remember his saying to me once, 'Yeats, when he was a young man, wore a beard and he never looked so beautiful as he looked with that beard. He used to come into my room in the early hours of the morning to say a new poem to me; oh, he looked so wonderful in that beard.'

Thirty years on, and O'Connor recalls one occasion when Yeats said something wounding to AE in company.

O'CONNOR: I saw that Russell was deeply hurt and I stayed on with him, when the rest had gone. He was very close to tears. 'Yeats has always been like that,' he said bitterly, 'always unscrupulous and always dishonest.' Naturally I believed him, and I went up to Yeats's house and, like the raw provincial youth I was, I told him that he'd been infernally rude. He took this reproof very meekly and said, 'I must smooth him down.' He'd just been reading a novel by Austin Clarke, one of the young writers whom Russell admired and he'd been reading it with genuine admiration, so he wrote to Russell to congratulate him on having been the first to recognise Clarke's genius. 'As usual you were right and I was wrong,' he wrote. Russell was always pathetically grateful for any little tribute from Yeats, so he rushed straight round to my house to read me the letter. 'I think that's very noble of him, don't you?' he said.

GIBBON: You realise, of course, that AE and Yeats had quarrelled at one time. There's a nine years' gap in their correspondence. Why?

CLARKE: AE was, in the strict sense of the word, a moralist, and to this was due his gradual alienation from W. B. Yeats. George Moore and Yeats were collaborating in a play, *Where There Is Nothing,* the original idea being that of Moore. But they quarrelled over it, and came to AE and asked him to decide the right or wrong of the matter. He agreed to do so, but Yeats, without telling him, completed in haste his own version of the play and published it in Arthur Griffith's paper, *Sinn Fein,* in order to establish the copyright. AE was so shocked by that breach of faith and by the cunning shown by the Sligo man that their friendship was never quite the same again.

'I feel towards Yeats exactly as if he had stolen my spoons,' said George Moore. All this, however, helped to heighten the drama of Dublin life and gave distinction to Dublin letters. 'A literary movement,' said AE, 'consists of five or six people who live in the same town and hate each other cordially.' Yeats and AE remained devoted and necessary foes. Ernest Blythe –

ERNEST BLYTHE: Yeats, like all great poets, had a great deal of practical common sense. He was a more aloof man than Russell; he was incomparably a greater poet, a greater artist. On the other hand, he had not the interest in the immediate economic issue that Russell had. He was a prime patriot but his interest was in a different aspect of Irish affairs. I didn't find it as easy to talk to Yeats as to Russell.

TIERNEY: AE, I'd say, was a much more approachable man than Yeats; Yeats was far more self-centred than AE and although in some ways they were alike, fundamentally they were totally different, because AE was a dedicated believer in a way that Yeats never was. You couldn't exactly call AE a theosophist, although he was influenced greatly by Madame Blavatsky, but the basis of his very passionately held religion was a kind of theosophy and he identified that with patriotism in the most interesting way.

SALKELD: Behind all this mystic business AE was, to me, an extremely practical, hard-headed businessman who had served twenty or twenty-five years behind the counter in Pym's, where I think he'd become Manager before working as a backroom boy for Sir Horace Plunkett in the Co-operative movement.

AE had started his career in Guinness' Brewery. 'I gave it up,' he said, 'as my ethical sense was outraged.' Then for six years he was a clerk in Pym's

warehouse at thirty to sixty pounds a year. 'The happiest days of my life,'
he said, 'when we sat up to all hours talking about everything on heaven
and earth.' It was Yeats who introduced AE to Sir Horace Plunkett, the
apostle of agricultural co-operation, and there and then AE found his
lifework. From Plunkett House AE organised banks whose loans proved the
salvation of thousands of small farmers, founded co-operative creameries,
edited the Irish Homestead *and later the* Irish Statesman, *and talked*
pigs, poultry, poetry and metaphysics to the youth of Ireland. Ernest
Blythe recalls the impact of it all.

BLYTHE: When I was a young man and a member of 'Sinn Fein' and
of the IRB into which, by the way, I was introduced by Sean O'Casey,
we thought a great deal of AE. He was perhaps the only man outside
the movement whom we really esteemed. We thought of him as a
patriot, different from us and something of an economic prophet.
We, of course, looked at his pictures when they were on exhibition,
and we read his poetry, but we thought of him as a man who was trying
to reform the national economy.

CATHAL O'SHANNON: It meant a great deal to a number of us young
fellows who were interested in the minority movements and were
wanting things to do, but I would say, speaking for myself, that AE's
influence, his real influence, was outside the Co-operative movement.
It was an intellectual and spiritual influence, on thinking people, not
only young people but people of various ages and of various classes.

> No blazoned banner we unfold –
> One charge alone we give to youth,
> Against the sceptred myth to hold
> The golden heresy of truth.

That was AE. 'I exist in Ireland,' he said, 'because it's my duty to leave
as many heresies in its literature as possible. The seeds I scatter will
come up in the next generation.'

POWER: He was a spiritual liberator and it is true to say also he was a
political liberator.

O'SHANNON: He was stirred very much by the great 'labour wars', we
called it the great lock-out of 1913, and he had a number of the
intellectuals of the time, W. B. Yeats, Seamus O'Sullivan, Padraic
Colum, P. H. Pearse, James Stephens, and others, lined up with

people in Liberty Hall who were fighting against the 404 employers. *Dr Tierney recalls the meetings with AE in Plunkett House.*

TIERNEY: I used to turn up every Friday afternoon to the gathering in his big office that he had painted himself at the top of the IAOS building in Merrion Square. We used to have tea there and all sorts of interesting people used to turn up. Yeats was often there, and James Stephens, and people like Stephen Gwynn, and I remember J. B. Priestley, Kingsley Martin, and quite a number of other people. What I discussed mostly with him at these gatherings was politics and things that were on the fringe of politics, and perhaps economic questions.

'Look what you've drawn me into,' said AE to Yeats. 'It seems odd,' he added, 'that a person like myself, originally shy, should get caught up with labour or economic movements.'

O'SHANNON: There was no question about that when he put pen to paper, particularly if he was fighting, as he nearly always was, for independence of thought and for the right of people to express themselves and to stand by what they had feelings for. That I think was one of the things that drew him to James Connolly. He described Connolly, in a letter to one of his friends, I believe, as the strong man and the intellect of the Rising of 1916.

It was AE who designed the banner for Connolly's Citizen Army – 'The Plough and the Stars'. Who else would have thought of it?

O'SHANNON: It was as symbolic of AE as it was of the Citizen Army. It was on a green background with the seven stars of the constellation on it. It was an actual plough of the old wooden type. The plough itself was in yellow with three stars of the constellation in the handles, and the four stars in the other part of the plough. The men of the Citizen Army called it 'The Starry Plough'. It wasn't easy to carry, especially if there was a high wind.

It was this banner that the Citizen Army carried in the Easter Week Rebellion, this device that later gave the name to Sean O'Casey's famous revolutionary play, The Plough and the Stars. *The gentle AE had put his hand to more than he knew.*

POWER: Naturally, as a spiritual man he didn't believe in physical force, and I think that the 1916 Rebellion, though he admired it, came in a sense as a shock to him.

The greatest shock was the execution of the leaders of the Rising. AE wrote a poem to them.

O'SHANNON: It was entitled *Salutation*, and started off with a first verse addressed to Pearse, and another to Thomas MacDonagh. The one to Connolly naturally struck me particularly because of my close association with him.

> The hope lives on age after age
> Earth in its beauty might be won
> For labour as a heritage.
> For this Ireland has lost a son.
> This hope into a flame to fan
> Men have put life by with a smile.
> Here's to you, Connolly, my man,
> Who cast the last torch on the pile.

I got to know AE much better in 1918 when I came to live in Dublin. Then I found that he was tremendously impressed by the 1917 Revolution in Russia.

But not over-impressed, as a letter to James O'Reilly indicates –

Dear James,
I don't know why you want to go to Russia when you can get all the character attributed to that country in your own with more variety. Remember Blake, 'To see the world in a grain of sand'? Ireland is a grain of sand in which any intelligent person can see the whole Universe.

Was politics a fundamental interest with AE?

TIERNEY: What was fundamental to AE was his own special brand of mysticism. He was a genuine mystic and believed in his visions. He had a very fully thought-out and well-articulated theory about the world and about Ireland's place in the world. He thought that Ireland was really alive, a living goddess of which we were all parts.

As for the rewards of political life when it came to the point of decision, it was Yeats who accepted a Senatorship. AE refused.

MERVYN WALL: When the first Free State Senate was being set up, the President of the Executive Council and the Government, that is Mr Cosgrave, sent a higher civil servant up to Rathgar to ask AE whether he would consent to accept membership of the Senate. This man arrived late at night (apparently the matter had to be hurried because lists had to be got out the following day) and AE came to the window after some time and just shouted out, 'What do you want?' This higher civil servant put the proposition to him, and he said, 'I'll have to consult the gods,' and banged down the window. Now this civil servant had to wait for about half an hour in the street and then finally AE pulled up the window and shouted out 'No.'

'My dear boy,' wrote AE. 'A man's success or failure is with his own soul . . . I don't care in the least for recognition.' 'The two great needs of life are good talk and plenty of solitude.'

O'REILLY: He did a great part of the talking in his own house. I think he only listened when he was tired, because after all Dublin is not a city of listeners; the only listeners in Dublin are tired talkers.

'I am nothing but an artist,' wrote Yeats to AE, 'and my life is in written words. You are the other side of the penny, for you are admirably careful in speech, having set life before art, too much before it, as I think, for one who is, in spite of himself perhaps, an artist.' All the same, it was Yeats who insisted that no visit to Ireland was complete without an interview with AE just to hear him talk.

O'REILLY: Rather curiously I had got to know W. B. Yeats well when I was an undergraduate at Oxford and he had returned to Dublin in the spring of 1922. I went to Dublin just after I had gone down from Oxford. I had by chance met Lady Ottoline Morrell at Garsington and she sent me a message to Mr Yeats. I delivered that message, and he said to me, 'Do you know AE?' I replied, 'No, I have never met him.' He said, 'Nobody comes to Dublin without meeting AE,' and gave me a card of introduction to him. That's how I met him. At that time Mr Yeats was living at number 82, I think, Merrion Square, and Plunkett House was second door to his house.

There is a well-known Dublin cartoon of Yeats and AE passing each other in Merrion Square on their way to visit each other – AE with his eyes on the ground, Yeats looking up to the heavens; the plough and the stars. Was Yeats right? Was AE's ploughboy journalism at Plunkett House a waste of life and of letters? 'He is doing a hundred times more useful work where he is than he would be by writing poetry,' said Sir Horace Plunkett. 'But one man in every thousand,' said Lord Dunsany, 'could have done the economics for that agricultural paper quite as well as

AE did; while if among the four million in Ireland there is one who could do AE's other work, I shall be very glad to hear of him, but doubtful of the news.' The one thing AE really cared about was his poetry.

GIBBON: Do I think he was a good poet? I don't know. I think he wrote a particular kind of poetry rather well. To judge his poetry he should really be here to chant it himself. Not that he did chant it very much, he chanted Yeats, he chanted one or two favourite quotations from Whitman. I wish I could give you AE chanting his favourite bit of Whitman – with a slight Armagh brogue and his hand moving up and down rhythmically:

> Come, lovely and soothing death,
> Undulate round the world serenely arriving, arriving,
> In the day, in the night, to all, to each,
> Sooner or later, delicate death.

PADRAIC COLUM: AE, whose memory was prodigious, knew all his poems by heart – most of Yeats's too. He chanted his poems, swinging from vowel to vowel. Yeats did not quite approve of this method. Once when AE was repeating a poem he said to me, 'I wish to heavens someone would give him a harp.' There was a chant in Yeats's mode of recital, but it was not as marked as in the incantation of AE. I can hear him, with his hand lifted, as he recites some of the later poems. They were closer to declamation than incantation:

> 'Put off that mask of burning gold
> With emerald eyes.'
> 'O no, my dear, you make so bold
> To find if hearts be wild and wise,
> And yet not cold.'

AE had a fund of enthusiasm that buoyed up a young poet, while Yeats was quick to have one check on any vagueness of expression. A young poet was apt to graduate from AE to Yeats. A poet was launched by AE, but given direction by Yeats.

'The greatest pleasure I find in life,' said AE, 'is discovering new poets.'

COLUM: Well, there was James Stephens, myself, Seamus O'Sullivan and, later, Fred Higgins and Austin Clarke.

TIERNEY: One of the most striking characteristics to me about AE was the very kindly way in which he sought after and did his very best to help young writers. He was a real patron and inspirer and encourager of young writers in a way that Yeats hardly was at all. Yeats threw everything on the great compost heap on which he grew poetry; nothing really mattered to him except his own poetry, and I don't think Yeats was nearly as friendly to younger poets, for example, as AE was.

'AE listened to you patiently,' said Monk Gibbon, 'Yeats swept you aside.' The fledgling poets of Dublin did indeed take shelter under the warm wing of AE from the cold, Olympian, hawklike Yeats. 'AE's canaries,' Yeats called them mockingly.

GIBBON: Yeats was quite definitely jealous of the affection which AE inspired in the younger men. I think it would be absolutely wrong to suggest that Yeats was anything but a friend of AE, but I do think that there was this unconscious or subconscious jealousy that made him take it out on AE a little bit.

'The antagonism which is between you and me,' wrote Yeats to AE, 'comes from the fact that though you are strong and capable yourself, you gather the weak and not very capable about you, and that I feel they are a danger to all good work. It is, I think, because you desire love.'

GIBBON: Quite definitely Yeats seemed to hate. If he could wean one of the younger poets away from AE he would – now I don't say he weaned Fred Higgins away because Higgins remained a great admirer of AE – but there was something in Yeats that wanted to steal AE's disciples. That's absolutely definite, and I think that Padraic Colum is the first instance of the thing.

'Colum,' wrote Yeats in his diary, 'is one victim of AE's misunderstanding of life that I rage over.'

COLUM: He shows disappointment in the fact that he raged over me. You see, I had left the theatre he was so impelled to use. That left me out of Yeats's circle and Yeats's influence – I had deviated. AE had urged me to stay with the theatre, that has now become the Abbey Theatre.

James Joyce submitted his earliest poems for AE's scrutiny. 'Young man,' said AE, 'there is not enough chaos in you to be a poet.' But in a letter to Yeats he wrote, 'I want you very much to meet a young fellow called

Joyce . . . who belongs to your Clan more than mine, and more still to himself . . . and I think writes amazingly well in prose.'

SALKELD: AE was undoubtedly the kingmaker as far as poets went. For example it was to AE and not to Yeats that F. R. Higgins went. My mother introduced him there and at the end of the evening AE in his paternal manner said, 'Have you brought anything with you?' F. R. Higgins produced the little sheaf of poems and stood up and read them out. As a result of this some of them appeared in the *Irish Statesman*. They were probably the first poems of his that were published.

CLARKE: AE edited the *Irish Statesman*, the liberal weekly subsidised by Irish well-wishers in the USA. But in the New Irish Free State it caused irritation and offence, for its columns were open to every shade of modern opinion. Poets, novelists, critics, contributed to the *Irish Statesman*, which was the only intellectual periodical in the country, the first indeed of its kind. The circulation was limited and eventually, owing to an expensive libel action over a rather indiscreetly worded article, the paper had to close down. A howl of primitive delight greeted its disappearance. Young writers, whom AE had discovered and helped and even found publishers for, quickly transferred their allegiance to W. B. Yeats who held a literary gathering once a week in his house in Merrion Square, a few doors away from Plunkett House where AE had edited the *Irish Statesman*.

O'REILLY: It was a terrible loss to Ireland, the loss of that paper. There has been nothing like it since and in the seven years that the *Irish Statesman* existed it produced very remarkable work and certainly would stand up to criticism. There has not been any Irish paper of that type comparable to the *Statesman* since it died in 1930. It produced many poems of Mr Yeats, a number of AE's and James Stephens's poems, and so forth – Bernard Shaw wrote for it, and there was a whole galaxy of talent at the time writing for it.

It was AE who first published the poet, Patrick Kavanagh.

PATRICK KAVANAGH: He was the first man who published and paid for a poem of mine, and I was astonished when I got a guinea from him, from the *Irish Statesman*. I didn't meet him actually when he was editing the *Irish Statesman*, I met him after it closed. I met him as a country gobdough, rather pretending, and I didn't meet him honestly, sincerely, though I recognised him as a great and holy man.

It was the first time I ever came to Dublin. I went up to see him as a country boy, which probably I was, without knowing it. He received me marvellously, with great kindness, considering that he wasn't altogether very well at the time. He was very good to me, quite friendly. He made tea for me. I admired the fact that he was a good man, and I know that there is a tendency now to make little of him on account of his work, but I think he himself was a great work. I never met Yeats but I would say AE was a much holier man. I'd say greater in every way, except that Yeats was a very fine writer, but I liked AE. I think that any man who contributes virtue, goodness and that kind of nobility which really is something, produces a union of hearts far more than any Wolfe Tonery.

If I have held a light, even for a little, it is something,' said AE. To Frank O'Connor one night he confided that he had a premonition of death.

O'CONNOR: He told me he wasn't in the least afraid of death, but he was afraid of the pain and humiliation that preceded it. I remember well the phrase he used, 'The immortal soul being kicked out of the world like an old sick dog with a canister tied to his tail.' I did my best to comfort him, but I wasn't very successful. We talked about the immortality of the soul and what life after death might be like, and gradually he began to brighten up. 'I know the fellow I want to meet when I die,' he said, laughing. 'I have lots of questions to ask Socrates about the things Plato makes him say. Now who do *you* want to meet? – Tolstoy I suppose. I don't think I could stand Tolstoy, you know.' Curiously when he left that night, I saw him home and he was in the highest spirits again; somehow or other he had talked himself happy. But a week or two after that I was seeing him home again and I quoted a verse I'd just written which began,

> A patriot's frenzy enduring too long,
> Can hang like a stone on the heart of a man,
> And I have made Ireland too much of my song,
> I will now bid these foolish old dreams to be gone.

He stopped dead and he threw his arms in the air in a frenzy, 'That's exactly how I feel! I have to get out of this country before it drives me mad.' A week or two later he told me he'd made up his mind to give up his Dublin house and take a flat in London

CLARKE: Sean O'Faolain and other writers are certain that AE left Ireland in a mood of despair, having decided to settle down in London, but there were practical reasons for his action; after the death of his wife, Violet, he found it difficult to live at 70 Rathgar Avenue by himself.

AE decided to give up Dublin and to give away his possessions.

O'CONNOR: Of all the men I knew, Russell was the most a creature of habit, and for him to give up everything – the house where he lived, his books, his pictures, his friends – was already a sort of death. Whatever it was against which he'd built up those defences of habit, whether it was loneliness or despair, they'd been breached at last. I'd have done anything I could to comfort him, but how can you comfort a man who can't weep, who maybe himself doesn't know what it is that he wants to weep about? He asked me to come to his house and take whatever I wanted of his things. I couldn't face the thought of taking things that I knew he'd loved. Then one night he sent Higgins for me. Higgins himself was very close on tears. He said, 'You'll have to come, AE will be hurt if you don't, and the man is hurt enough, God knows.' So finally I went. Russell's face was like a tragic mask as he showed people about his rooms and offered them his little treasures. By this time I was as bad as Higgins – wanting to cry only made me angry. I said I didn't want anything of his, but he replied in a broken voice, 'But you mustn't leave without something; look, I put aside these Jack Yeats Broadsheets. I know how you admired Jack Yeats – do please take them.' I stayed on and Higgins stayed with me and we made casual conversation as we might have done at a wake, only on this occasion the corpse was one of the company. When we left the pubs were shut or I think we'd have got blind drunk.

Austin Clarke went to see AE in London.

CLARKE: I found him in very good form. He told me that with the earnings of his lecture tour of the United States he had enough to live on in a modest way for the rest of his life.

'It is quite easy to be poor,' said AE. 'My fixed income is about £100 a year, and am I unhappy? Good God, no. I feel like Swedenborg's angels who were continually advancing to the springtime of their youth!'

CLARKE: A month or two later I came up to visit him again and was shocked at the change in his appearance. We began to talk of Ireland which to him was still the blessed Isle of ancient gods and heroic legends. The evening sunlight shone through the window and against it his face seemed emaciated and longer, giving him a rather startling resemblance to the older Tennyson. He told me that he had not long to live and added, 'Death would be an exciting adventure.'

A few weeks later he died at Bournemouth. He was buried in Dublin. Frank O'Connor gave the funeral oration.

O'CONNOR: When he died, Yeats, for some reason, refused to make the last speech over his grave. 'I should have to tell all the truth' is the excuse that Higgins reported him making, and what that could mean I don't really know. Yeats asked me to make the speech instead.

'We are never satisfied,' said Yeats, 'with the maturity of those whom we have admired in boyhood, and we remain to the end their harshest critic . . . I demanded of Russell some impossible things.' At the graveside –

O'CONNOR: Yeats stood behind me, an old man who looked as though he didn't have long to live himself, and opposite me on the other side of the grave was Mr De Valera; in those days it wasn't considered a mortal sin to attend a Protestant funeral. I don't know what nonsense I spoke over the grave, I suspect it was all very youthful and very literary – all I should say now was that this was the man who was father to three generations of Irish poets, and there is nothing more to be said.

'OLD IRELAND FREE'

On Easter Monday 1916, a body of armed Irishmen occupied the GPO and other strategic buildings in Dublin, and proclaimed Ireland a Republic. This is the recorded story of that Easter Week. It is told by some who took part in, and by some who saw, the Easter Rising.

> 'Twas early early in the spring
> The small birds whistled and sweetly did sing,
> Changing their notes from tree to tree,
> And the song they sang was old Ireland free.

CECIL SALKELD: We got up at seven in the morning on Easter Monday morning, and what struck us all was that there was no dawn chorus; there were no birds singing, except when we got to the top there were some larks very high in the air. And the Rising must have been under way.

That was Cecil Salkeld, a boy of ten at the time, staying on the Hill of Howth, overlooking Dublin. He and the generation before him were brought up on the songs of their Motherland. Sean T. O'Kelly, later President of the Irish Republic –

SEAN T. O'KELLY: The songs meant everything. My mother used to sing patriotic songs, my father wasn't very vocal. My mother was preaching to us children (she had seven children) that we should be Fenians and stand for Irish Independence.

MAJOR-GENERAL PEARCE BEASLEY: I was reared by a father and mother who had the same ideas. I was brought up on the story of Ireland and the spirit of the nation. I had a love of all languages, but especially Irish for patriotic reasons.

DENNIS MCCULLOCH: My mother, who came from the County Down, was an extraordinarily fine woman. I had three brothers. She taught us all that a man had only two duties – the first one was to God, and the second one was to your country. You came afterwards yourself if you were lucky.

LIAM O'BRIAIN: I was born in the city of Dublin; my father a city man, my mother a country woman, very Gaelic in her background, from a few miles north of the city. My earliest politics were being instructed, when I was six or seven years of age, to recognise the tune of 'God Save the King', to keep my hat on or my cap on if it was on, to put it on if it was not on, and to sit down if I happened to be standing up and to remain seated. I did not know why, but that was so.

These speakers later took part in the Easter Rising. But what were the years of growing-up like? The excitement of learning the Irish language, of discovering the Irish people? Liam O'Briain –

O'BRIAIN: Oh well, you're going back a good while now. In 1908 I made my way west for the first time. Wonderful experience at that time to go to the Gaeltacht, these Irish colleges. It was the nearest thing to heaven really. I couldn't explain it. There was no conception. And to meet this language of your country again, hear people speaking it. The first peasants that I heard coming out with all the verbal forms – the irregular verbs, the affirmative forms and the negative forms, that I'd learned out of a book at school, to realise they were alive! And I heard this old fellow, I could have gone down on my knees and worshipped that man.

Cecil Salkeld felt the wind of change:

SALKELD: I grew up in Ireland during the Gaelic Revival at a time of great tension, and excitement and gaiety. Everybody was interested in learning the language, and my mother was particularly interested that we children should learn Irish as our second language. There seemed, in that sunny time of childhood, to be an inordinate number of festivals going on everywhere. The area that I remember best was one at the Rotunda in, I think, the summer of 1913. It was a wonderful day of sunshine, and the wind blew the dust over hordes of screaming children. There were tents everywhere with lemonade and liquorice bootlaces; there were planks mounted on trestles to form platforms for the young girls to dance, there were people singing. But the kernel of the meeting, the centre, was the massed meeting which was being held in the Round Room of the Rotunda. Then Eoin McNeill, I think it was, came out and called for volunteers. And after a lengthy speech the volunteers were asked to take one pace forward. And I saw the three first men who stepped out. One of them I did not know. He was a countryman with a darkly-burnt face and a light-coloured cap. The second was a tall young man whom I had already encountered as teaching me Irish down in the west – that was Eamonn de Valera. The third was a cousin of mine, Douglas French-Mullen, who afterwards became captain in the 4th Battalion of the Irish Volunteers. All this took place in an atmosphere of great hilarity. I remember Gerard Cross singing a song which brought enormous applause from everybody. Surprisingly enough, I remember the words of the refrain, which were:

> 'Oh, won't Mother England be surprised,
> Whack fol the diddle fol the di do day.'

The sunshine, the dust, the children and the music went on and around and around, while in the distance the enormous figures of the Dublin Metropolitan Police stalked past quietly and went into the snugs of Parnell Street to peer out and watch what was going on.

It was, in fact, a turning-point. At the Rotunda meeting that day, John MacNeill, Professor of Early Irish, founded the Irish Volunteers in answer to the Ulster Volunteers.

RICHARD MULCAHY: After sixty years of activity according to the English rules to get Home Rule – and the Irish people were about getting something from their agitation – the English changed the rules. In these circumstances Volunteers were called into being.

By 1915 there were 10,000 Volunteers. Not an insurrectionary force at first. Florrie O'Donoghue –

FLORRIE O'DONOGHUE: But behind all these movements we had the Secret Irish Republican Brotherhood. A very small organisation numerically, not more than two thousand strong in the whole country and Britain, an organisation without military training, without arms.

The hard core with a secret council of its own and a secret aim – insurrection. So there were two elements in the leadership of the Volunteers. There were the insurrectionists like Pearse, McDermott, Kent, Plunkett, Clarke, MacDonagh; and the anti-insurrectionists like MacNeill and Hobson. There had to be a show-down. Bulmer Hobson –

BULMER HOBSON: As far as following is concerned, MacNeill was the person who had following in the Volunteers. I was aware, probably early in 1915, that the Supreme Council of the IRB had passed a resolution by a majority, that they would stage an insurrection before the war was over. I was in the position of being General Secretary of the Volunteers, and Chairman of the IRB in Dublin. It was a position that could put a spanner in the business. We were aiming at making the British government in Ireland impossible, and developing a guerrilla business. That wasn't dramatic enough for Pearse and Connolly, who wanted a splash – they wanted to go out in a burst of glory. They organised the Military Committee with the utmost secrecy. It was like a secret organisation inside the IRB, with anybody who didn't fall in with the thing carefully kept in the dark. Dennis McCulloch, who was chairman of the Supreme Council, was kept in the dark. I was kept in the dark.

MCCULLOCH: Bulmer was a lovely character, except if he didn't have his way he'd break up an organisation, and I had the devil's own job keeping him in line. He was a tremendous factor.

Was it to be a process of attrition? Or a rebellion?

HOBSON: In 1915 I tried to ginger MacNeill up to taking a definite line. We were either going to do one thing or the other. MacNeill was an extraordinary person. He was a fine scholar, a first-rate mind, and a very charming person. He would do anything to avoid a showdown or a fight. And when it came to the end of 1915 O'Connell, FitzGibbon and I demanded from MacNeill that he should draw up a memorandum stating Volunteer policy, and that we would hold a special meeting and would demand, 'You either assent or you dissent', and we'd know where we were. After the meeting started I saw MacNeill quietly slip the memorandum into a drawer, and then there was a general discussion. But both Pearse and McDermott explicitly stated that we had low, suspicious minds, that they would never go behind anybody's back. The next thing that happened was the insurrection.

Easter Monday, 1916. John MacNeill's daughter, who was eleven years old at the time, says –

MRS SWEENEY: I remember waking one night and hearing a motor-car coming up the avenue. I got up and went down to where I could see the hall from the staircase. It was the night of Holy Thursday, Good Friday, when my father first heard of the intended Rising, and I know now that the other men in the hall were Bulmer Hobson and

Ginger O'Connell. I can't remember how we were told of the Rising. I've no memory of hearing artillery, but I remember hearing the elders of our house going up past our bedroom, through the attic to the roof, from which they could see the flare of Dublin burning.

'Both MacNeill and we have acted in the best interest of Ireland,' said Pearse in his last dispatch from the burning GPO. 'No dishonour,' said MacDermott, 'should rest on MacNeill's head.' Indeed, no.

What kind of men were the leaders of the Insurrection, the seven who signed the Proclamation of the Irish Republic – Pearse, Connolly, MacDonagh, Plunkett, MacDermott, Clarke, Kent – who were afterwards executed? Bulmer Hobson recalls Patrick Pearse, poet, school-master, patriot, instigator and Commander-in-Chief of the Easter Rising.

HOBSON: Pearse was a very odd person. He was full of theories, of the necessity for a recurring blood sacrifice to keep the national spirit alive. And he talked about being the scapegoat for the people.

McCULLOCH: Pearse was a dedicated man – I wasn't a dedicated man. I didn't want to die, to tell you God's truth, unless I had to.

Desmond Ryan was a pupil at Pearse's school, St Enda's.

DESMOND RYAN: He never incited to insurrection. Only on one occasion, in 1910, did he ever mention it to us, in an English class – I forget how it came up. He said there is only one lesson in history, that freedom is only won by force.

O'BRIAIN: Pearse wrote a wonderful poem called 'A Vision' – 'a vision of beauty naked I saw there before me, and I closed my eyes and concentrated my eyes on the patterns before me. On the road I am going and on the death I'll die.'

HOBSON: He kept moving more and more rapidly to the left and I swore him into the IRB at the end of 1913. Six months later I wasn't nearly revolutionary enough for him.

RYAN: If you met him for the first time, you would think he was the last man who would be a revolutionary. He himself said he was a harmless literary nationalist.

HOBSON: His father was English and his mother was County Limerick.

His mother, said Desmond Ryan, looked on him as a young god.

RYAN: She lived in this atmosphere, you see; these famous three wishes that he wanted to have – he wanted to start his bilingual paper, he wanted to start his famous bilingual school, and he wanted to head an insurrection. His mother realised the Rising was on and that the movement was going ahead. The Volunteers were armed, and spied on by the detectives. Pearse didn't know a detective in Dublin: there was a man who must have walked on Pearse's heels all the time, for years. Pearse said, 'But who is following? I've never seen the man in my life.' He took great precautions against being followed – he had a sword-stick, and a glove in which he kept an automatic revolver. Willie and he slept at the top of the house, there was a rope-ladder, a bicycle in case of a raid, and all this atmosphere. And you got used to it. He was a terrific Gaelic scholar; he had a wonderful power with boys and he could make you learn anything.

HOBSON: Pearse had great qualities in certain directions – he wrote very well and he delivered a number of outstanding orations. And, of course, Pearse's orations were carefully written out, learnt by heart, rehearsed in front of a mirror and delivered perfectly.

O'KELLY: Pearse was a very superior person – intellectually, oratorically. He would prepare himself for any occasion, where he had to make a public speech, and the most famous speech that he ever made was the one at the grave of O'Donovan Rossa in Glasnevin Cemetery, and I'm sure he gave tremendous preparation to that speech; he had it perfected and memorised and he acted the part – he was capable of doing that.

'They think they have foreseen everything,' cried Pearse, ' . . . but the fools, the fools! – they have left us our Fenian dead, and while Ireland holds these graves, Ireland unfree shall never be at peace.'

RYAN: I once said to him, 'Why do you make these violent speeches, why do you write so much – don't you think the British will tumble to it?' 'Good God, no,' he said, 'that's the last thing they'll tumble to.' But Joseph Plunkett didn't approve of that; he said, 'The British are not such fools as *you* think.' He said, 'For God's sake keep quiet and keep your wild young savages at St Enda's quiet. They're always talking about when we're going to put up the barricade; tell them to stop.' So this was the eve of the Rising, this was a bit dangerous, I admit. Pearse sent for me and said, 'When you are outside this house, will you please shut up.'

To his Irish students, Pearse, on the eve of the Rising, said, 'Always remember if ever you're free, it's the son of an Englishman who will have freed you.'

RYAN: Oh yes, it was a schoolmasters' Rising, it was a poets' Rising. It certainly was a poets' Rising. General Mulcahy was the one man who voiced that feeling of the hidden poetry of the pre-Rising or the Rising itself. He said, 'On the eve of this great adventure of ours,' – this is the gist of it – 'we could feel a great wave of hope through the land, we could feel the violets springing up from under our feet.'

Pearse, Plunkett, MacDonagh – the three poets of the Rising.

O'BRIAIN: MacDonagh was a lecturer in University College, Dublin. He was irrepressible. He's written some very good poems. He read a lot, read widely.

HOBSON: MacDonagh was a complete puzzle. He was clever, witty, good-humoured, a delightful companion, married with two children. He wrote a play years before which was put on in the Abbey, in which seven men ran an insurrection. It seems Plunkett and MacDonagh and the poets attached a lot of importance to seven and, as MacDonagh said, he foretold the whole thing in this play.

O'BRIAIN: I was in the Abbey Theatre from the very first. It was revolutionary in Dublin to have plays up there with actors with genuine Irish accents. At least they set my blood on fire I must say. There was Lady Gregory, Cathleen ni Houlihan and there was Pearse.

And Yeats . . .

RYAN: Pearse had a terrific admiration for Yeats, he wouldn't stand any attack on Yeats, wouldn't tolerate it. He said to me once, 'You know, as the years pass, in days to come, people will say that this was the age of Yeats.'

> *'I lie awake night after night*
> *And never get the answers right,*
> *Did that play of mine send out*
> *Certain men the English shot?'*

asked Yeats, in later years. Senator Michael Hayes taught with Mac-Donagh, and fought beside him in the Easter Rising.

SENATOR MICHAEL HAYES: He was entirely a theoretical soldier in the sense that he had no military experience of any kind; he studied and he gave lectures on street fighting and tactics and all that kind of thing – none of which I must say I ever attended.

HOBSON: One day, he came into my office and he pulled out a book, put it down on my desk, and said, 'Hobson, did you ever read that?' I picked it up; it was Caesar's *Gallic War*. I said I had read it a good many years ago, what about it? 'But,' he said, 'don't you carry it about in your pocket?' 'No,' I said, 'why should I?' 'Well,' he said, 'you can't understand strategy without it.' But MacDonagh was quite ready to have an insurrection at any time.

And the other leaders? Had Edmund Kent a touch of poetry?

O'KELLY: I liked Kent. He was a stern fellow – a man of principle, a very determined Irish Republican. I once heard him play before Pius X at the Vatican in Rome. He played the pipes there and there was a public audience for the Irish. And then he marched into the Council Room, dressed in a green and gold Irish costume that he had fashioned for himself. Nobody in Ireland ever wore it before. He marched up and down and played Irish tunes – 'O'Donnell Abu' and a few other things like that; then he marched out again after playing for about ten minutes. Oh, of course, the Irish all naturally cheered him and cheered him and cheered him again as he marched out.

What about Tom Clarke?

O'KELLY: Well, there's no greater man amongst them than Tom Clarke, who had spent fifteen years as a convict in English prisons.

HOBSON: The penal servitude for the political prisoners at that period was quite ghastly. About forty per cent of them were mad within the first six months.

O'KELLY: And to think of a man coming out after the terrible sufferings he went through, and coming out as determined as ever to carry on the fight.

HOBSON: He was a man of extraordinary sincerity and a good character.

He was a tireless force, and his small tobacconist/newspaper shop in Parnell Street was a focus for rebel plots and plans and hopes.

DOMINIC O'RIORDAN:

> As evening falls in Dublin,
> And twilight gathers round Parnell Street,
> I have a vision of a quiet man
> Looking and gazing at the Post Office,
> Distance some hundred feet.
> So he must have waited,
> So have been his desire,
> To send the word out of that building
> To awaken Ireland with a house on fire.

Clarke and MacDermott met for the first time in that shop in Parnell Street.

To set Ireland on fire; to raise her on stilts of insurrection. What was MacDermott like?

RYAN: I met MacDermott, I liked him. He was a great organiser – that was his real power – and he was Tom Clarke's left hand. He was very much hampered by an attack of infantile paralysis, but he was a very brave man.

BEASLEY: Sean MacDermott – there was no other man had so much influence over me. He was a most lovable type. A beautiful type of man. He was full of fun and humour and at the same time very much in earnest about the Cause. He liked the ladies and the ladies liked him, and all the young men adored him too. Five foot eight, dark, oh dark, white skin, black hair and grey-blue eyes.

CATHAL O'SHANNON: He was the most lovable of the whole lot.

MRS O'KELLY: I was too young to be consorting with Tom Clarke, but I wasn't too young to be whispering with Sean MacDermott, of course. He always had a nice word for every girl.

MRS MULCAHY: He was a marvellous person in his way. He wasn't what you call a very well-educated man, but he had all the books. Everything on Ireland, that's the only thing that interested him. He got on awfully well with everybody; he could play cards; he could drink a bit; he could go to ceilidhes and so on, although he was very disabled. He was full of fun. And although I knew him intimately really, and saw him very, very often, he never gave away a single thing to me about what they were doing. Not one thing.

It was Dennis McCulloch and Bulmer Hobson who had persuaded MacDermott to join the Irish Republican Brotherhood, in Belfast.

MCCULLOCH: We talked to him and he was very suspicious about it. We were a kind of secret society, and he didn't like that. He was an extremely religious fellow at the time. We cured him of that. We convinced him that we were not after his soul.

By 1916 MacDermott was Secretary to the Supreme Council of the IRB. Tom Clarke was Treasurer, Pearse was Chief. The fuse was now laid to the powder-keg of insurrection, and the trail led from Clarke, says Sean T. O'Kelly –

O'KELLY: Next to him I would put Pearse. And then the next person I would put as the person responsible for the Rising taking place, Sean MacDermott. And I would maybe be wrong in saying 'after' him – side by side with Sean MacDermott I put James Connolly.

It was Connolly – and his Citizen Army – who put the match to the fuse. Who was Connolly? And what was his Citizen Army?

HOBSON: The last time I met Connolly I was having tea with Sean Lester in the vegetarian restaurant and Connolly came in and joined us – and we were arguing about the necessity or non-necessity of an insurrection; Connolly said, 'The working class is always revolutionary – somebody's just got to strike a match – it goes up like powder.'

BEASLEY: Connolly was a first-rate, thoroughly sincere man. He didn't know what fear was. He was a practical revolutionist, a practical soldier.

RYAN: Very few people knew Connolly – I don't know that anyone knew him. He was a mystery. He could keep his own council, but he was terrific – he was like iron. But he was a relentless man, twice as tough as Larkin any day. Connolly was very hard to like. He had too much intellect – and slightly suspicious or more than slightly. Pearse got on with him very well.

Owen Sheehy-Skeffington recalls his father's friendship with Connolly –

OWEN SHEEHY-SKEFFINGTON: They were both in the Socialist Party of Ireland which had a total membership of about thirty-three or something like that, and they were very close. Connolly was an older man but my father had a deep admiration for him.

And what about Connolly's Citizen Army?

SKEFFINGTON: Curiously enough, the Citizen Army started as a kind of peaceful citizens' group for the purpose of ensuring that strikers and the working-class movement could hold meetings without their being broken up by strike-breakers. And so a little bunch of people were called together at the Mansion House. At this very first meeting the Lord Mayor got cold feet and refused them the room at the last moment, and Robin Gwynn, who was a very strong and also a very saintly man, said in his quiet way, 'Well, won't you come down to my rooms in Trinity College and we can continue this discussion?' They did, and the Citizen Army was founded in Robin Gwynn's rooms in Trinity College. At that first stage it was a peaceful, non-violent movement. When it became an army in the full sense, and resorted to rifle and drilling, my father broke his association with it.

JUDGE LYNCH: Connolly gave us all lectures on street-fighting and how to get barricades . . . secure your water supply, secure food for your men and the people within your area.

HELENA MALONEY: Connolly was very keen on absolute equality between men and women. If a girl could handle a gun she was given a gun. If a man could cook a meal he was expected to cook it, and not feel in any way degraded by it. Wherever their capability lay, everyone had to do that work for Ireland's sake.

CATHAL O'SHANNON: Connolly, of course, drew people to him – particularly in the Labour Movement. He was very cool-headed – not in any way a demigod but a very fine speaker. Pearse apparently did not draw very many personally towards him, he seemed to be in some ways cool. Connolly, to many people, seemed very cool too, and a bit distant, but he wasn't – certainly not among his friends. But a sort of fellowship developed between Pearse and Connolly through the years.

SKEFFINGTON: They did, in fact, like each other very much. One of the things that my mother used to say was that Pearse was coming more and more under the intellectual spell of Connolly, and that, if they had both lived, Pearse was quite clearly going more and more towards a Socialist outlook.

Pearse and Connolly, the Irish Nationalist and the Irish Socialist, a strange conjunction. As a well-known Natural History of Ireland says,

'The Carrion Crow has mated with the Hooded Crow in County Dublin on two occasions, probably on account of the impossibility of finding a mate of its own species.'

DOMINIC O'RIORDAN: One of the most interesting things about the Rising is that in it Pearse, a Republican and an Irishman, and Connolly, a Socialist, met for the first time in all history the dialectic of modern life: Connolly said, just before the Rising, 'The Socialists will never understand, they'll forget that I am an Irishman.' But it was Connolly who taught Pearse the fact that Socialism was the only important development in this world, and it was Pearse who taught Connolly that a nation should be one thing, one thing apart, that the Irish language is a spiritual dynamite.

Between the two of them, poet and proletarian, they blew the notion of a tame and timid Ireland sky-high. Connolly forced the pace, called the tune.

O'SHANNON: Connolly got sharper and sharper, and more or less came to a decision that if there was no rising by the Volunteers, he and the Citizen Army would certainly take up arms and begin an insurrection.

MCCULLOCH: Bring out the Citizen Army – the folly of that was too majestic. Because they hadn't more than two hundred men altogether.

So, early in 1916, Pearse and Connolly met and came to an agreement.

O'SHANNON: On the date they had fixed for the insurrection, Easter Sunday, 1916. I think it was a big strain on Connolly himself; he was absent for two or three days and when he came back he wouldn't tell anybody, not even his closest friends, where he had been or what he'd been doing.

HELENA MALONEY: I asked him where he'd been. 'Oh,' he said, 'I've been in hell, but I don't want to talk about it.' And that's all he said.

The date was fixed. The stage was set. The players rehearsed. Sunday after Sunday, Pearse's Volunteers paraded openly through Dublin on manoeuvres, and Connolly's Citizen Army marched forth from Liberty Hall, headquarters of the Socialist Party, under the banner of the 'Plough and the Stars'.

MALONEY: For many weeks beforehand, Connolly had a scheme which worked very well. There was a very big blackboard, six feet by three, outside the front door of Liberty Hall, on which every Saturday there were flamboyant notices chalked. 'Assemble tomorrow, full equipment, for an attack on Wellington Barracks.' The next week it would be 'Assemble fully armed for attack on Dublin Castle.' I said one day to Connolly, 'Why do you put out these notices, that don't mean anything?' And he smiled, and said, 'Ah, did you never hear the story of wolf, wolf, wolf?' We drilled and marched in the Hall. And I had some time before bought a revolver for myself. So I had my revolver and I taught the girls to shoot.

Before Easter came Connolly's and Pearse's orders for mobilisation.

RICHARD MULCAHY: Pearse came in for a short time to speak to us; he spoke to us on the importance of the manoeuvres that were going to take place on Easter Sunday; the necessity for everybody being there, having all their equipment and bringing a couple of days' rations, and that was that, very important. Then he proposed to dismiss us; Con Colbert at the back spoke up and said, 'Commandant, what about men who, if they come out on Sunday, are afraid of losing their jobs?' And Pearse just looked very detachedly down over us and said, 'I don't think any man should come out on manoeuvres on Sundays that's afraid of losing his job.' And we were dismissed.

Michael Hayes, Military Secretary to de Valera:

HAYES: De Valera, a teacher, was the Commandant. On Holy Thursday night, 1916, he inspected the battalion, and it was obvious that something serious was going to happen on Sunday; we were told to parade with all the weapons we had. As far as my memory serves me they were expecting about four hundred men and they had about two hundred and fifty assorted weapons. It seemed to me a very dismal lookout. On the Saturday night, I went to confession. There were a great many men going to confession, many more than usual on a Saturday night.

Richard Mulcahy had intended to go on a religious retreat.

MULCAHY: You got a room to yourself with a fire that sparkled on the ceiling all night. No one spoke to you for four nights and the intervening days. You quietly listened to some lectures in the church and you walked the grounds. I was thirsty for a rest and for the breath of the spring air down over the limestone country of Clare, and I saw all that thing going smash. On Thursday morning I knew that a Rising was going to take place on Sunday at four o'clock.

On Saturday night there was a secret meeting at Edmund Kent's house.

SALKELD: They had had their tactical discussions and military palaver, and were now relaxing – some of them – over a bottle of stout. But most of them, as you can imagine, over lemonade. Or a cup of tea. I'm remembering that Douglas was the famous pianist. 'Come Douglas. Come, play something apropos.' And he sat down and played Chopin's Funeral March. That was on the Saturday evening.

The dream was ended. The reality had begun. Connolly and Pearse had put their hands to the plough, but their star was not in the ascendant. Roger Casement had been arrested in Kerry. The German ship that was bringing them much-needed arms had been intercepted and scuttled. And yet hopes were high in Dublin and eyes were starry.

MULCAHY: Under all the influence that was going on, I remember one old porter who would always come out and show you the sky, and tell you, at about twelve o'clock, 'There's Mars, and there's Venus, and there's the Plough; and when you come out in the morning 'twill be turned round.'

SALKELD: I remember my cousin, Douglas French-Mullen, coming in late in the evening in a raincoat, and under this he had his officer's uniform on. Of course, we knew nothing and he told us nothing – that mobilisation had already been called. And he, being an insomniac, did not trust himself to wake up early enough to call his men. So he came down to borrow a book. And I've remembered the book. It was *A Child's Book of Stars.*

On Easter Sunday morning came calamitous and confusing news for Pearse and Connolly. John MacNeill, the head of the Volunteer Movement, had countermanded their orders and cancelled the Rising.

BEASLEY: We were to have been out on the Sunday and the thing was called off. Then Sean MacDermott came over to me, 'We've decided to call off for the present,' he said, 'but keep your men together ready for further word.' He asked me to act as bodyguard for Tom Clarke.

So I went out and escorted Tom Clarke. 'It's heartbreaking,' he said, 'this thing has spoiled everything. I feel like going away to have a cry.'

MULCAHY: Most of the people in the place had heard of the cancellation order except myself. But I was living such a quiet-minded life out there that I didn't look at the *Sunday Independent* that day. I got home to Sutton, and at Dublin at that particular time there was a place where I had a sing-song now and then. I wasn't much of a singer. I always had about one song. And my song at that time was 'Let Me Like a Soldier Fall'. I can tell you I was not going to sing my one song that night, and I didn't. And I realised what a fraud of a song 'Let Me Like a Soldier Fall' is. So the following morning I came into town early and Thomas MacDonagh came along to me with his cape swinging from the shoulders in a jaunty kind of a way. He said, 'Strike at 12.' And in the second section of Lower Gardner Street, strolling down as if they were having an after-Mass ramble on a Sunday, were Sean MacDermott and Tom Clarke.

Sean MacEntee came to Dublin that same Monday morning for orders. At Liberty Hall he met Pearse and Connolly.

SEAN MACENTEE: I remember the phrase which Mr Pearse used, 'We strike at noon.' It was arranged that I should catch a train back to Dundalk. When I got there the train was leaving, so I came back very crestfallen to Liberty Hall and met Connolly and told him what I'd done. I said, 'Not my fault – I went by the clock,' pointing to the clock on the wall. 'Oh,' he said, 'doesn't everybody know that that clock is always five minutes slow?'

Time had called them into the Centre. The clock was about to strike – at Liberty Hall. They came from all parts of Dublin. Poets, teachers, civil servants, clerks, shopboys, labourers. By bicycle, tramcar, on foot. One of the last to arrive was O'Rahilly in his motor-car. 'I've helped to wind up the clock,' he said, 'I might as well hear it strike.' Yeats's poem, 'The O'Rahilly' –

> Sing of the O'Rahilly
> That had such little sense
> He told Pearse and Connolly
> He'd gone to great expense
> Keeping all the Kerry men
> Out of that crazy fight;

> That he might be there himself
> Had travelled half the night.

The weather was golden, when at twelve o'clock they marched off to occupy the GPO and other key points in Dublin. 'Rebellion weather', they called it. Paddy O'Connor got news of the Easter Rising late.

PADDY O'CONNOR: It was at dinner-time when I came home; my mother gave me my dinner and told me, 'Eat up and eat plenty,' and, says she, 'I'll get your taps ready,' and she did. She put the rifle beside me and other gear she thought I'd require. 'Mother,' I said, 'I mightn't be coming back any more.' 'Oh,' she said, 'I understand that all right, but you see, go on now like a good boy, and God bless you and do your best,' and that's all she said. Oh, a great mother.

John MacNeill, head of the Volunteers, got news of the Rising from Liam O'Briain:

O'BRIAIN: He said, 'I must go home now, put on my uniform and join in.' That was his first impulse.

Helena Maloney of the Abbey Theatre marched –

HELENA MALONEY: I marched with 1st Company under Captain John Connolly. No relation to James Connolly.

O'SHANNON: That was the John Connolly who played in the Abbey.

MALONEY: Yes. And we marched to attack Dublin Castle. It was part of Connolly's plan that the first shot should be fired at Dublin Castle, because he said the effect of that, if it was heard through the country that Dublin Castle had been attacked and taken by the rebels, would be that the whole of Ireland would lift its heart up and come and join us.

Yeats's poem, 'Three Songs to the One Burden' –

> Come gather round me, players all:
> Come praise Nineteen-Sixteen,
> Those from the pit and gallery
> Or from the painted scene
> That fought in the Post Office
> Or round the City Hall,
> Praise every man that came again,
> Praise every man that fell.

MALONEY: We came to the Castle Gate, and then Connolly said, 'Get in, get in.' But the sentry at the gate, quick as lightning, banged the gate in our faces. Connolly said, 'Get into the City Hall.' We went up into the City Hall and got up on the roof. About one o'clock we were on the roof – several men and I and some girls, and John Connolly, and he was struck by a bullet. There was firing, you see, from the Castle.

> Who was the first man shot that day?
> The player Connolly,
> Close to the City Hall he died;
> Carriage and voice had he;
> He lacked those years that go with skill,
> But later might have been
> A famous, a brilliant figure
> Before the painted scene.

MALONEY: I said a prayer into his ear as he went and he was dead.

Another play was billed to open that day in Dublin.

SALKELD: It was at the Hardwicke Street Theatre, and the play was August Strindberg's *Easter*, scheduled for Monday, 26 April 1916. And the main characters were P. H. Pearse, William Pearse, Thomas MacDonagh, my mother, Nell Burn, and myself. The piece produced by John MacDonagh, the brother of Thomas.

That play never went on. The three main players, the Pearses and Thomas MacDonagh, were engaged elsewhere in the drama of the Easter Rising. Sean McGarry was in the GPO and saw the leading players.

SEAN MCGARRY: Tom Clarke, his eyes sparkling with elation, MacDermott in joyous mood, Connolly, happy as a schoolboy at a picnic; Plunkett who was very ill on Sunday seemed to have taken on a new life, and Pearse, as usual, was in high humour. The garrison, to a man, were enthusiastic. Only about half an hour after our entry we saw the lancers advancing towards us from the direction of the Rotunda.

Mrs Mulcahy went to the GPO.

MRS MULCAHY: And we came down O'Connell Street, and the first thing we saw that was revolting was a horse, dead across the street. It seemed the Lancers came. The first thing we noticed over the post office was the flag, the tricolour, I'd never seen a tricolour before. Connolly was standing outside the door.

During that week of siege Mrs Mulcahy and her sister were in and out of the post office. They saw O'Rahilly:

MRS MULCAHY: He'd dressed up in a great green uniform and a hat which cocked up at the side, and he was very much keeping control.

They saw Pearse:

MRS MULCAHY: Pearse said he'd like to send a message to his mother. He gave us two messages to take out, in writing – one to his mother and one to the country. Sean MacDermott then told me that Tom Clarke would like to have a talk with me. So Tom was brought up some time in the night. He was quite gay, you'd think he was out on a spree or something. He sat down and said, 'I'd like to tell you a few things because we here, of course, will be completely wiped out, but you and some others may escape. And I want to tell you why we have come out here now, so that the people of Ireland will at least understand our motives. I had to keep a serene face, and a lot of my friends were in there, including my brother, 'wiping out' so to speak. And really it was most extraordinary because I felt so unreal myself that I couldn't believe anything could happen. You know they made you feel like that. Gave you the sort of feeling that nothing could happen.

'We're going to be slaughtered,' said Connolly. It all seemed so non-chalantly done. Liam O'Briain met a friend, Harry Nichols, on Easter Monday.

O'BRIAIN: It was a lovely morning. We stopped and looked at the Gate of Stephen's Green barricaded, and some lads down on the ground, rifles sticking out of the railings. There was a man in the magnificent Citizen Army uniform parading up and down. Lieutenant Bob de Court – 'Me father was a Frenchman, I know all about revolutions.' And he was addressing the passing mob, 'If you're any bloody good, come in here and fight for Ireland.' So we went over to him, 'We're Volunteers; we're looking for our own Company, to join up.' 'If you are Volunteers, isn't this as good a place for you to fight as anywhere else?' At that instant a burst of fire occurred further down the street; so Harry Nichols said, 'I'm with you boys.' He flung his bicycle away and started to climb the railings and joined in. So I had to follow him. There I was among the Citizen crowd whom I didn't know, except one of the women. And she got me a shotgun and this pocketful of cartridges. I'd never fired a shotgun in my life before.

Twice a day the firing stopped, to let the park-keepers feed the wild ducks.

O'RIORDAN: The Citizen Army had taken all the grand pianos out of Frederick Mayes Piano Shop and stretched them across the road. All the old women had taken bottles of wine, bottles of stout, bottles of whiskey from Smith's Shop, nearby, and they put them on top of the pianos and there they were with the bottles of whiskey on top of the pianos and they were thumping, dumping, bumping away on the pianos with one finger.

O'BRIAIN: The Citizen Army was supposed to be Communist at the time. In fact they were ordinary poor Dublin labouring men and they were all very good, strong Catholics, and they'd all been to Confession before the Rising; indeed during the Rising, a priest was there. At least one day I was out in the sort of outpost we had and I ran across a street to a doorway, a back door that led into the College of Surgeons; I banged on this door and there was firing up and down the street and I was in a hurry. They took their time inside before opening the door for me, and two old men were there standing with guns in their hands pointing at me when I came in, so I was very annoyed and I said something like, 'Why the devil didn't you open the door before now, the damn door?' One of them said to me, 'Give over with that foul language now, and we all after being to the priest and trying to keep good.'

And what about the Countess Markievitz?

O'BRIAIN: She was a Second-in-Command in Stephen's Green when I went in there. She was dressed in the Citizen Army green, which was a darker shade to the Volunteer green – a sort of South African-style shirt with knee-breeches and bootees all in green, and a slouch hat and a big revolver which used to be called the Peter the Painter. She could use it too – she was supposed to be a dead shot. She was not there as a woman, she was there as a combatant. The men all worshipped her. They all remembered what she'd done during the strike three years previously when she'd been washing and cooking and bringing swarms of children home to her house, you know, all through that strike – so much so that her husband, poor old Count Markievitz, used to say,

'I can't get into my own house. My wife has the house full of children. She said to me, "Go away, go away, there's no room for you here tonight. Go somewhere else." ' Oh, the Countess was really a great one.

Charles Duff was in Ireland on leave from the British Army.

CHARLES DUFF: That Easter of 1916 I was in the British Army and had gone home to Northern Ireland to spend a few days' leave with my parents. On my way back to England I reached Amiens Street Station in Dublin just about noon on Easter Monday. When we reached the Mara Restaurant in Trinity Street, the old waiter was out in the street putting up the shutters. The waiter seemed flurried and then came over and said, 'The trouble's started. Take my tip and get out of the city as quick as you can, for there's going to be holy murder. Listen, sometimes you can hear the shots over there on the other side of the Liffey.' We heard the shots all right and took his advice.

Down by the Liffey Paddy O'Connor was entrenched behind a barricade, when a motor-car drove up to it.

O'CONNOR: To our amazement, we saw a very tall officer emerging – he had a gun in his hand and he was armed – that was the difficulty, because we wouldn't have shot if there were no arms or anything like that. He turned, he was getting away, and three or four shots rang out – they were determined not to let him get away, you see, they had to get him. So I was very sorry to see he was wounded about the eyes, and I heard afterwards that it was Lord Dunsany, and personally I felt very sorry to see that he was wounded, on account of his love of literature and all that, and I thought it was a great pity.

The most tragic shooting was that of the pacifist, Frank Sheehy-Skeffing-ton, by a British officer. His son recalls –

SKEFFINGTON: My father, who was a pacifist as well as a feminist, and a socialist, published an open letter to Thomas MacDonagh, in which he said that he had been on a platform recently with MacDonagh – whom he greatly admired – but was shocked to hear him looking forward to bloodshed, to military feat of arms. If you resort to arms you are in a sense failing to think beforehand of your aims. Also if you resort to arms you tend to find yourself at the end with the gunmen, the military men in charge, who don't know anything about running the social and economic matters. All the men that my father admired –

the Connollys and the MacDonaghs, and the Pearses, were doing something by means which he disapproved, though he approved of the ultimate aims. What could he do? Well, what he did do seems quixotic and foolish, but he just couldn't sit still and do nothing. What he did do was to go down town and try to organise a Citizens' Defence Force to prevent looting. It seems odd because he was not concerned with private property; he was a socialist and something indeed of an anarchist, but what he was concerned with was that the name of the Irish revolutionary should not be blackened. And so he successfully organised a little band of a kind of Citizens' Defence Force. Tuesday evening my mother came home as usual, but my father didn't. We didn't know what had happened to him. He had, in fact, been arrested at Portobello Bridge walking up the middle of the street, had been arrested and taken to Portobello Barracks. He had later that night been taken out by Bowen-Colthurst, who was I think then a Captain, and used as a hostage. He was brought back to barracks, and the following morning Bowen-Colthurst, first consulting his Bible – he was a very religious man – read, somewhere in the Bible, something that seemed to him to indicate that he should take out my father and two other journalists who were in the cell at that time and have them shot. This he did; he formed a firing squad and had them shot on the Wednesday morning. My father had been shot and buried in quick-lime.

O'BRIAIN: Of course, Paul Colthurst was just a mental wreck, shell-shocked in the retreat from Mons. His mother was simply prostrate.

And how had Charles Duff fared?

DUFF: I was far too early for the boat and killed time just by wandering about, only to be stopped by Military Police who, having satisfied themselves about me, led me off to their office nearby. In that office I was told to join a group of men like myself in uniform and on leave. From time to time a non-commissioned officer opened the door and called out a name and the man went out with him, not to return; my turn duly came and I was escorted before an officer, a major. He told me that as they were very short of officers he wanted me to take charge of some men for any job that might be going. I asked him whether this meant that we were liable to be put with the troops engaged in putting down the rebellion. Indeed that was so. But my mind was already made up, and I informed him that I was sorry but I could not do that, for I had joined the British Army to fight the Germans. I joined as a volunteer in Ireland and did not want to kill any of my fellow countrymen. The major did not look up from his papers, but remarked very quietly, 'Refusing duties, eh? Well, you know what that means in these circumstances. Is your mind made up?' I said, 'Yes.' He rang a bell, and I was escorted out into another room where I found a score of highly excited Irishmen, and within a minute I knew they were in the same boat as myself. More men arrived, the story was the same and so it went on until the early hours of the morning when the Sergeant came in and shouted, 'Collect your kit. Follow me!' We were hurried into lorries and taken to the Holyhead boat. There must have been over two hundred of us. We duly returned to our units.

And to France. Charles Duff to Passchendaele. For five days the Dublin insurgents, outnumbered twenty to one, held the GPO. Sean McGarry was in it.

MCGARRY: The building shook again and again as the shells exploded, and they were falling on Liberty Hall. And the whole street became a mass of flame. Machine-guns sprayed bullets on us and the roof became dangerous. This was the pattern of the day when Connolly, going out to place an outpost in Liffey Street, was wounded. Finally a fire-bomb struck us and started a fire which could not be put out. The roof had to be evacuated as another bomb struck. The flames grew worse and the fire worked downwards. The wounded were evacuated to Jervis Street Hospital. With them, after much argument, went the Commandant and the nurses; and later came the order to line up for evacuation. We formed up in the yards and exits to Henry Street, which we crossed into Henry Place. We had several wounded here and O'Rahilly was killed at the corner of Moore Street.

Yeats's poem, 'The O'Rahilly' –

> What remains to sing about
> But of the death he met
> Stretched under a doorway
> Somewhere off Henry Street;
> They that found him found upon
> The door above his head
> 'Here died the O'Rahilly.
> R.I.P.' writ in blood.

There was bitter fighting with the English Tommies in North King Street.

LYNCH: About a dozen of the soldiers – who appeared to be very stupidly led – turned into Cuckoo Lane at the double. This was just completely under our fire, and these lads were wiped out in no time. It was a tragic thing in many ways. One had to be sorry for them. They were only very young boys, and in fact Lieutenant Shouldice told me that when he went to collect the rifles he said that he heard one lad saying, 'Oh mammy, mammy,' which was terrible.

McGARRY: We then broke into a shop in Moore Street and tunnelled towards Parnell Street where we found we were completely surrounded. The chiefs went into conference and after what seemed to me an eternity, McDermott called me and with tears falling said, 'We are going to ask the lads to surrender. It would have been far better to go down in a good fight, but it is too late now.' We went aimlessly from room to room, just waiting. We did not talk; we just looked at one another in a kind of 'it cannot be' style, until the order came to line up in the street. Slowly and with leaden feet, we went into Moore Street, formed up under a white flag, then marched into O'Connell Street, where we were surrounded with what seemed to be hundreds of soldiers, and we sorrowfully laid down our arms. So that was the end.

RYAN: And the soldiers on the other side said, 'We're glad you stopped, but you won't 'alf catch what for.'

At Stephen's Green the Citizen Army Group surrendered.

O'BRIAIN: The last man going in was a lad who had come over from London to fight. He was born and raised in London. His name was O'Leary, but he spoke with a tremendous cockney accent. I got hold of him and I said, 'O'Leary, you can beat off.' 'What do you mean?' he said. 'We're surrendering.' I said, 'We're going to surrender. What's going to happen I don't know – we may be shot – but you have what we none of us have, you've a perfect passport. You go out and say you're an Englishman. You've only to open your mouth and you'll be believed. Say you're an Englishman here on your holidays.' 'You think that'd be right?' he said. 'Yes,' I said, 'it will be all right. Go on. Give me your stuff.' So I took his things, sent him away like that and he got away. He didn't thank me for it. Twenty-five years later I met him and he said, '*You* all went to jail. You were kept by His Majesty's

Government for eight months after that. But I had to go and get a job and work for my living.'

On Sunday, Thomas MacDonagh surrendered at Jacob's factory.

MRS MULCAHY: He came in with his big cloak on him, and he was very nice to us and then he said, 'I'm afraid, ladies, I'll have to ask you to leave. I'll have to consult my staff about a very serious matter.'

HAYES: MacDonagh went away then in uniform with a British Brigadier-General Lee, then came back and summoned a meeting of officers. He had seen Pearse, and he proposed to give the order for a general surrender. He was a very vivacious, lively, active-minded man and that speech was quite different from his usual manner. It was clear that whatever happened to us, he would probably be executed.

SALKELD: The entire centre of the city was gone. Dublin had been levelled as I've only seen Berlin levelled. O'Connell Street was gone, with the exception of the GPO and Nelson's Pillar, and everywhere there was smoke rising for weeks afterwards.

Pearse's sister could hardly believe the sight.

O'RIORDAN: His sister, coming down O'Connell Street after the Rising, saw all the twisted, tumbled, wrinkled buildings and said, 'But Paddy was a nice boy. He wouldn't hurt a fly, would he?'

How did his brother, Willie, feel about surrendering?

O'RIORDAN: Sean McGarry told me this story: Willie Pearse began to insult a young man, a young English officer who was very polite, very courteous altogether. So Sean McGarry brought him aside and he said, 'For God's sake, will you ever shut up or we'll all be shot.' And Willie Pearse, the brother of Patrick, said, 'Listen, I cannot go home to my mother without Paddy.'

Both brothers were executed a few days later. Clarke, MacDonagh, Kent, Plunkett, MacBride also. MacDermott and Connolly were the last to be shot. Frank Thornton –

FRANK THORNTON: Sean MacDermott shook hands and said, 'I'll be shot, and it'll be a bad day for Ireland if I'm not. You fellows will get an opportunity, even if in years to come, to follow on where we left off.' Well, Sean was shot.

Mrs O'Kelly and her sister, Mrs Mulcahy – the Ryan sisters – saw him before his execution.

MRS O'KELLY: A terrible experience – we were driven through this awful dark night, through the city, across to see him in this awful cell with candlelight and soldiers sitting in the corner. He talked to us for quite a long time, and he seemed to be almost as gay as ever, you couldn't imagine that he was a man going to die.

MRS MULCAHY: He had a uniform on and he cut the buttons off; it was very difficult for he couldn't get anything to cut them with. He cut them off to give to various people.

MRS O'KELLY: He was telling us how happy he was that the Rising had come off, that it was the greatest dream of his life and if he lived he only wanted to do the same thing all over again. And we said good-bye to him and that was that. We came home and we knelt down and said our prayers for him. I remember weeping, weeping, weeping, weeping at the thought that I'd lost the greatest friend I ever had and he . . . and he was lost like that; he was executed.

SKEFFINGTON: Connolly was the last to be executed. He was strapped to a chair and taken out and shot; he had been badly wounded. But before he died, his wife and Dora Connolly visited him. He knew he was going to be shot but he felt that a blow had been struck and that the awareness in the conscience of the Irish people had been awakened. As his wife was talking to him rather sadly, he said, 'There are plenty of good men left, and there are good Socialists; there are people like Frank Sheehy-Skeffington,' he saw a cloud on his wife's face and he said, 'What's the matter, has something happened to Sheehy-Skeffington?' And she said, 'Yes,' and she told him, and without a word he turned his face to the wall.

The cost of the Rising was almost too great. Sheehy-Skeffington, 'The most absurdly courageous man I have ever met or heard of,' said James Stephens. Pacifist and Patriot. Connolly's conscience. The good men who might have been spared, gone. Yeats's poem, 'Easter, 1916' –

> Too long a sacrifice
> Can make a stone of the heart.
> O when may it suffice?
> That is Heaven's part, our part

To murmur name upon name,
As a mother names her child
When sleep at last has come
On limbs that had run wild.
What is it but nightfall?
No, no, not night but death;
Was it needless death after all?
For England may keep faith
For all that is done and said.
We know their dream; enough
To know they dreamed and are dead;
And what if excess of love
Bewildered them till they died?
I write it out in a verse –
MacDonagh and MacBride
And Connolly and Pearse
Now and in time to be,
Wherever green is worn,
Are changed, changed utterly:
A terrible beauty is born.

Ay, they were great days to be young in. The stir there was. And the hope there was. And maybe a little of the heartbreak too.

BIOGRAPHICAL NOTES

On Some of the Contributors, Compiled by Harden Jay

BRIAN AHERNE: Abbey actor who later left Dublin to take up film work in America.

SYLVIA BEACH: Published the first edition of *Ulysses* at the Shakespeare Press, Paris, in 1922.

PEARCE BEASLEY: Leading member of Irish Volunteers, friend and biographer of Michael Collins.

DR RICHARD BEST: Born 1890s. Distinguished Gaelic scholar and linguist, he was long associated with the National Library. A well-known Dublin character and friend of Joyce and Gogarty, he appears under his own name in *Ulysses* (the National Library episode).

CAPT. DICKY BIRD: Well-known race-goer and Dublin character. He was a close friend of Smyllie (q.v.) of the *Irish Times* and George Moore.

MR BLAKE: A friend of Joyce's from the National Library.

ERNEST BLYTHE: A member of the Irish Revolutionary Brotherhood (IRB), to which he was introduced by Sean O'Casey, he joined Sinn Fein and held many important government posts including the Ministry of Finance. At present Director of the Abbey Theatre.

DR THOMAS BODKIN: Born in Dublin in 1890s. After association with Dublin's National and Municipal Galleries, became Curator of the Birmingham Art Gallery during the 1930s. An intimate of Dublin literary and artistic circles. He also published a book of verse including several translations from the French.

MONSIGNOR PATRICK BROWNE: Born 1890s. Cleric, scholar, poet, bon viveur and wit, at home in Dublin's literary and artistic circles from the Yeats - AE - Gogarty days onwards.

FRANK BUDGEN: Painter and friend of Joyce, he produced the first major critical work on the novelist, *The making of 'Ulysses'*.

MRS BUTLER: The Dublin woman whose house Gogarty escaped to after his famous swim across the Liffey.

JOHN CHICHESTER: One of Dublin's most amiable characters. Frequenter of the circle which met in O'Neills of Merrion Row and the Palace Bar. Naturalist and journalist.

AUSTIN CLARKE: Born 1896. Regarded by many as Ireland's premier living poet, he also wrote an autobiography and many verse plays. A Foundation Member of Irish Academy of Letters, he became its President in the 1950s.

JOHN COLBERT: Friend of Cathal O'Shannon (q.v.) and member of the Palace and Pearl Bar circles.

PADRAIC COLUM: Born 1881. One of Ireland's best-known poets, contemporary and friend of Yeats, Lady Gregory, etc. Among the first to write for the Abbey he also produced several books on folklore and a life of Arthur Griffiths. Member of the Irish Academy of Letters until his death in 1971.

BRENDAN CONSIDINE: A leader of the Republican forces in the Civil War and (for a short time) Gogarty's captor.

WILLIAM COSGRAVE: Politician and statesman. First Taoiseach (Prime Minister) of the Irish Free State.

CON CURRAN: Dublin barrister and author of several books on architecture, including one on the Bank of Ireland. A close friend of Joyce from the early Dublin days onwards, he was the recipient of much correspondence from Joyce after the latter had left Ireland.

CHARLES DUFF: Ulster-born author and journalist, friend and contemporary of George Moore and Gogarty.

MRS ELLIS: Wife of Dr Ellis, resident surgeon at the Civic Guard Depot in the Phoenix Park to which Gogarty made his escape.

ST JOHN ERVINE: Belfast-born (1883) playwright, dramatist, critic and novelist. Came to Dublin in 1915 and was for a time Manager of the Abbey. A member of the Irish Academy of Letters.

PADRAIC FALLON: Poet, born Co. Galway 1906, who joined Customs and Excise Service. Reluctant to publish in volume form, much of his poetry appeared in the *Dublin Magazine* during the 1950s. Also author of plays for radio and stage.

DAVID FLAHERTY: Journalist friend of Gogarty's in New York.

NINO FRANCK: Italian painter and friend of Joyce during the Paris period.

MAJOR FREYER: Close friend of the Gogarty group from the early days onwards. Conversationalist and eccentric, he retired to the West of Ireland to live on Achill Island with his extensive library.

HANS GASSER: Zürich friend of the Joyce family and Frau Giedion.

MONK GIBBON: Dublin-born (1896) poet, and author of two autobiographies. An adherent of the Yeats – Gogarty circle. He was also an intimate friend of Michael Farrell, editing the MSS of the latter's epic novel *Thy Tears might Cease* after the author's death.

FRAU GIEDION: A friend of the Joyce family (James and Nora) in the Zürich period.

LORD GLENAVY: Wit, financier (Director of the Bank of Ireland) and patron of the arts. With his wife Beatrice the centre of a literary circle comprising not only Irish but English literary figures.

LADY GLENAVY: Under the family name of Beatrice Campbell she wrote an extremely successful book of memoirs of the literary circles she had known, *Today we will only Gossip*.

NOLL GOGARTY: Well-known Dublin lawyer and wit, son of Oliver.

OLIVER ST JOHN GOGARTY: Born 1878. Distinguished wit, poet, novelist and surgeon. An intimate of both Yeats and Joyce, he appears in *Ulysses* as Buck Mulligan. Senator of the Irish Free State, 1922–36.

MRS GRIFFIN: Galway-born sister of Nora Barnacle, Joyce's wife.

ARTHUR HANNAH: Proprietor of Hannah's Book Shop in Nassau Street, and friend of Yeats.

LADY HANSON: Patroness of the Arts and friend of the Shaw family, she held a literary salon in the Gogarty days.

SENATOR MICHAEL HAYES: Secretary to De Valera. Prominent Member of Fianna Fail Party and for a long time speaker in Dail Eireann.

MRS MARY HIGGINS: Widow of the poet Frederick Higgins. Born 1896.

BULMER HOBSON: General Secretary of the Irish Volunteers and Dublin chairman of the IRB. He was also a close friend of Roger Casement.

JOE HONE: Yeats's first biographer, member of well-known Anglo-Irish family distinguished for their contribution to the arts and literature.

DENIS JOHNSTON: Dublin-born (1901) major Irish playwright (*The Moon and the Yellow River*). Director of the Gate Theatre 1931–6. He has also written a celebrated biography of Swift.

MARIA JOLAS: Editor of *Transition*, with her husband. She first published Joyce during the Paris period.

EVA JOYCE: James Joyce's sister.

STANISLAUS JOYCE: Younger brother of James, best known for his book on Joyce, *My Brother's Keeper*.

PATRICK KAVANAGH: Born Monaghan 1906. Considered Ireland's major poet since the death of W. B. Yeats. His two novels are both regarded as classics. A contradictory and invigorating character, his influence over the younger generation of Irish poets is inestimable.

ANNA KELLY: Well-known Dublin journalist, at one time secretary to George Moore and then to Michael Collins. For many years she ran a column known as 'Kelly's Corner' in the Irish Press.

DR KERRIGAN: A contemporary and friend of Joyce, he was a Medical Student at UCD in Joyce's days there.

MME LEON: Widow of the lawyer M. Leon and close friend of Joyce during the Paris period. Still an occasional contributor to the *Irish Times*, she writes under the pen-name of 'Noel'.

FATHER LEONARD: A priest who became an intimate friend of the Shaw family through his interest in music.

DR 'CON' LEVENTHAL: Dublin-born in the 1890s. Lecturer in Departments of English and French, Trinity College, Dublin. Friend of Joyce in the early Dublin days and member of Dublin – London – Paris literary and artistic circles. A close friend of Samuel Beckett. Most of his work consists of critical essays.

JUDGE LYNCH: A friend of James Connolly and prominent member of the Citizen Army. He defended St Mary's Abbey in Church Street during the Easter Rising.

MAUDE GONNE MCBRIDE: Great beauty. Daughter of a well-known Anglo-Irish family and an ardent and active Nationalist. She was the constant inspiration for Yeats's finest love poetry. Married John McBride, shot for the part he played in GPO at the Easter Rising. Mother of Iseult Stuart and Sean McBride (both q.v.).

SEAN MCBRIDE: Son of Maude Gonne McBride and prominent Senior Counsel at the Dublin Bar. One-time Minister of External Affairs, then became Secretary of the International Commission of Jurists in Geneva. A founder member of Amnesty International.

DENNIS McCULLOCH: Active Republican and owner of McCulloch's Piano Shop on Stephens Green.

MARTHA McCULLOCH: Friend of Gogarty, to whom she introduced W. R. Rodgers in 1969.

DONAGH MACDONAGH: Born 1912. Poet and playwright of repute. Co-editor, with Lennox Robinson, of the *Oxford Book of Irish Verse*. Best known for his verse plays he was also a broadcaster and District Justice.

SEAN MACENTEE: Born 1899. Poet and politician, took part in the Easter Rising, later elected Sinn Fein member for Monaghan and continued a distinguished political career, holding many ministerial posts until the 1960s.

SEAN McGARRY: Helped in the defence of the GPO during the Easter Rising with Connolly, Pearse, and the other signatories of the Irish proclamation of Independence.

NORAH McGUINNESS: Distinguished Ulster-born artist and frequenter of artistic and literary circles. A close friend of Yeats family. Lives in Dublin.

ROGER McHUGH: Dublin-born (1908), contemporary of Flann O'Brien and Niall Sheridan (q.v.). At present Professor of English at UCD, he has written two plays produced at the Abbey. The bulk of his work, however, is historical and critical.

SIR COMPTON MACKENZIE: Born 1899. Well-known Scottish novelist. Friend of Yeats, Gogarty, Lord Dunsany, etc.

BRINSLEY MACNAMARA: Pen-name of John Weldon, born 1890. Novelist and playwright, Nationalist, Volunteer and friend of Yeats. Joined Abbey Theatre in 1909 and left three years later to devote his time to writing. Produced his first and most controversial novel in 1918. Later he became Director of the Abbey and wrote several plays performed by the Company.

MISS MACNIE: Member of the Yeats – AE circle. Famous caricaturist of literary figures under the pseudonym 'Mac'. Some of the finest examples of her work are to be found in the Dublin Arts Club, of which she was a founder member.

SEAN MACREAMOINN: Gaelic scholar, wit and conversationalist, he first left the Department of External Affairs to become a producer on Radio Eireann in the late 1940s and is now with Telefis Eireann. A regular contributor to the *Irish Times*.

W. K. MAGEE: School friend and contemporary of Yeats, later a friend of AE and George Moore. He was associated with the National Library.

HELENA MALONEY: Abbey actress in the early Yeats – Lady Gregory period and active republican sympathiser and friend of James Connolly.

ADRIENNE MONNIER: Business adviser to the Shakespeare Press and friend of Sylvia Beach (q.v.).

LARRY MORROW: Ulster-born (1903), he wrote for the *Manchester Guardian* and the old *Freeman's Journal*. He then became a producer on Radio Eireann and contributed to the *Bell Magazine* under the pseudonym of 'The Bellman'.

GENERAL RICHARD MULCAHY: Republican, statesman and enthusiastic supporter of the Gaelic language. After the death of his ally and friend Michael Collins he became head of the Free State Army and later leader of the Fine Gael Party in Dail Eireann.

MRS MULCAHY: Wife of General Richard Mulcahy. Active Republican sympathiser during the Easter Rising.

ALEC NEWMAN: Assistant Editor of the *Irish Times* and Editor in the 1950s. A member of the Palace and Pearl Bar circles and close friend of Higgins.

MICHAEL NOYK: Dublin solicitor of Republican sympathies, friend and contemporary of Cathal O'Shannon (q.v.) and member of the old IRB circles.

LIAM O'BRIAIN: Distinguished scholar, broadcasting and television personality. Professor of Romance languages at University College, Galway. Was involved in the Easter Rising 1916 (Stephens Green).

SEAN O'CASEY: Born in Dublin 1884. One of Ireland's premier dramatists, he revived the reputation of the Abbey in 1920s. Also Secretary of the Irish Citizen Army under James Connolly. Left for England after quarrel over *The Silver Tassie* with Lady Gregory, Yeats, and Lennox Robinson.

FRANK O'CONNOR: Pen-name of Cork-born (1903) Michael O'Donovan. Best known as a master of the short-story form, he also produced several novels and was a distinguished translator of Irish poetry. A director of the Abbey during the 1930s, two of his plays were produced during this period.

PADDY O'CONNOR: Republican fighter in Easter Rising.

ROBERT O'DOHERTY: Dublin lawyer, wit and close friend of Gogarty, whose solicitor he was.

FRED O'DONOVAN: Well-known actor in the early days of the Abbey. He took the part of Christie Mahon in the first production of Synge's *The Playboy of the Western World* in 1905.

SEAN O'FAOLAIN: Writer. Born in Cork in 1900 and fought on the Republican side in the Civil War. He returned from America to Dublin in the 1930s to make his reputation with several collections of short stories, novels, plays and historical biography.

SEAN T. O'KELLY: Second President of the Irish Republic.

MRS O'KELLY: Wife of President O'Kelly.

EOIN O'MAHONEY: Lawyer, born in Cork in the 1890s. He was one of Dublin's most celebrated characters, known as 'The Pope O'Mahoney' because of the infallibility of his replies to any given question. Wit, scholar and geneologist, he had the entrée to all circles – literary, artistic, political and social – from the Yeats – Gogarty days until his recent death.

SHELAGH O'MAHONEY: Sister of Eoin, journalist and broadcaster.

LEO O'NEILL: Proprietor of O'Neill's Public House in Merrion Row, a meeting-place of the Dublin literati from the Gogarty days onwards.

JAMES O'REILLY: Close friend of W. B. Yeats. Renowned Dublin wit, known to his friends as 'Blasket O'Reilly' after the Blasket Islands in the west of Ireland.

DOMINIC O'RIORDAN: Writer, broadcaster, and public relations officer for the GPO in the 1940s.

CATHAL O'SHANNON: Born 1890s. Ardent Republican and prominent member of the IRB. He was also a journalist who contributed regularly to Dublin's leading newspapers.

KEVIN O'SHIEL: Old Republican friend and contemporary of Pearce Beasley (q.v.). He published a life of Collins.

SEAMUS O'SULLIVAN: Pen-name of James Sullivan Starkey, born 1897. Founder of the famous *Dublin Magazine* (1923), he played a prominent part in the Irish literary revival. A friend of Yeats, AE, Gogarty, Joyce and Arthur Griffiths; member of the Irish Academy of Letters.

SEAN O'SULLIVAN: Well-known Dublin artist, born 1906. Member of the Royal Hibernian Academy.

ARTHUR POWER: Born 1890s, painter, writer (one book on Old Waterford) and frequenter of literary and artistic circles in Dublin from the early days of Yeats, Gogarty, etc., onwards.

FRANÇOIS QUINTIN: Maître d'hôtel at Fouquet's, Joyce's favourite restaurant in Paris. Joyce presented him with a first edition of *Ulysses*.

SHELAH RICHARDS: Actress at both Abbey and Gate Theatres. Took the part of Nora Clitheroe in the first Abbey production of O'Casey's *The Plough and the Stars*. Formerly married to Denis Johnston (q.v.), now produces for Telefis Eireann and Abbey.

GEORGE ROBERTS: Publisher, director of the printing firm Mounsell & Co., he was the first publisher of the works of J. M. Synge and many other prominent writers of the period, including Joyce, the first edition of whose short stories, *Dubliners*, he destroyed.

LENNOX ROBINSON: Born Cork 1886. A distinguished dramatist, he was chosen as Manager of the Abbey by Yeats in 1910 and went to London to study theatre with Bernard Shaw. Resigned to work full time but became organising librarian for the Carnegie Trust in Ireland. Returned as Director of the Abbey from the 1920s to the 1950s. His most successful protégé among the many dramatists he encouraged was the young Sean O'Casey.

DESMOND RYAN: Born 1890s. Scholar and historian. Author of a biography of Patrick Pearse, *A Man Called Pearse*.

CECIL SALKELD: Artist and well-known Dublin character. Best known for his paintings (see the murals in Davy Byrnes Public House, Duke Street), conversationalist and wit. His daughter, the actress Cecila Salkeld, became the wife of the late Brendan Behan.

EILEEN SCHAUREK: James Joyce's sister, married in Trieste where she went to visit her brother.

OWEN SHEEHY-SKEFFINGTON: Scholar, senior lecturer in French, Trinity College, Dublin, and long-time Senator in Dail Eireann. Well known for his radical and liberal ideals and forthright speech, he was the son of the pacifist Francis Sheehy-Skeffington, shot during the Easter Rising 1916.

NIALL SHERIDAN: Senior Executive in Telefis Eireann. Attended UCD with Flann O'Brien and Roger McHugh, who, with several others, made up the brightest College set since the days of Joyce. Poet in his own right and one-time Editor of *Comthron Feine*, he appears as 'Brinsley' in Flann O'Brien's *At Swim Two Birds*.

BERTIE SMYLLIE: Born 1919. Editor of the *Irish Times* for a lengthy period. Best known for his encouragement of young writers, many now established as leading authors, whose work he first published in his newspaper.

EDWARD MILLINGTON STEPHENS: Nephew of J. M. Synge and owner of the Synge family papers, many of Synge's letters and MSS, etc.

JAMES STEPHENS: Born 1882. Celebrated Irish novelist, best known for *The Crock of Gold*, and author of poetry, criticism, short stories, etc.

L. A. G. STRONG: Born 1896, well-known poet and novelist. Broadcaster in early days of BBC. Also wrote on local history (*The Hill of Howth*). Member of the Irish Academy of Letters and a Fellow of Royal Society of Literature.

ISEULT STUART: Daughter of Maude Gonne McBride (q.v.). Frequented artistic and literary circles in Dublin and London. Married novelist and playwright Francis Stuart.

MRS SWEENEY: Daughter of Eoin MacNeill, founder of the Irish Volunteers.

LADY THOMSON: Widow of the Chairman of the United Arts Club.

DR MICHAEL TIERNEY: Clerical scholar and writer. For many years President of UCD.

MRS TYRELL: Mother of Lady Harrison (q.v.) and friend of the Shaw family in the Synge Street days.

MERVYN WALL: Dublin-born (1908) Civil Servant, employed in Unemployment Exchange, who became Programme Assistant in Radio Eireann in the 1940s, and Secretary of the Irish Arts Council from 1957 onwards. Best known as a novelist, he has also produced several plays and short stories.

DUDLEY WALSH: Dublin solicitor and man about town.

HARRIET WEAVER: Wealthy American patroness, of the arts in general, and Joyce in particular, who first published Joyce's *Portrait of the Artist* in instalment form in her progressive Parisian review *The Egoist*.

MRS BRENDA WILLIAMS: Gogarty's daughter and distinguished sculptress.

DOSSY WRIGHT: Abbey actor from the early Yeats – Lady Gregory period onwards. Frequenter of Dublin literary and theatrical circles, he was a well-known wit and raconteur.

ANNE YEATS: Daughter of W. B. Yeats for whom he wrote the poem 'A Prayer for my Daughter'. Distinguished artist and associate of Royal Hibernian Academy. Lives in Dublin.

MRS YEATS: Wife of W. B. Yeats; born George Hyde. Influenced his poetry through her interest in spiritualism (see Yeats's 'A Vision').